The Hotel Hokusai

by T. Y. Garner

To Frank,
Best wishes!

Ringwood Publishing
Glasgow

Issued in 2024
by
Ringwood Publishing

Flat 0/1 314 Meadowside Quay Walk, Glasgow
G11 6AY

www.ringwoodpublishing.com
e-mail: mail@ringwoodpublishing.com

ISBN: 978-1-901514-98-8

British Library Cataloguing-in Publication Data
A catalogue record for this book is available from the
British Library

Printed and bound in the UK
by Lonsdale Direct Solutions

Praise For Hotel Hokusai

"The Hotel Hokusai is a beautifully realised portrait of Yokohama in the late 19th century, where characters historical and fictional are weaved together in a compelling whodunnit inspired as much by the Japanese literary 'I-novel' as the golden age crime stories beloved by eel-chopping protagonist Han. A wonderfully engaging way to imagine the reactions and exploits of the real Glasgow Boys as they encountered Japan for the first time, while examining the often shady Western influence on the recently opened country. Garner himself views his subject with an artistic eye every bit as sharp as those he writes about and the result is fit to go up on the wall with the best of them."

Callum McSorley, author of *Squeaky Clean*

"Evocative and atmospheric, The Hotel Hokusai brings the colourful, bustling world of 19th century Yokohama to life. Packed with memorable characters, drama, mystery and humour, this is an impressive and ambitious debut from a talented new voice."

Iain Maloney, author of *The Japan Lights*

"Garner expertly captures the essence of what it feels like to end up alone to foreign country. Adapt or die. A compelling debut novel."

John Gerard Fagan, author of *Fish Town*

Dedication

To all who've had to start from scratch
in a strange country
wherever that may be

Like an eel swallowed
in a basket of eels,
the line amazes itself

eluding the hand
that fed it

– Seamus Heaney

"A twenty-year old girl, a resident of Tokyo, was found drowned in Yokohama harbour on Sunday. She lately applied for a post in the Telephone Exchange and her failure in this essay is supposed to have brought on suicidal mania."

– *The Japan Weekly Mail*, May 13th, 1893

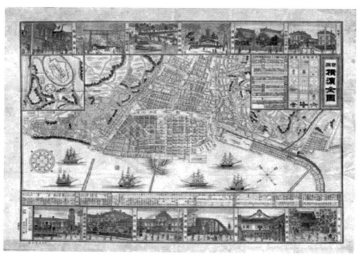

– The Foreign Settlement, Yokohama, Japan, 1893

Part One - The Worker

One

Hakone, Kanagawa, 1903

From where I am writing I can see both my past and my future in this country. My past hangs on the wall: a charcoal sketch of two figures at work on a waterfront eel stall, given to me by a man who came into my life for a short time and then disappeared, not just to me but the whole world. There was a brief surge of interest in his fate, some scurrilous rumours, and then the dust settled.

Why have I not attempted to resurrect Archie Nith before now? Well, for a long time I was not sure how I felt about what we did together in those months. But more than that, I was concentrating on my present and ensuring my future, which I can see now: it's the rise and fall of the hemispherical curve of my wife's belly, rising and falling as she dozes. It will not be long now until I am a father. Me. Han. The idea is frightening, I will not deny it, and will be even more so if it turns out to be a boy. Then I will be the model to copy, the one whose flaws are reproduced. Shit! *Kuso! Ssi bal!* Though why should a girl not copy me as well? She might become an Asian Arabella Hawk, a woman who acts like a man, travels across the world, writes plays, and gets men to dance to her tune. Not like her mother at all, so if that is to happen the influence would all have to come from me. Yuki would fight against it. Will fight. *Kuso! Ssi bal!* Shit! What are we doing?

But I am getting ahead of myself. The first consideration is language. Yuki knows I am considering this, but not on what terms. She thinks there is a duality of choices when in fact there is a … a what? *Ssi bal!* Shit! *Kuso!* – I don't know the word. A triality? Is that even a word in English? Well, if it is not, I don't know one in any of my other tongues, and it's a logical possibility, so I will hazard it. I'll trial a triality, ha! That's one of the lessons I will teach her, or him: based on what you know, hypothesise, then hazard a guess. We cannot all be Sherlock Holmes, but we can do our best with what grey matter we have.

Another lesson: know the questions you want to ask. My first one is this: is there space in a baby's brain for two languages, never mind three? Or will it only befuddle if one parent talks a different tongue to the other? Should I speak only in Japanese, to avoid confusion, at least until an age where he, or she, can discriminate between different tongues? But then when that stage is reached, what second one to introduce? No doubt English will afford the greater opportunities in commerce, science, medicine, literature; while Korean is the language of nothing but my heart, childhood, my mother and my sister. Of the time before the Reverend Hare. But is that time not exactly what I want to give my child? Yes, I think it is.

There, I have made up my mind. Japanese with Yuki, and at work; Korean – assuming I can remember it – with the baby; and English, until the time seems right, only here, in this story. Call it an experiment in triality. Perhaps it will work, perhaps it will fail. At the very least it will keep my brain sharp, as honed as Yamato's knife glinting on the chopping block waiting to be used.

*

Have you ever seen a basin full of eels? Just the sound of them slithering over one another makes you shiver, but you have to ignore it; grab one next to the head and pluck it out. It's as thick as undersea telegraph cable and it thrashes as

4

you slap it down on the board. Before it knows a thing, you whack the knife down and through, an inch below the eye. Do this hard enough to still the thrashing body, but not so hard that you sever it. Next, you nail it through its eye to the wooden block. It's still flicking back and forth, so press it down. Now slice it through the middle from tip of tail to gaping neck. Lay the two lengths side by side; with the flat of the blade nuzzle out bones and innards. Then slice into segments just the right size that Yamato can thread his lattice of skewers in and out the flesh. You can get onto the next one, while he will daub them in soy as black as ink, and plunge them in the oil bubbling in the pan above the charcoal. Five minutes crackling and sizzling, then they're ready for his loyal customers. Maximum freshness is part of his pitch. He thinks when people stop to watch it's to make sure the eels are as freshly killed as advertised. This may be so, but perhaps they simply can't resist the act of killing: as Horney says, the public are bloodthirsty bastards.

I remember the moment when I told the artists I planned to become a writer. We were at one of the teahouses on the coast road towards Honmoku, sitting at a table outside under the canopy. A waitress poured green tea. Horse-drawn carriages passed on the road in front of the ocean. Crickets screeched their song. It must have been late August or early September, 1893. My 16th year. Edward Hornel, always the most financially astute of the three, gave one of his bullish snorts:

'If you want to write, crime is the thing, and if you don't know which to choose you ought to go straight for murder.

Deciding not to tell Hornel that I knew this already, I enquired why it was so.

'Because', I can still hear his condescending baritone, 'the public are bloodthirsty bastards, aren't they!'

George Henry, less abrasive, more ironic, and the hardest

even for my English skill to follow, questioned whether it was 'not a tad cynical to deploy a fellow's demise as narrative device?'

'Any more cynical than painting coos, KG?' Horney retorted.

Henry was nicknamed KG, short for King George. Half-mocking respect for his age – he was 36, they were both 30. They used to joke about his claim to be next in line for leadership of 'The Glasgow Boys' – that's what they called the group of artists they belonged to. They were from Scotland – did they ever stop mentioning it? – and only in Japan for a year, all reasonable expenses paid by their dealer, who stood to make part of the profits from their work. Henry and Hornel (Horney, they called him) were always trying to outdo each other.

But Nith tended to exist on a different page altogether.

'The problem with crime stories is they peddle this myth of innate evil,' Nith spoke up. 'Most criminals are just desperate people ruined by the system.' This was a favourite Nithian theme and he would have carried on, but Horney cut him off with a pun:

'Call him Conan Doyle or Conman Doyle, you still have his stories by your bedside don't you!'

But it was not Horney's advice that made me want to write a detective story. The blame for that lay with what happened a month or so prior to that afternoon in the teahouse. I was still working then near the waterfront, and all it took was the wake from a departing launch, churning the shallow waters of the harbour, and up she came. Her navy-blue persimmon-patterned *yukata* clung to her body, but her face already held the pallor of death when the salvager pulled her from the water. Sunlight glittered on the wet muscles of the man's back as he climbed the ladder. He reached up to grip the rail with one hand and the girl's head flopped over his shoulder. My

6

mouth dried up when I saw the two freckles on her neck just below the ear, and the way her eyes still stared, but now with a dreadful emptiness of comprehension. In that first moment of recognition, I made the parallel with my father, who had drowned while attempting a misguided swim when I was too young to remember. I assumed the girl too must have died an accidental death, and when I looked up at Yamato, my boss and mentor, it was not at all with suspicion, but to seek some explanation from him as to why she would take such a foolish risk. I remember he was staring, transfixed, at the corpse and muttering words under his breath. It sounded like a prayer, like the one he had recited when he took me to the temple and an absurd thought occurred to me: could she have been another acolyte of the Dragon King, Ryuo, who had taken her worship too far and met her end searching for his palace on the seabed?

The salvager passed the girl up to two other men, who guided her gently down onto her back on the quayside; by that time in the morning already warmed by the sun. One of the two fellows rose to his feet and turned to face the semicircle of gawkers that had assembled. He was Japanese, but like many officials, wore Western clothes.

'Does anyone here know who she is?' he barked in Japanese-inflected English, before repeating the question in his mother tongue. He must have been one of the intellectual elites who had been sent abroad to study, and come back full of Western ideas – in his case – of how police work should be conducted. Again, I looked at Yamato, expecting him to speak up, but he said nothing; only clamped his hand to my shoulder.

'Does anyone have any information?'

'Looks like she drowned,' some local Sherlock piped.

The policeman ignored the comment and went on.

'If you hear anything come to the police station tomorrow.

For now, we need to do our job and you need to do yours. So, if you would be so kind, shift your arses.'

'Shouldn't we tell him?' I hissed at Yamato, but he only swore at me and dug his fingers even more tightly into my shoulder. We dispersed along with the others: a few sailors, dockworkers and seafront strollers, a typical port settlement mix. When I asked Yamato if we would go to the police station later he growled at me:

'Shut up, *bakayarou*. Do you want us to be suspected of killing her?'

I was stunned into silence and my own feverish thoughts. As we returned to the stall to start the day's work, another Japanese man clattered past us in the opposite direction. His arms were loaded with equipment that I would come to recognise as tripod, camera, and flashbulb. From behind the stall I stole glances between chops of eel, a risky business for reasons I will explain. However, I had already made up my mind at that point that I would carry out my own investigation into her death, and for the short time remaining until she was covered and taken away, I tried to fix what she looked like at the end in my mind as sharply as if I possessed the image myself.

Two

Time, like an eel, is slippery – especially when you try to trace it back. Was it three or four months earlier when I had been seen on board a ship, waved out of Busan harbour by my proud tearful mother and the Reverend Hare, upright as the cross at her side? Was it after five or after six nights at sea that I arrived in Yokohama? What I do know is that I had nothing but the brass-buttoned black suit I had been given for my new life, a pouch of Japanese *yen* that 'would do me until my next stipend', and my letter of recommendation to the College of Christ's Soldiers in the East. When I came ashore I wasted no time in locating the rocky bluff from whence – the Reverend Hare had assured me – this famous college blazed forth its righteous torch. But though there were grand European style houses, cafés, shops, and – offering momentary false hope – a church at the top of the hill, there was no college that I could find. Eventually, I asked an attractive woman in the midst of plastering a paper to a noticeboard outside a brick building. After recovering from the shock of hearing me, an Asian, speak perfect English, she informed me that an institute for religious teaching had occupied a building further down the street until a few years earlier, but it was now a milliners.

'Excuse my ignorance, Ma'am,' I said. 'But what is a milliners?'

She smiled, benignly. I could not help thinking she was pleased to find there were limits to my language ability.

'A hat shop, dear.' She lifted the beribboned straw boater on her head in case I had not understood.

'I see.'

She was not unperceptive and realised that I was in need of consolation.

'We have a theatre up there,' she pointed back up the hill. 'Come and see *Frankenstein* at Hallowe'en.'

I stumbled away, wondering who or what *Frankenstein* was and what it had to do with the festival the Reverend Hare had described to us as the time when God held a lottery for the evil spirits languishing in Hell, the winners being rewarded with a night back on earth amongst the living. At some point in my aimless wandering I walked past the church again and went in, but when a man told me the times of the services – whether through shyness or some instinct to avoid another Reverend Hare – I only thanked him and walked away.

*

How would anyone feel if they arrived, young and alone, with very little and knowing no one, in a strange city? I don't think my reaction was unusual. First, you are stung by the jellyfish called panic. You think you are done for. Then you realise you are only paralysed, and slowly the effects of the sting wear off. Your body starts working again, but you are a subtly different kind of animal; the kind that makes quick, rough plans based on what you need to survive for the next four, six, twelve hours.

You manage the first night – even sleep. Then, on the second day, you wake up, and this may be the worst moment of all: when you realise it starts again. From morning to nightfall, the same challenge, a battle you'll face alone, with no one to help you, and no prize for winning except the right to keep fighting another day. But survival instinct will carry you far. Like any creature thrust into a strange environment, you realise that you must adapt or die. And if you're wise

10

you will count any blessings you can find: for example, the consolation that nobody is trying to nail you to a board with a stake through your eye.

For two days I had been hanging about at the waterfront, the first day speaking to no one, only trying to scent out possibilities. The second day I forced myself to make enquiries. In the morning I approached some dockers unloading crates off a ship and onto carts to be taken to one of the warehouses that lined the port side. I asked them what I needed to do to get a job working with them. At first they ignored me, until one who spoke English said I was too scrawny and wet behind the ears, but if I wanted to waste my breath I could ask their boss. When I asked where I would find that person, the man who had spoken to me wiped his brow and made a gesture with his finger, explaining that the boss was never in one place for long. I was about to turn away when he added, taking pity on me, that the man did have certain habits, one of them being that he obtained his lunch at Yamato's eel stall at one o'clock every day. Consulting his timepiece and informing me that I had an hour to wait, the fellow pointed me towards the stall. I set myself up a short distance back from it, atop some crates against the side of a warehouse.

Thus, it was that I had a grandstand view of the accident that set me on this course. Before Yamato's chopping boy began screaming, I saw his finger left sitting on the block like a gentleman's cigar waiting to be lit. I saw the knife clatter to the ground and two English sailors in white uniforms passing, one of them demonstrating some boxing moves, the other laughing. Like Yamato, who had been in the midst of skewering, they turned at the zing of steel on stone. The boy, who was Japanese, had sunk to his knees, clutching his hand. His head had dropped onto his chest and he was making indistinct mewls like the kitten the Reverend Hare had brought home in a box one day, having – he claimed –

11

saved it from a woman's dinner plate.

Yamato was on his knees too, peeling off his bandana and wrapping it tightly around the injury to staunch the flow of blood. The sailors had gathered round to watch and – out of blind instinct – I ran over and stood behind them. Yamato was muttering into the boy's ear, perhaps telling him that it was only a finger, the pain would pass and in time he would not miss it. The blonde officer who had been throwing punches took a couple of steps to the side and bent to retrieve the digit from where it lay absorbing eel juices. He began examining it, turning it over like it was a piece of jewellery for sale in a shop.

'Hnnn … Clean cut,' he said, as detached as the thing he was looking at.

'Could get Sawbones to sew that back on,' said the other.

I would be lying if I said my pity lasted longer than it took me to sense the potential of the moment. Quite aside from what desperation will do to anyone's morality, mine was formed from a unique interpretation of the Bible. Take the Reverend Hare's version of 'Jonah', crying for his release when the great cetacean washed up on a beach. Just as he was on the point of suffocating, the movement of his foot kicking out against the wall of the stomach was seen, the blubber was sliced open and Jonah slipped out through its guts onto the sand, gasping: 'Thank you, Lord, O thank you for in your goodness you have spared me!' But, in fact, his liberators were a tribe of cannibals who preferred man to whale, and from there we had the expression: 'Out of the whale and into the stewpot'. But before he was consumed Jonah was able to use his skill in oratory to convince the tribe firstly that whale meat was in fact very tasty and good for the brain, and secondly that they would burn in hell if they did not accept the word of God, who as proof of His almighty power, had sent Jonah to them inside a whale. And so instead of their pudding he became their pastor, and the moral was that you had to use the resources God had put on your plate.

The blonde officer tapped Yamato on the shoulder, and my future boss looked round with a face like a cat caught dragging a dead bird into the house. The finger of his employee was being pointed at him, and he surely thought he was being accused of some form of negligence, though what the dark-haired officer was saying was only that they would take the boy to a surgeon. Yamato, not understanding English but wishing to appease them, gave a little bobbing bow and, releasing his grip on the tourniquet, cupped his hands into a bowl ready to receive the digit with the reverence it deserved.

'Ah – a,' the blonde officer pulled it back. 'How do I know you won't sell it as an eel fritter?'

The second officer crouched and mimed the action of sewing it back on, until finally Yamato got the message and pulled the boy to his feet, firing a volley of Japanese into his ear. Through the shock of his pain, I could see doubt on the boy's face as he looked up at these foreigners who were offering to have magical acts of healing performed on him. 'Come on, lad,' the blonde one ruffled his hair. My predecessor gave a last glance at Yamato, who motioned with his hand, encouraging him to go. Then the threesome were off up towards the pier where a British frigate was moored, the boxing fan pulling the boy by his fully intact left hand, the other replacing Yamato's sweat-encrusted bandana with a pristine, white handkerchief he had extracted from his pocket.

Three

The previous night I had been crying, but silently, so no one would find out that I was not a man and a Christian ready to make his own way in the fast-turning world, but a lost boy who missed his mother. This was in the sleeping room of the lodging house, surrounded by the grunting, snoring, farting forms of the cheerfully unbaptised Chinese labourers who were its typical residents. I had been guided to this sanctuary as evening descended at the end of my first day. After seeing me try to lay my head down on a bench in the shorefront park, a kindly Chinese woman had told me to come with her. I was hesitant, wary of being conned, but desperation led me to accept her offer. I did not realise at the time how lucky I was. Miss Miura, the owner, was Japanese, but one of the few believers in Pan-Asian fellowship. She spoke Chinese, and even a few words of Korean. Later I learned she had been married to a Chinese man, who had gone back to his country, leaving her with a source of income which gave its residents exactly as much luxury and privacy as you would expect for three *yen* per week. In fact, when you considered morning and evening meals were thrown in, this was cheap. There were twenty futons upstairs in the large room we all shared, ten against each wall, with me at one end.

Though I had a bed, I always struggled to sleep in that room: my recurring memory is of lying awake, listening to my neighbour emitting rhythmic grunts, watching the rise and fall of the distended belly on which his hands were laid. There was always someone else awake, and I took care not to let my tears transmit into any telltale snuffling. These efforts to conceal my misery caused me to resent all the

14

more the tranquil repose of the man beside me, who seemed to demand no more from life than the right to earn money, satisfy his most basic needs, and sleep ready to earn again.

At some point the friendliest of the Chinese men explained to me with a mixture of gestures and English that most of them worked at the docks loading and driving carts. Their labour took them out in the morning and afternoon, and they spent the evenings in the lodging house, gambling their earnings over a game they played with black and white tiles on a square board pitted with notches. One of them had offered to teach me it, but though he dragged me once into their circle of players I did not stay long, and with the excuse that I was tired, retreated to my own futon. The game was called *Go*, and its rules are not as complex as they first appear, though becoming good is another matter. I have always been quick at picking up games, so why, I wonder, did I not join the Chinese and learn this one, whose infinite possibilities for strategy would surely have appealed to me?

I think the tiles the players used must have reminded me too much of *gonggi*, which at that time represented everything I had lost and longed to go back to. *Gonggi* is the game of pure nostalgia. Even now to think of it takes me instantly back to the time before the Reverend Hare. The dusty square of earth in the centre of our village, with the well and the hot sun and the crickets screeching. Though all of that could be in a Japanese village like this one where I live now and am writing these words, except for the game, which I've never seen Japanese children play. All you need are five pebbles, and then for hour after hour you can sit in a circle playing, totting up the points. Pick a pebble up, toss it in the air, pick up another and catch the first in the same hand before it falls. It sounds simple but isn't. So much skill is required, and judgment, of how high to throw, which pebble to go for. But the last round is pure technique and a bit of luck, where you have to throw up all five, turn your hand over and catch as many as you can on the back of it. Usually most of them skitter away into the dust.

That was my childhood, a Korean childhood, before the Reverend Hare came and began steadily turning me onto his path, which had led me to that boarding house full of snoring Chinese men, feeling utterly lost, with my story yet to start. This writing of it has been rather similar, if I am honest, but now I am into my stride, and as I write, I find I am remembering afresh and even learning new things. I have realised, for example, that I will teach my child *gonggi*, and that this, as much as language, will make them grow up with a Korean part of their soul. The part the Reverend Hare tried to cleave from mine from the moment he decided that, of all the women in our village, the one he wanted most was my mother. Never mind that she already had two young children whose father had drowned in a foolish attempt to swim the Han River. Give him his due, my adoptive father was open-minded about who to indoctrinate. I did not have to be his own flesh and blood to merit his special attention. But then maybe he would have preferred his own, but wasn't able, though I am sure it was not for want of trying.

*

Was it perhaps a month before my first night at Miss Miura's that he had spoken to me man-to-man? He had been out on his weekly run of baptising and burying converts in the countryside around our village, and Mother had already given us our portions of rice when he came back, whistling a hymn as he usually did. Removing his hat and wiping the sweat from his face with his handkerchief, he sat down at the table built in the carpentry style of Joseph of Arimathea. With the precious silver fork given to him on his visit to Bethlehem, he blessed the rice mixed with egg yolk which my mother set in front of him. We watched him chewing each grain, mindful of the Lord's role in creating it. When

16

he had finished he wiped his beard and moustache carefully, leaned forward with his elbows on the table and his chin resting on his knuckles. This was our signal to steeple our palms, shut our eyes and listen while he thanked the Lord for providing sustenance. 'Amen,' we all said with a single voice, and opened our eyes. I found him grinning at me, his blue eyes glittering like sapphires in a royal crown.

'You arrre rrripening, boy,' he said, rolling his r's, a habit which it took me a long time to shake, having learned it from him and assuming it to be a standard feature of English. I nodded, knowing the literal meaning of ripen and being able to guess what it meant in reference to me. This was his habitual manner of address, constantly stretching me with metaphors and idioms.

'I think it's time you and I had a talk about your future.'

Mother and my sister, Yoona, went through to the other room, which the Reverend Hare had created using his God-given funds to extend into the yard, although it gave the chickens less room to peck. I could hear the beginnings of another of Mother's stories, the kind I used to like but had now outgrown. I stayed sitting opposite him with the table bulwarked between us and we fell into the usual routine as night descended on the fields outside. He brought out his tobacco pouch, packed some down into his pipe, and lit it. The bitter scent infused the air between us.

'Tell me what you learrrned in school today.'

He knew the answers because he had taught the class, but I had to prove I had absorbed his teachings.

'Astronomy, Sir. The order of the planets.'

'Which is?'

'Mercury, Venus, Earth, Mars, Jupiter,' I was counting them off on my fingers, and moved to the other hand. 'Saturn, Uranus, Neptune.' I released my breath.

'Verrry good. And what is the way you remember that?'

'"Most very elegant men jump ship unless nobbled."'

'Good. The sea is no place for dandies to be trapped. And what do we call that method of remembering?'

'A menonic?'

'A mnemonic. M – N – E – M – O – N – I – C. Spelling is very important. As Christ reminded Peter before his crucifixion, he would not tolerate a gospel littered with spelling errors.'

'No, Sir.'

'The only way to learn to spell is to practice writing from dictation. That is why I have never given you the Bible to read, because I wanted you to hear the words and write them for yourself.'

'I wrote out the story of Jonah, Sir, as I remembered you tell it.'

His already wide mouth stretched further into a grin.

'Good. How many b's in cannibal?'

'… One.'

'That's right. One b, or one being!' If mother's laugh was a mountain stream in spate, the Reverend Hare's was the wheezing of a rusty well pump; his larynx quivered like a seaweed polyp, and his mouth would remain agape even after the sound had died. With his mane of red-gold hair he looked like a lion in full health, but inside his mouth was a vandalised cemetery. A few months before that conversation, in a moment when his guard was down, I had plucked up the courage to ask him about these gaps.

'I wagered my gold teeth,' he let slip.

'Gold teeth, Sir?'

My amazement at the notion of teeth made of gold outweighed my shock that the Reverend had wagered, even

18

though we had heard the parable of 'The Racecourse at Jerusalem', when Jesus freed the horses from their chariots and miraculously hitched the Jewish bookmakers to run in their stead. But even after a brief lesson on dentistry, he seemed to feel for the first time the need to justify his behaviour to me.

'I was not always on the path of Christ's teachings,' he confessed. 'For long years I strayed in the wilderness, in the company of sinful men. Men without the guiding light of woman at their side, or the moral leash of home to constrain them.'

I think on this occasion also we were at the table, pipe smoke filling the air between us. Mother and Yoona must have been in the other room again, at their sewing maybe, or praying, or sleeping.

'Coarse brutes,' he growled.

'What did they do?' I whispered, my fear equalled by my curiosity to find out. Suddenly he reached across the table and plied my lips apart, invading my mouth with his fingers and thumb. He yanked a molar, and I felt a slight discomfort but the tooth did not budge.

'Well-attached, aren't they?'

I nodded mutely up at him, wondering if punishment was coming for my impudence.

'But no match for a wrench,' he muttered, letting go.

Then he told me what a monkey wrench was, even sketching one for me in my notebook of new words. Later, in secret, I drew a picture of the three brutes holding him down, two forcing his mouth open while the Most Evil of them all worked away at the gold molars, as the Reverend issued mute howls of protest. In my sketch I rendered my best guess as to what a ship's cabin would look like. There was a table with cards left lying on it – he had described for me the four suits – and three loose stacks of coins. The

19

Reverend's pile had been reduced to nothing, and instead of leaving the game he had staked three of his own teeth on the outcome of the cards. Why the absence of women or home would cause him to make such an offer I could not then begin to fathom.

It was this picture, from a few months earlier, that was in my head as I listened to the Reverend's words on that evening of the talk. He had moved on from Jonah and was telling me that the point was that just as you could only learn to spell from listening and practice, not merely the copying of words, the same was true of the greater picture. To learn about life, you could not merely copy one man's example, excellent and correct as it may be. It was necessary to venture afield, to listen to the examples of other men and derive from these multiple examples the best formation of your character.

'Do you underrrstand my meaning?'

'Yes, Sir,' I said, although my thoughts wandered elsewhere. What if other men were not good men, but gambling, teeth-pulling brutes, and that reading books rather than listening to them could be a more effective way to perfect my spelling? The Reverend Hare should know that, I thought, since it was he who had given me the books that taught me how to spell and to write. And I did not have to copy, for I had the images of the words in them printed in my mind. My favourite, which I had read five times or more, was *Treasure Island.* There were whole passages in that book that I could have written out from memory, with each of the words spelled correctly. But I did not say any of this.

'You are to go on an adventure,' the Reverend was saying.

'Like Jim Hawkins?'

He pulled a fold of skin on my cheek, 'That's right, like Jim. But your treasure will be the word of God ...'

And he went on about the journey to Japan and the College of Christ's Soldiers in the East, where he was already arranging to have my fees sent on ahead. But as he was informing me about that great institution, my thoughts were already racing after the fees. I pictured myself looking out on the waves from a storm-tossed cabin, being tied up by pirates, marooned on an island or swallowed by a whale. Eventually, Mother and Yoona were called into the room, and together, the Reverend and I told them of the plan for the next stage of my education. I clasped Mother tight as her tears flowed onto my chest, but held firm – 'as upright as the cross,' to quote the Reverend's advice on good posture – and in our own language told her this was the path the Lord wished me to follow. I would come back of course, armed with the tools to follow in our adoptive father's footsteps and preach the Word to our own people.

Four

'I can do that,' I said in Japanese, and bowed low to the ground, smelling eel guts and sweat. When I raised my head to Yamato I had to shield my eyes because the sun was high in the sky behind him. He was looking at me suspiciously. I was sure what I had said was correct, having heard it from one of the Chinese who always offered to help Miss Miura clear the table after everyone had drunk their bowls of broth from the communal pot.

'*Nani?*' Yamato growled, which I knew meant 'what?'.

I repeated what I had said, more slowly this time, and he screwed up his already wrinkled face, running a greasy hand through his hair, wild without the bandana to contain it. I pointed at the few eels still wriggling in the crate and made chopping motions with my hand. The sun was beating down overhead, the sweat was dripping off me, and the endless passage of men and goods along the waterfront must have been going on as usual: potential customers and profit that Yamato was losing. But he continued to stare at me as if I were a rare beetle who had unwisely scuttled out from under a rock. I was wearing a cheap white vest that I had bought in a shop selling garments for workers, but with my smart trousers and shoes my lower half was still more fit for the college. On the chopping board the knife glinted, and finally Yamato picked it up. He examined the blade, perhaps testing its sharpness, or wondering whether there was enough boy blood on it to be worth wiping off. He must have decided there wasn't, because he turned it round in a ceremonial fashion and offered me the handle.

'Let's see then,' he said, with a shrug. He stood with his arms folded and his lips curled back, watching me, waiting. I approached the table. I had watched the process and thought I knew what to do. I reached into the crate and, overcoming my repulsion, grabbed an eel round the neck and lifted it out. Its tail whipped against my forearm but I forced the head down onto the board, and taking up the spike in my left hand, focused on the glaring, angry eye. I tried to summon the courage of Jim as he faced Long John Silver, but I was too tentative; the implement did not go all the way through, and the creature, no doubt in some form of serpent agony, almost slipped out of my grasp. I heard Yamato mutter something dismissive, and hurriedly drove the stake the rest of the way in, until it made contact with the board. But no matter how hard I pushed, the stake would not penetrate the wood. Without the head firmly anchored, I would never be able to gut the flesh in the right way. I worked the implement with my wrist, and with each sideways twist the hole in the unfortunate creature's head gaped wider, exposing more pinkish gore of eye socket and whatever brains an eel has. The tail was flapping more feebly now. How long could it survive this? How about if I just waited until it expired before going on? But Yamato's arms appeared over my shoulders. He spat some words out as he wrenched the impaler from my grip and yanked it out. I began to lift my other hand from the neck but no sooner did I raise it a centimetre than he forced it back down. I understood what he said meant 'hold it'. Then in the next second the implement flashed down with great speed, *thunggg*, and the point was embedded deep in the wood. He pushed me aside. '*Mo mirre!*' Now watch. I stood back, and this time I realised what a difference it made to see things from the actor's point of view, rather than the spectator's. Before, I had merely thought I knew what to do. Now I could imagine my own arms replicating Yamato's movements: the half severing of the head; the slipping of the blade the length of the body; the peeling back of the creature's flesh; and then the trickiest part of all, the sideways dance of the blade to remove the innards. Yamato worked swiftly, violent and delicate all at once. In no time at all the two halves were emptied of bones and sliced into small lengths. Contemptuous, he looked down at me. 'Like that,' he said.

'Yes, *sensei*,' I said.

'I'm not your teacher,' he spat back.

The next hour was endless. I could not understand many of Yamato's words, but I could catch the derisory batter they were wrapped in. At any moment I expected the dismissal to come. Then when it did not, I began to wish it would. Instead, Yamato only observed as I battled with the slimy flesh, interrupting my attempts with bursts of ridicule, and every time I threatened to ruin an eel completely, snatching the knife out of my hand for a fresh demonstration. All this in public, with a constant stream of passers-by: dock workers and customs men going for lunch, sailors strolling ashore, women on their way to the park. And whether they stopped or not, I felt their stares crawling over me – the humiliation of an employee must be a compelling spectacle – a theatre that was real and didn't cost a *sen* to see. We did business as well – the popularity of Yamato's battered eel was undeniable – and he somehow still managed to see to customers with a servile charm that made his treatment of me seem all the worse.

But as the sun slid round the sky, the number of eels in the crate kept diminishing until there was just one left. Pity for the creatures had not entered my head – I was far too busy concentrating on the technique of slaughtering them – but seeing this lone eel struggling in the shallow water at the foot of the crate, I wondered what it was thinking. Did it know what was coming? Did it have the same urge to live as me? I regarded it for a few seconds before I grabbed it by the neck, making a silent prayer for God to absolve me of what I was about to do. Then I slapped it down on the board with enough force to stun it, lifted the nail above the eye and impaled it expertly, or so it seemed to me. I risked a glance at Yamato as I wiped the blade for the hundredth time on my filthy trousers, then sawed into its length. I could feel his critical gaze and tried my utmost to replicate the motions I had seen him perform. 'At least let me finish this one by myself,' I was thinking, the object of my prayers having quickly changed from God to Yamato. And he did, grunting in a way that I knew meant he was surprised, that I was better than he had thought. When the last segments were taken from the oil, I had to help him lift the pan off – even at the edges it was almost burning to the touch, but I did not flinch and copied his steps to the side where we set it down. Yamato removed the metal drum from the cart and placed it next to the pan, which we then lifted, tilting until the batter began flowing into the drum in a steady stream. My arms were aching but I forced them to keep working; to drop my side of the pan now would be a disaster.

When the last of the precious fluid was syphoned into storage and we set the pan down, Yamato tossed me a cake of soap and a rag. I missed my catch and the soap skidded away across the quayside. I went to fetch it and following Yamato's instructions, first I soaped every greasy inch of the pan, then wiped it with methodical sweeps of the rag from bottom to top, so that any solid residue came to the rim and could be scraped off into the palm of my hand. The last stage was the soaking. I carried the rack down to where the long promontory of the pier began, and a set of steps led down to the water's edge. I descended these and lowered myself to a squat on the bottom step. Wavelets lapped over my filthy shoes, soaking them and chilling my feet as I scooped the bowl into the ocean, angling it so that when I lifted again the water spilled back out, a slick of grease and a froth of soap bubbles now floating on the surface.

Yamato watched me place the bowl on the top of the cart. He had already stashed the oil drum and left the knife and tools to soak in a jar of soapy water. There was nothing more to be done. The work was finished for today. I stood before him, head bowed, awaiting my fate. I was thinking nothing at all; what I called 'my self' had been temporarily extinguished by the work.

Five

My sister, Yoona, used to have an old doll made of straw that our mother had made with bindings to separate the various body parts. The straw was noosed tight into a tiny neck, and after a long, thin face with watermelon seeds sewn on for eyes, it was bound again near the top, leaving an inch or two of straw bunching out so the hairstyle resembled the fruit of the gardenia. Because we called that fruit *chija*, this became the doll's name, and like a plant she managed without a nose, mouth or any clothes. Soon after the Reverend Hare came among us, he found Chija lying on the floor of the room where we all three then slept.

Through the doorway I watched him – it was a fascination for me, watching him when he didn't know he was being watched – as he picked her up and examined her. He turned her over and even smoothed the strands of straw that passed for her hair. He was smiling to himself, and I proudly thought it was at the care and skill with which the doll had been fashioned by my mother. Years later – perhaps a year before I was put on the ship – another incident made me remember this first one and see it in a new light.

We were playing. Or I was not playing, I was too old for that. But it was a wet afternoon and I was keeping Yoona entertained by the elementary game of hiding Chija, who had long since been surpassed by a proper doll which the Reverend had brought back from a rare trip to the capital. This was a smooth-cheeked, glass-eyed creature in a lace dress, human enough to be baptised with the Reverend's approval. Susan reigned supreme at my sister's bedside, but Chija, who could be stuffed anywhere and contorted into various positions, still had her uses. Having exhausted the hiding places in the house, I decided to take her outside and place her at a corner of the window, hiding 'in plain sight'. While Yoona closed her eyes and counted, I opened the front door silently and ran round the side of our wooden dwelling – straight into our Protector and Benefactor. I backed away, clutching the doll tight to my chest, and began stumbling out some explanation as to why I had not been studying.

'Ah-ah,' the Reverend held up his hand. 'Excuses do not excuse.' This was one of his favourite admonitions in the classroom, but when he said it he was never truly angry, and I could see from his faint smile that this was the case now.

'You are off to perform some voodoo, I suppose?'

I must have looked confused, because he bared his teeth and plucked Chija out of my hands. 'This,' he said, holding her up by the ragged bunch of stalks on her scalp, 'reminds me of the brrranch of witchcraft known as voodoo.'

I knew something of witches and witchcraft – he had told us before how in his country, many years ago, people used to believe that certain women worked with the devil, they were accused of being witches and burned at the stake. The accusations were false, he said, there was no such thing as witchcraft, although there were undoubtedly women who believed in it.

'Voodoo, Sir?'

'It is a practice of certain Caribbean islands, on the other side of the world from here.'

'How does it work?'

'One makes a model of one's enemy – usually a crude doll such as this,' he waggled Chija in my face. 'Then … Let me see …' He dug in the pocket of his blue waistcoat and extracted one of the sharp little wooden sticks he was always fashioning to poke food out from between the wreckage of his teeth. 'But anything sharp will do. Now, you have to focus on the face of your enemy, and say what is it that you want to happen to them … perhaps warts on the face or a rash on the stomach, or braining by coconut. Then, jab in the requisite place.' He stabbed his toothpick into Chija's stomach. I flinched and he laughed.

'Don't look so alarmed, boy, it's all prrrimitive superstition and nonsense!'

I lay awake in the dark that night, a few feet from my sister's sleeping form, remembering the first time I had seen him looking at Chija. So, it had nothing to do with love and admiration, I thought – only amusement at our primitive state. He was our minister and teacher and, as mother always reminded us, the father we never had before. The thought that there was something about him I did not like was dangerous. I knew this, but in spite of it I found myself fantasising about making a Reverend Hare doll, and sticking sharp sticks into it, especially the thing that dangled between his legs. I wanted this appendage to burst into flaming warts, dry into a hard crust, and then break into flakes like a piece of wood on the fire. It was to punish him for the noises he and my mother made at night, on the other side of the thin wall when they thought I was asleep.

*

I could not make a voodoo doll of Yamato – only imagine one, and jab it with mental pins: 'Give me the job,' I willed him. The seconds crept by. I glanced up and met his glittering dark eyes still bearing down on me. '*Ashita kimasu?*' I said. My Japanese was primitive – 'I come tomorrow?' – and perhaps this was what amused him and made up his mind. He directed my eyes to the large clock on the side of the customs building, the fingers of which read half past two. 'Ten o'clock,' he said, putting his fingers to the angle of the clock hands in case I had failed to understand.

I bowed again, then cupped my hand out before him and

said simply, because it was all I knew how to say, the Japanese word for money. His forehead creased, his eyebrows arched like caterpillars, and he began making a creaking sound that I realised was laughter. '*Okane*', he repeated, creaking, and then again, as if the word 'money' itself was a joke, or the concept of being paid for the work you did. But he dug his hand into the pocket of his stained pantaloons, pulled out a leather pouch, and extracting a handful of coins from it, held them out in his palm.

'How much?'

Had I misunderstood? Had he really asked me how much I wanted? I had not considered the question of remuneration at all. What was a fair wage? What was enough for me to survive on? I had no idea. If I asked for too much, would he give me less? I was tongue-tied for so long that eventually he lost patience, said something I did not understand, and counted out a few coins into my hand. Not knowing enough at that point either about Japanese currency, or Yamato's character, I assumed he had given me a pathetically small amount, less than my predecessor received. I burned with anger at myself as I stumbled away down the pier, merely putting one foot in front of the other, anything to escape the scene of my exploitation, to which I had agreed to return the next day for more.

Six

I had been with Yamato for a month and my technique was now much honed by practice. Thought barely interrupted the smooth repetitions of my arms, the muscles in my biceps and triceps as I worked the blade. I had a routine now: as soon as Yamato and I parted ways, I would rinse my vest in the ocean to rid it of the reek of fish guts and sweat, then sit on the quayside waiting for it to dry while eating my lunch which was, naturally, a portion of eel.

When this was done, I would pull on the still damp vest and take a walk along the seafront, watching out for the ships that were coming in and out of port, as well as the human traffic on the promenade, always busy with sailors, foreign and Japanese, merchants and their carts. I had forced myself past the stage where I still thought constantly of attempting to communicate with my family. In our village, we did not conceive of things such as addresses, and the Reverend had assured me that I would receive correspondence from him, care of the College of Christ's Soldiers, containing notice of how I should respond. Perhaps there was a point at which I could have presented myself to a police station or an embassy, and they would have helped me, but that ship had sailed.

We made a brisk trade. Every day the sun beat down and – after a minute or two – Yamato and I would be glistening with sweat. He was still a slavedriver, but I was starting to feel a strange affection for him. It came with the last of the lunch rush, when we stood side by side in the heat on the quayside, panting, both stinking of fried eel, my arms aching from the gripping and the chopping. At first, the clear-up had to be done straight away, but gradually a pause was introduced. I don't remember when it happened, but there was a point when Yamato did not just bark orders and abuse, he actually talked to me. By listening to him, my Japanese improved rapidly, and soon I could string together a few sentences without faltering. As I had memorised Stevenson by heart, I now lay in bed at night running over Yamato's monologues, spat out in a husky growl, litanies of outbursts punctuated by the *ro* suffix with which Japanese men mark their linguistic territory.

'There they go. Fed for another day. Dunno how lucky they are, the half of them. Y'ever gone hungry, boy? Yes, you have, I can tell. You've got the eyes of a *kojiki*.'

'What's a *kojiki*, Yamato-san?'

Yamato was growing into the role of language teacher; he now understood that when I did not know a word, he had to engage in some pantomime, or search for simpler terms in which to explain it. Behind his sighing and eye-rolling, I could even sense that he enjoyed this process.

'Someone who has no home. Like a *yaken*.'

'What's a –'

'Bloody useless you are. *Yaken* is a lost dog. WANWAN! A hungry dog with no home. You get it now?'

And I would nod, pocketing the words. I have learned since that most people's word pockets have holes in them. Perhaps it was the age I was, but I only needed to hear a word once and it became mine for life. This did not, of course, help my reading and writing of Japanese. Like many an immigrant, I became fluent in the language as it was spoken by the workers, while remaining for a long time, near-illiterate, and baffled by the more elevated forms.

'Yes, you and I are scavengers both. I was your age when I first saw the sea. Mountain village boy I was. Ran away one night with just the clothes on my back. Turned up in

32

Yedo with nothing but my *kinniku* and my *atama*. And my son, of course.'

I no longer needed to see Yamato cup his own gleefully, to know that by *musuko*, he did not mean his son, but the slang for penis. The other words were new to me, however, and I asked him what they meant.

'These, boy' – his fingers squeezed my upper arm, now taut as a rope with new *kinniku* – muscle – 'and this' – he tapped my *atama*, signifying the brains inside. 'Yes, you and me both, we could handle a knife and we're smart, not like half these city kids. I picked up work in the fish market ...'

And so I learned, drip by drip over the weeks and months, both a language – at least in its oral form – and the story of Yamato's rise from penniless waif to Emperor of Eels, King of the Waterfront, Feeder of the Modern Nation, and – strangest of all – loyal acolyte of the Dragon King, Ryuo, to whom, on his monthly visits to the shrine atop the hill at Motomachi, he dedicated his prayers.

'The sea's been a father to me, boy. It was the sea that pulled me here, and the sea that looked after me. You know the story of Urashima Taro?' I did not, but I knew that I was going to hear it from Yamato's lips. Long ago, a young man called Urashima Taro had rescued a sea turtle from the attentions of cruel children, then ridden on its back under the green waves to the Dragon King's palace on the seabed. Here, he was rewarded with a feast and beguiled by the Princess. Two nights later he was returned to the surface, swam ashore and walked back to his village, only to discover that 50 years had passed, his parents were long dead, and he was an old man. Except this is not to do justice to Yamato's telling, the woebegone look in his eyes when he described Urashima's return – the way he gripped my arm, as tightly as if it were an eel for the block: 'The lesson is what, lad?'

What was it about me that drew these kinds of men

with their crazy lessons to find me? I had come from the Reverend Hare's parables to this. Out of the whale and into the stewpot, as Jonah would say.

'When you've escaped once, don't ever go back to where you came from!'

'Yes, Yamato-san,' I bobbed my head in the deferential bow which was fast becoming my habit.

*

I was not skilled, then, at distinguishing between white men. To me, they all resembled the Reverend Hare: tall, invariably moustachioed figures with noses as sharp as shark fins, and eyes that seemed sure of their right to shape the world. Whether it was into the shape of God or the Devil I still could not make up my mind. I could not bring myself to accept that our family's saviour had deliberately packed me off on a ship, hoping never to see me again. Even after I had verified beyond reasonable doubt that the College of Christ's Soldiers in the East did not exist, there was still a part of me that expected salvation to appear with a European face.

The other part was now sure that the Reverend was of Satan's party, disguised with Luciferian cunning in the garb of the holy. Either way, my experience had given me the conviction that the White Man held designs on me, and the hardest thing to face was that since arriving in Yokohama, neither The White Man, nor The White Woman, had given a hoot. Not a single one of the prosperous Europeans or Americans, who strutted about as if they owned the whole of Japan, and not just a tiny settlement on the coast, seemed to care about or even to see me. After my initial, futile enquiries after the college, I had not addressed any of them. Instead, I would follow, getting as close as I dared, seeking out groups of two or three, the more animated in conversation the better. From the start, I was amazed to find that I could pick out much of what they were saying. In that sense the Reverend had been authentic: the language he had spoken was undoubtedly the same that I heard from most – though not all – of the Europeans: the barbed and convoluted babble of English. And I was its master: I had the knowledge of it.

At first, I thought the dark-haired man with the moustache was one of the non-English speaking ones. He was taking an excessive interest in the process of eel cookery, watching Yamato turn the skewered fillets but without making any of the gestures to indicate he wanted one. Instead, endeavouring to look Yamato directly in the eye – never a good idea – he produced a series of foreign sounds. Yamato glared sideways at me: he knew by now that I understood the language most of the foreigners spoke. But I only shook my head as the customer repeated the same queer sounds that I knew were not English, but which did not sound like the nasal tones of French either. As he repeated the utterance with a hint of desperation, it dawned on me.

'He's trying to speak Japanese, Yamato-san. He's asking how much.'

'*Hai, hai,*' Yamato growled, as if he had understood this all along. Clearing his throat as if he were about to deliver Hamlet's soliloquy, he proclaimed the one English phrase he had committed to memory, '*Wan eeru huif-ti sen,*' which equates to 'One eel, fifty *sen,*' butchered by the Japanese accent.

The customer smiled, gave a miniature bow, and responded with a mispronounced *arigatou*. Yamato looked at me and hissed, 'Does he want the bastard eel or not?' I shrugged and continued filleting, secretly enjoying the comedy of it. The stranger continued to watch us with unnatural closeness, then jabbed a finger almost into the brazier itself, saying in Japanese, '*nani?*'

Yamato instinctively raised his skewer in self-defence. I

explained to him that the man wanted to know the Japanese word for eel, which I passed on to him. The customer repeated the word, *unagi*, as if he were tasting the real thing, then said, no doubt more to himself than to either of us, 'Have you never thought to put it in a pie?'

As Yamato's brow darkened further, I could not resist stepping in. I knew about pies as the Reverend Hare had instructed mother on the making of them.

'If you're in search of pies, Sir, there is an English bakery on Motomachi Street that does them.'

Now it was the customer's turn to be surprised. He had not expected to be understood, far less given a coherent and sensible reply by a chopping boy. But he recovered his poise quickly.

'Oh, I know. I have two friends who are never out of that place. Personally, I should far rather try the local specialities.' Turning back to Yamato he said 'Two,' this time mercifully raising the right number of fingers to confirm his order. My master obliged, grudgingly, and when the transaction was complete and this strange fellow finally turned his back on us, he turned the vicious side of his tongue on me, as if I were to blame for the awkward situation in which he had found himself.

Seven

The next day the odd gentleman was back, but earlier, while we were busy preparing for the midday rush. While he waited for Yamato to fry his portion, I could feel his eyes pouring over everything: my working of the blade; the eels writhing in the tub; the charcoal glowing in the brazier. It was as if he hungered, not for a length of flavoursome eel, but the knowledge of our trade itself.

The day after that, along with the two bronze five *sen* coins, he handed Yamato a rolled sheaf of paper. Protesting, Yamato tried to return it, but he had already turned on his heel and was striding off behind a cart loaded with bundles of silk. Muttering, 'crazy foreigners,' Yamato tossed the roll down behind our stall, indifferent to what it was or whether oil spattered it. When we were done cleaning up, I asked him if I could see it and at Yamato's nod I rolled the paper flat on the hot, hard stone of the quayside.

At first glance it was nothing but a tangle of black marks, like a mass of complicated *kanji* characters, but on closer inspection they fused together to depict Yamato and I at work. The first sketch showed us from close up, concentration etched on my face as I raised the knife to behead another poor impaled eel; Yamato with his brush, applying his soy glaze to the fillets. The other sheet showed us from a distance, an alchemy of quick charcoal strokes which came together to form an impression of us at work, backgrounded by the sun-bleached side of warehouse number three. I looked up to gauge Yamato's reaction. He was scowling down at the paper, as if it were an abusive letter complaining about the quality of his batter or the size of his fillets.

'Foreign artists,' he spat. 'Could do better myself.'

'Can I keep it?'

He snorted. 'Wipe your arse with it if you like, or I'll use it to light the coals tomorrow.'

I took the sketches back to my lodgings, another new possession to add to my scant collection. There was a shop where all the dock workers purchased their clothes, where I had bought an overshirt to change into after work, out of my vest, which rinsing in the ocean never really cured of the stink of eel guts. In the same shop I had bought a pair of sandals made out of bamboo fibre, so now all of my good clothes – the suit and the leather shoes which the Reverend Hare had bought me in Busan – stayed in the lodging house, wrapped in a bundle on my futon. My most precious possessions – my copy of *Treasure Island*, my notebook, and a letter from Yoona in her still uncertain Hangul script, were placed underneath the mattress. It was to this collection that I added the artist's unsolicited gift.

*

I was visited by a recurring nightmare in those days and weeks: I was swimming in an enclosed pool with others who slithered and writhed against me. Repulsed by them I tried to escape, but I could not surmount the vertical edges of the pool: a hand always reached in, wiry fingers tightening round me, plucking me out, slapping me down on a hard surface where white sunlight dazzled me. A human form loomed over me, a glint of something in its hand, then the awareness that one part of my body had just been severed from the other. I would wake up, then, in the stifling heat, gulping stale air, tasting the blessed relief of being all in one piece; a feeling immediately tempered by the fetid odour of too many men sleeping too close together. I would wriggle my body free of the sweat-soaked sheet and sit up to pray for God to protect Mother and Yoona, Korea, and myself. I asked Him to forgive me for butchering the eels, and to take pity on their serpentine souls.

Each afternoon I would return to the lodging house after another hard day, the endless chopping guaranteed to infect my dreams. Always the same route: leaving the waterfront behind and onto the Motomachi road that ran beside a little creek. To my right, across the stream of brownish water, stood the narrow precincts of Chinatown, with the vermillion temple rising above the darker roofs of the houses. To my left, the light-coloured European villas clustered up the bluff, the rocky outcrop overlooking the bay. The bluff side of the street was lined with tailors, cobblers, bakeries; all sorts of shops catering to Western tastes. Up the creek banks, Chinese children scampered through the long grass, crying out in their singsong tongue. I recognised the game of bandits against soldiers they played; their ferocity in these mock battles belonging to the childhood I had left behind in another country. Soon I would turn right, cross a bridge and through the gate into Chinatown, past the temple with stalls clustered in front of it selling amulets and bracelets for good luck, then left along a street of rough wooden two-storey houses, of which the third, after a laundry, had the Chinese characters for a boarding house painted above its entrance.

At that time in the afternoon Miss Miura would usually be sitting in the alcove behind the arm-waving cat on the wooden counter. She knew that when I came in I liked to go upstairs to the bathroom to wash – I would fill a zinc basin with water that ran at a trickle from the tap, then strip naked, using my soap sparingly to clean my body. Dried and changed, I would then go to rest a while on my futon, before coming down to the common room to eat. Usually it would be only me and a couple of the Chinese men, most of them having gone out to eat somewhere else. I would sit alone at one of the two long low tables with a newspaper and a notebook, and if she had time, Miss Miura would tell me the meaning of the *kanji* characters which I would copy into my notebook, using Japanese if we both knew the word, or gestures if we did not. It was a haphazard method at best – sometimes the characters I copied were obscure, and she tried to teach me what she thought were more useful ones. Once, as a surprise, she made me *tteok guk*, the broth that we Koreans eat at New Year. I remember her kneeling beside me, beaming after she had placed the bowl down in front of me on the table, waiting to see my reaction. I was to tell her, she said, if it was the way my mother made it, and if not, she would make it right the next time. The Chinese workers in the room feigned outrage at the favourable treatment I was receiving, and I felt embarrassed, though I attempted a smile at the same time as chewing a hunk off the disc of sticky rice cake. The glutinous mass resisted separation, stretching out between my teeth and the chopsticks which held it. Miss Miura had made a very good *tteok guk*, but it was not like Mother's, and early summer was a strange time to be eating our New Year dish. Remembering all those New Years at home made tears well up behind my eyes, and I was grateful for the steam rising off the broth that gave me an excuse for blinking them away. Instead of feeling gratitude, I am sorry to say that I resented Miss Miura, and only muttered a desultory thanks, scant acknowledgment for her efforts. Yet I am sure she would not have held it against me, understanding my desperate loneliness, against which I thought my best defences were my dog-eared copy of *Treasure Island* and my precious notebook.

Still, if I were to give advice to any young person finding themselves alone in a foreign country, I would say that the friendship of an elderly landlady is good for you, only in small doses. Do not refuse its offer, but believe me, you are better off in the evenings to venture outside. I would put on my smart suit and leather shoes, as if I were an apprentice pastor going out to study. In reality, although I walked with purposeful strides, I had nowhere to go other than up and down the waterfront as the evening cooled. Yet, probably because I had a bed to go back to, I liked this time. I liked how the water gained a translucent shimmer as the sun sank and the light made everything appear sharper and more defined. On these aimless walks, I would observe the boats moored in the bay, whose comings and goings I had begun to keep careful track of. There was a practical purpose to this, or at least I told myself there was: I had begun to consider the possibility of a boat as my escape route, not to return to Korea, but for embarking on a life at sea. In fact, the more I thought about it, the more it seemed the logical thing for me to do.

At sea, my rootlessness, my hybrid identity, would be an asset rather than a handicap. I was not so naive: I knew that real seagoing would not involve following secret charts to buried chests of treasure. I was gathering information about the different types of craft, learning to distinguish whalers with their high foredecks for the harpooner; the fast three-masted clippers that carried cargos of silk and tea; the low, metal-hulled gunboats waving a dance of flags between their funnels. Of these, it was on a whaling ship that I saw myself. I had an idea that my route onto one would involve befriending some of the sailors who came ashore in raucous gangs, staggering into and out of the bars of Bloodtown, singing songs whose meaning I could only catch in snatches. On such a ship, out on the open ocean, I would truly detach myself from the past. I knew it made sense, yet I was held back by the thought that if I took to the sea I would be throwing myself afresh into the unknown, potentially at the mercy of men like those who had parted the Reverend Hare from four of his teeth.

These were the conflicting thoughts I wrestled with, and usually, by the end of my evening stroll, I had convinced myself that the sea was where my future lay. But then, the next day, as I walked home from work with the coins from Yamato tight in my pocket, my mind would veer in the opposite direction. I would gaze upwards at the clouds stretching across the sky like tendrils of egg white in boiling water towards the line of purple hills on the horizon, and think Japan was offering itself to me as a land I might one day call home. That day beside the creek I was thinking exactly these thoughts, when I heard a voice at my shoulder that startled me out of my reverie.

'Hullo there, remember me?'

I veered to the side, convinced that I was going to turn around and find the Reverend Hare had come for me. But though the accent was similar, it was not my adoptive father. It was the moustachioed artist, his eyes glittering with friendly interest. He wore a loose red shirt spattered with paint, the sleeves rolled up to his elbows. Under one arm he carried his folded easel; over the other shoulder he had a canvas bag out of which poked rolls of paper like the one he had presented to us. My brain struggled to formulate a reply, and I could produce only the one word: 'Yes.'

Unperturbed, he fell into step beside me and began to talk.

'That eel of yours tastes divine – I hope the old man pays you well. If not, you'd probably prefer to be tipped the old-fashioned way. Just my bad habit to use these,' he pulled a few paintbrushes out of a pocket of his shirt, waving them under my nose as if I had asked for proof. The brushes were slim, far more delicate than the one Yamato used to daub our fillets with soy before plunging them into the batter.

'You understand everything I say, don't you?' I nodded again. He let out a whistle to express his admiration. 'Been trying to learn Japanese myself. Bloody impossible. I'm too old, I think.'

'Anyone can learn,' I said. As soon as I had spoken, I

held my breath. I had never contradicted the Reverend Hare without being rebuked. But I need not have worried: he was curious, intrigued.

'How?'

'I listen to Yamato-san all day.'

'Yamato-san – he would be your boss?'

I nodded.

'So, you are not Japanese yourself?'

I shook my head. 'I am Korean.'

He raised an eyebrow. 'Korea. Would you believe it, I've made it to 30 and never met a Korean. You're my first! I'm Archie Nith, from Scotland.'

I had shaken the hand he offered, and was about to tell him my name, but at the mention of Scotland I broke free of his grasp. 'The Reverend Hare's country!' The words were out before I could stop them.

He laughed. 'The Reverend Hare! Who's that?'

'My second father,' I replied, the answer I had long since learned to give to other children in the village.

'Well if that's not an answer to demand another question I don't know what is.'

I said nothing. We had come to the wooden bridge across the creek that would take me into Chinatown. I knew that he would be heading in the other direction, up the hill to the European houses. We stood facing one another, each filmed in sweat, our clothes dirtied by the work we did.

'I still don't know your name,' Nith said.

I told him, and we shook for the second time. I was prepared for the moment when this man too would turn his back on me, and I would be alone again.

Then he said: 'Han, the feeling I have with you is almost uncanny. I can only describe it as a sense that destiny, fate,

43

call it what you like, has drawn us together.'

Two emotions were competing within me. On the one, hand I was unwilling to trust a man from Scotland again, after the Reverend Hare's betrayal. On the other, I knew that he was right. Whether I liked it or not, I had a connection to him: we were both outsiders in Japan, and I sensed that he wanted to help me.

He took me to the house they rented, on a lane leading up the hill, backing onto the Westerners' burial ground. It was half hidden from the lane by a low, stone wall made higher by a bamboo trellis. You entered through a wooden gate set into this wall, over which the bamboo curved in an arch. Now you found yourself in a small garden: a lawn, dwarf pines, a maple tree, flat moss-covered stones leading up to a door in the European style with the number 38 on the front in shining brass. The walls of the house were made of white-painted wooden slats. The roof was gently sloping, with red-brown tiles, ridged along the centre and jutting out at each corner. Because it was built on a hill, on the seaward side the land dropped away, and two thick wooden corner posts supported a veranda. At the back was a narrow strip of well-tended lawn, then a bed of flowering plants. A stone wall separated the house from the graveyard, and high fences of bamboo hid it from the neighbouring houses up and down the slope. It was a little world all in itself, a dream of privacy and seclusion the likes of which I had never imagined.

'And now I'll show you inside,' said Nith, once the tour of the garden was complete. 'Then you can decide if you want to buy us out or not.' It took me a few seconds to realise he was joking. I had a few *sen* from that day's wages burning a hole in my pocket, and my meagre savings stuffed into the lining of my mattress at the lodging house. He must have seen the dismay on my face because he patted my shoulder before opening the door to reveal a low entrance then a step up to a darkened hallway.

'Here we are. Home, boys!' he yelled. 'As you'll see, we live Japanese style,' he bent to remove his shoes, indicating to me a row of slippers tucked under the step. A voice answered from another room – I couldn't catch what it said. Suddenly a lightning streak of white darted past our ankles and out into the garden. 'Tsuki! Tsuki! Empress! Oh, suit yourself. Drat these slippers, why are they always the wrong way round!'

The artists' house had a Japanese-style interior. There was *tatami* matting on the floors, thin walls of wood up to knee height, then rice paper fitted between a framework of wooden slats. The doors slid open and shut along smooth grooves. Nith unslid one on the left at the end of the hallway and I followed him, flapping in a borrowed pair of house slippers into the room. I was frozen in my tracks by a glare that told me I was about as welcome as a cholera-carrying rat in a restaurant kitchen.

'The only creatures I hate more than children,' growled the glarer, standing just to the side of an easel, 'are adolescent boys. You'd better have a bloody good reason for bringing him here, Nithy.'

Another voice, softened by amusement, cut in: 'Don't worry about Auld Horney, lad. He's just having a spot of geisha trouble.' My gaze flicked across to its owner, also behind a wooden frame, slighter of build and altogether less threatening. The first man retorted with an oath I had heard the Reverend Hare mutter when he had cut himself or banged his leg or encountered someone he hated. Whether it was directed to me, or the other painter, I did not know. I looked over my shoulder for support and found Nith right behind me.

'Meet Han, boys. Linguistic genius who chops eels for a living. Han, meet the two finest, dandiest painters this side of Montmartre.'

'George Henry. Pleased to meet you, Han.' The painter on the left came forward, light on his stocking feet, a twinkle in his eye, and shook my hand. As he did so, he cocked his head at the other painter, who did not acknowledge me but continued scowling, stabbing ferociously at the canvas with his brush. 'That's Edward Hornel, or to give him his proper title, Auld Horney, or just Horney for short. We suffer him because, despite appearances, he's game for a laugh. And he knows more stories about beasties and bogles than pretty much anyone on God's earth.'

I nodded. Horney seemed unimpressed by this description, but Henry carried on regardless. 'And what's Archie been telling you about us? All scurrilous lies, I'm sure. You'd be better off asking him what he's doing hanging about with eel salesmen like yourself when he should be busy painting perfect geishas like the pair of us.'

I had the sense they were picking up an argument that had been going on for some time, the nature of which I couldn't hope to understand.

'I'd like to think I could find prettier ones than you two,' Nith joked. 'But I'm starting to think there's as much of Japan in the sweat off an eel seller's brow as there is in those damn geishas.'

'That may be so, Archie, but not the Japan Alec Reid wants. Now sit down, Han,' Henry urged me to the floor. 'We're going to do what we call 'acting like the natives', and partake of a cup of tea in the torture position. Kettle on, Horney, I believe it's your turn.'

From my low vantage point I looked up at the purple-faced Hornel who fumed at Henry, hurled his brush against the wall and stalked out without giving me a second glance. Nith also left the room 'to refresh himself', and, at Henry's invitation, I watched him decorate a geisha's kimono with red-petalled flowers. In a soothing, humorous voice, he told me a little about the process of oil painting – how you had to lighten and darken your colour to show the tiny variations of light and shade caused by the human form under the fabric. I was absorbed, and hardly noticed the time pass before Hornel returned with a tray bearing a teapot and four black lacquer cups decorated with gold leaf patterns. He set it gently on the floor before easing himself down after it with a grunt. Nith came back in wearing a clean white shirt.

'Looks like tea is served,' Henry said. 'Let's take our well-earned break from these blooms.'

'Well, have you discovered the linguistic genius's secret?' Hornel said to Henry.

'I learnt English from Mister Robert Louis Stevenson,' I added, coolly, if not quite truthfully.

Horney's ruddy and habitually frowning face cracked into a rare smile.

'Well, well. A Japanese lad with a Scottish accent. Wonders never cease.'

'He's not Japanese,' Nith anticipated me. 'He's Korean.'

'Of course, he is. My apologies.'

Henry's turn: 'So tell us, Han. How does a Korean brought up on Stevenson end up selling eel in Yokohama?'

I told them, leaving little out except the parts where I was miserable and missed Mother and Yoona. It was not difficult: all I had to do was cast it as an adventure, like *Treasure Island*. Except, I realised, when I ended, long after Henry and Hornel had given up sitting cross-legged and taken to the divan, where they were joined by the returning cat, my story was only half way through. It was waiting for me to find my fortune and return to rescue Mother and Yoona from the treacherous Reverend Hare.

After eating with the painters, I strolled back down the hill to the lodging house under a crescent moon, a swagger in my step, carrying a volume of stories which Nith had assured me would keep me entertained. Arthur Conan Doyle – I had never heard the name. But it was telling my own story, or a version of it that pleased me, which had bolstered my confidence. Part of this was linguistic: in English, even more than in my mother tongue, I was able to express myself like a man. I had enthralled them with my tale, and even made them laugh with my impressions of the Reverend Hare's homilies and Yamato's fits of Japanese cursing. They had expressed wonder at my capacity for learning 'the language of our hosts' – as Henry kept calling it. Nith took great delight in explaining to me how they had been in Japan since April, in which time Henry and Hornel had picked up about a dozen words between them – 'and all of those mispronounced'. I smiled, recalling Horney's retort: 'Your problem, Archie, is that while you may be able to make the odd remark, you rarely seem to understand the answer.' As the three of them chuckled, Henry had then related an incident in which Nith had attempted to try out his Japanese while they were being shown around the shop of a local silk dealer. Nith had been convinced the man had asked if he wanted to buy anything. 'Only,' said Hornel, 'he had confused the word for "buy" with the one for "return". What the dealer had actually asked him was when we would return to our own country – to which he' – Horney pointed a finger at Nith who was smiling and shaking his head, 'replied that we couldn't as we hadn't brought our money with us. You can imagine what the poor fellow was thinking: "Good God, here we are landed with three Glasgow beggars who can't even afford their passage home!"'

'Horney's being a bit cruel,' said Henry, 'Archie did half redeem himself by understanding that the chap then very politely suggested we could sell some of our paintings.'

Hornel's grin grew even wider: 'To which he replied that we would sell them when we're back in Scotland.'

Nith seemed to enjoy the story even as it poked fun at him, and I would come to realise that the painters often talked to each other in this bantering style.

*

Sharing my living quarters with the Chinese men, and working with Yamato, whose words I was always concentrating to catch, I had forgotten the simple joy of taking part in a conversation without effort. I imagine it is like this for a master musician who has not played their instrument for a long time. Picking it up again, you are first astonished, then delighted, by the return of a voice you had almost forgotten you possessed. English felt as natural as a native tongue for me, though I did not like to think this was a measure of how much the Reverend Hare had succeeded in effacing my Korean soul. Once I met the artists, I was content to exist using only English and Japanese, with the consequence that I also began to think in these tongues, and less and less in Korean. In fact, amongst the babel of voices in the Yokohama of my first months, I did hear Korean spoken, not frequently, but often enough to make it unremarkable. And yet, I never approached the speakers and introduced myself as a compatriot. Why was this? I think the reason is that I felt, in some part of myself, that I was not a real Korean. This caused me to feel a strange mixture of shame and pride: there was a part of me that wanted to stand unique and separate, that did not want to become an ordinary member of a mass of immigrants from Japan's nearest neighbour.

But I knew even then that my gifts were a double-edged sword. Though they set me apart from other Koreans, most light-skinned people looked at me and saw only the characteristics of a race to whom they felt superior. I belonged nowhere. Crossing the bridge from Motomachi into Chinatown, I would often pause on the middle of it and look down into the water. I began to identify with that creek dividing the European and Asian parts of town, a mingling of influences flowing muddy and indistinct out into the waters of the harbour.

Eight

'Samoa!?'

'Aye, Han. A king, they say.'

'Does he still ...'

'Concoct his tales? Oh yes, I don't suppose he can stop now. Though they say it'll kill him in the end. He always was a sickly, slippery sort of a fellow. Spent a lifetime dabbling in ways to cure himself. I'm sure that's where Jekyll and Hyde came from ...'

I had devoured the volume of stories Nith had given me, all of which featured the enigmatic detective, Sherlock Holmes. Much as I admired the ingenuity of Conan Doyle's plots, Stevenson was my first love, and I had asked Nith if he had never turned his hand to the topic of crime-solving. Nith told me that the closest he thought RLS had come was the *Strange Case of Doctor Jekyll and Mister Hyde.* He did not have a copy with him, unfortunately, but he assured me it was a lurid piece of work published to get Stevenson out of financial troubles; my hero's true forte was travel and adventure, and he lived by these rules as well.

'Where is Samoa?' I pressed Nith.

'Somewhere in the South Seas, I believe. Why, are you thinking of seeking him out? Don't! In the stories – that's where you'll find him. No good ever came from meeting your heroes. He's probably an arrogant ass, puffed up on his own mythology. And too busy scratching away with the pen to chat to you.'

'Have you met him?'

'Not I, Han, No. Once, I made the mistake of encountering a certain James McNeil Whistler. This was in Paris … but enough. Tell me about the charcoal. Where does your Yamato-san acquire it?'

It was about a week after our meeting by the creek, and the second time I had met him since then. The other was an evening stroll along the waterfront, arranged in a brief conversation as he bought his lunch from the stall. Yamato had been suspicious after the unwanted gift. I had told him Nith had merely been asking what we had thought of the sketch, to which I had responded we would prefer our next tip in cash. Something told me that Yamato's dislike of Nith was such that if he knew I was meeting him, I might be in danger of losing my job.

That Sunday we had arranged to meet at the bridge. From there, we had walked up the Hundred Steps that led up the steep slope of the bluff, away from the shops of Motomachi and the cramped roofs of Chinatown. After a brief look at the shrine at the top, we had gone into one of the teahouses beside it. From the garden you could see right out to the West and the hills of Kanagawa. Peeking up beyond them, as improbable as a white rabbit from an illusionist's hat, was the snowy cone of Mount Fuji.

A slight breeze countered the humid afternoon heat. Wooden tables had been set up outside between pine trees whose needles scattered the ground. In the other direction sails sparkled in the sunlight out in the bay. The trilling of cicadas surrounded us. We sat opposite one another, sharing a pot of cool green tea poured by a Japanese teahouse girl. On my day off, my work with Yamato seemed a distant memory. I had paid 30 *sen* that morning to visit a public bath, and probably only carried the faintest whiff of eel juices.

Nith seemed to enjoy just listening to me talk, and so I found myself recounting the time Yamato persuaded me to give up my day off to earn an extra *yen* going with him on the charcoal run. We had pushed the cart covered in empty sacks miles inland along the Tokyo Road. The route was lined with blacksmiths, timber merchants, tailors, teahouses, temples and the practices of medical men. Small tracks branched off it with rough houses backing onto fields of rice, cabbages and *daikon* radishes. Some, Yamato told me, led to the grand residences of illustrious Lords who still employed samurai to protect them. The road was always busy with a steady stream of travellers on foot or in the saddle, heavily loaded carts coming to and from the port. In several places, workers were hacking away vegetation or filling in ditches to widen the road further. We had turned up one of those lanes branching off, and I realised how the port and settlement of Yokohama was a world apart. These dusty tracks between wooden shacks with fields behind them were not so different from Korea. No wonder the Japanese were so busy lining their coasts with cities full of high buildings and bridges. They did not want foreigners to know that just a few miles away, the interior was still a land of peasants. Yamato went up to the door of a house and knocked. A woman appeared and when he talked to her she directed us round the side where charcoal was piled up under a rickety shelter. I was instructed to load the sacks while Yamato bartered and paid. When they were as bulging full as they could be, we returned to Yokohama with them piled on top of the cart.

Nith was intrigued by every detail of this: 'This charcoal seller. She sounds promising – perhaps I should paint her. Han, you wouldn't happen to know a fellow called Jules Bastien Lepage, would you?'

I pronounced back the name to him as best I could.

'No, I do not know him,' I said, after considering all I had learned in books and classrooms about the history of the world. Nith chuckled and I began to feel a little annoyed with him. I had had enough of the feeling of being toyed with by white men.

'I'm sorry, you wouldn't have. Lepage is an artist like me, someone who has a clear idea of what we should do. He thinks our role is to paint common folk going about their jobs, like your charcoal seller,' he paused. 'I believe everyone, at a certain time in their development, needs someone to act as a guiding light, the person we wish to emulate. You have a gift for narrative, you know. If you were to write, I imagine yours would be a certain Scottish exile living in Samoa.'

It had never occurred to me that I might wish to try my hand at writing. In truth, the idea did not displease me, but I resented Nith for presuming that my hero would be one of his countrymen.

'My hero is Yi Sun Shin,' I said, feeling a wave of patriotic emotion rising from my throat into the well of tears behind my eyes.

'A Korean author?'

I don't think he expected me to recount with quite as much fervour the exploits of the greatest naval commander in the history of the world. Like every Korean, I had grown up hearing tales of Admiral Yi. Mother used to tell me about his legendary victories over the Japanese, for which he was never adequately recognised until after his death. I quoted what he had said before he died: '"The battle still rages. Bang my war drums. Do not announce my death."'

Nith, after hearing me out and expressing sufficient admiration, returned to his own theme.

'Well, Han, as Admiral Yi is to you, Bastien Lepage is to me. To us, I should say.'

'He is the hero of Scottish people?'

'No. Or only a small portion of them. He is an artist. A Frenchman, in fact and not the most famous. But he set out, by his example, a path for us to follow.'

A rhinoceros beetle had alighted on the trunk of the pine

tree next to our table, as if in answer to my invocation of General Yi. Nith went on: 'When you are a painter, you see, the greatest question, before you come to any matters of technique is simply, what shall I paint? Because if you think about it, there's a choice as terrifyingly great in number as the celestial bodies in the sky, or grains of sand on a beach. Anything that exists can be painted. And not only that. Anything that has existed, Admiral Sunshine for example, of whom I did not even know until now – or anything that has been recounted in books of myth or religion, or even, in more recent times, works of fiction. I might even try to paint Stevenson's Hyde, whose face contains ineffable evils, monstrous beyond description. Do you follow what I'm saying, Han?' He ran his finger around the rim of his cup, eyeing me intently for my reaction. I nodded, though I was somewhat lost, more annoyed at his mispronunciation of the name of Yi Sun Shin. Out of the corner of my eye, I registered the rhinoceros beetle's continued sap-sucking on the pine. If only a stag beetle would turn up, I thought, then we might see a battle.

But Nith went on: 'For many centuries, in Western Art, at least, the answer was provided by religion. And what results it yielded! The great masterpieces of Italian painting were all from the Bible. And yet, if you see the works of Leonardo da Vinci, Michelangelo, Caravaggio, their fascination was less with there,' he pointed upwards at the sky, 'than with this,' he indicated my torso. 'The human form itself. Bone and sinew – man in action. If I could show you, Han, a certain Caravaggio picture, you would think Christ's hand was reaching out of the painting to touch you.' He took a breath, drawing in the threads of his argument. 'With enlightenment, religion gave way to history and myth, scenes from great battles. You have heard of Napoleon, the General who took the reins in France once the revolution turned into a bloodbath? A tiny man. But he had himself painted on a rearing horse crossing the Alps.

Which comes first? The hero or the hero's pose? The wee tyrant realised it might be the latter. All this time you see, Han, art has been in the service of religion or the rich and powerful. I haven't even mentioned the portraits the rich commission of themselves, in their finery. *That's* been the bread and butter of artists through the ages!'

Nith's rush of words washed over me like the tide over a beach. It was only a couple of years ago, when I picked up an English book about the history of art in a Yokohama bookshop, that all this came back to me. At that time, my exposure to art had been all but non-existent, and his lecture was mostly lost on me.

'So why, Han? Why is it ever thus?'

My attention had been distracted again, this time by the entry into the tea garden of a striking couple. They were both Westerners, but of a different, almost Asian complexion, with slender limbs and delicate features. Both were dressed elegantly, the man in a suit, the woman in a pale green gown. Arms entwined, they moved up the path between the tables like gods who had taken on human form for the day.

'Why do you not just paint beautiful things?' I asked.

Archie emitted a strangled moan, covered his eyes with his hands and let his face fall to the table. I ventured to check his condition with a hand on his shoulder, and he lifted his head. He was smiling broadly and I understood he had merely made a performance of his horror.

'Please, God, don't tell me Whistler's ten o'clock lecture has reached even here. You'll accuse me next of membership of a cult, of having a strange vocation for the unlovely! Simply because I choose to paint the folk, who through their toil and labour, make this modern world of ours possible.'

I had not the slightest idea what he was talking about, and to give him credit, he did belatedly realise this.

'Han, you must forgive me. I have come at this too

quickly I can see.'

At that moment the spirit of Admiral Yi chose to rescue us from the conversation. With a tremendous whirring the great beetle lifted itself into improbable flight. Its horn upright like a lightning rod, it hovered over our table for an instant before rising over the roof of the teahouse, disappearing in the direction of the faint bluish horizon of the hills to the West.

'Now that is a beauty!' Nith cried.

For the remainder of our talk I kept glancing at the cloth obscuring the entrance to the teahouse. The celestial pair must have decided to drink inside, however, and soon Archie decided it was time he ought to be returning to his canvas.

Nine

My solitary evening walks lengthened in the week following that encounter, their range extended to encounter the full gamut of Yokohama settlement life. I would trace the various roads over the bluff, past the foreigners' villas with their large windows revealing glimpses of electric-lit interiors. Sometimes music would drift out from them across the manicured lawns to my pricked and eager ears. Then an hour later, I would find myself wandering the maze of narrow streets between the wharves and Chinatown, the part of the port known as Bloodtown, where sailors spilled out of dozens of drinking dens. As I walked past these I peered in through the windows to observe what scenes of Luciferian iniquity were occurring within.

One evening I summoned the courage to enter a tavern myself. Imitating the man being served before me, I asked for a whisky. The tattooed Goliath of a barman eyed me doubtfully, then shrugged and poured some of the amber liquid into a glass. I paid and perched myself on a stool at one end of the bar, from where I could survey the room and remain unobtrusive. A crew of young sailors sat around and on top of a large table dominating the centre of the room. One of them, sitting near to me, was boasting about his expertise with the harpoon. His crewmate made a remark that I did not catch, but the whole group exploded with laughter, stomping their feet on the wooden boards and raising a din like the drums of hell. I was considering who looked the most approachable to ask about joining their boat, when a voice growled at my ear. The barman was pointing at my untouched glass: was his whisky not good enough for me?

I assured him I did not doubt the quality of his liquor, and to prove it, I attempted to take a long draft. My reaction – gagging, spluttering and almost falling off my stool – was sufficiently dramatic to draw the attention of the whole bar. The landlord's arm saved me from further shame, gripping my head like a vice, propelling me to the door and ejecting me into the night.

I remember all this not because the shame of it still nags me, but because it was the same evening, shortly afterwards, that I saw Yamato's former employee leaning back against the wall outside a different tavern. He caught me looking at him, and I braced myself to be recognised. Perhaps he would be out for revenge on me for me stealing his job. But he ignored me and turned to some sailors who had just piled out of the tavern – three tall, bearded Europeans to whom he addressed a sales pitch in garbled English. Going up to them, he extracted a curious object from a cloth bag hanging over his shoulder. It was a ball, dark-brown in colour, that looked like nothing so much as a piece of animal dung. I watched from the shadows as the sailors, after the inevitable mockery of his accent, inspected the merchandise. One of them did this by sniffing the ball, licking his finger, rubbing it on the brown surface, then licking again. This test evidently produced positive results, for the sailor nodded at his crewmates and pronounced it 'proper dope'. He then enquired after the price, a question which even my predecessor understood, quoting them a figure that almost made me blow my cover by bursting into laughter. It would have been enough to purchase all the portions of eel we sold in a day, and I was hardly surprised when one of the men grabbed him by his shirt collar and thrust him against the wall. I feared I was about to witness another act of violence against this boy, when he piped up in English:

'I am agent of Jardine Matheson Company.'

This produced a remarkable effect upon the men. The

boy was released and given an exaggerated apology. Coins were handed over without further haggling and the men left in possession of their ball of dung. I followed them for a short distance until they entered another bar, then turned and retraced my steps to pass my predecessor one more time. He was still leaning against the wall outside the tavern, and I was able to confirm something else: he was still short of a finger on his chopping hand. Whatever surgeon the English officers had taken him to had been unable to perform the operation of reattachment. But did this matter, when he could make a whole five *yen* from selling what looked like a lump of animal dung?

Thoughts of this, and the beautiful woman I had seen in the teahouse, distracted me at work for days afterwards.

'What's wrong with you, boy? You're chopping eels not combing your little sister's hair. *Kono touri*! Like this!' Yamato snatched the poor writhing sea-worm from my grasp, slammed it down and filleted it himself with a speed and deftness that I could not hope to match.

'Sorry, Yamato-san. My mind is on a different page.'

'*Ja*, get it back on this one quick! Or your body might as well join it.'

He could be sharp, could Yamato. But as I have hinted, he had grown rather affectionate towards me. As we loaded up the cart that day, he spoke to me as tenderly as he knew how.

'Missing home, are you? I remember it. Every day, work, eat, shit, sleep. That's it. In here,' he prodded my chest, then said something which I hardly understood. He picked up the knife, 'It's like this,' running his finger along the blade, 'when it loses its edge, what do we do? We sharpen it. But how? Three things, boy. Three things guaranteed to sharpen a working man's soul. It took me years to find out but I'll save you the time. Can you guess?'

In a flash of inspiration, I wondered if Yamato could be

60

talking about the things I had seen for sale outside the bar – for that price sharpening a soul seemed a fair expectation.

'Little brown balls? What foreign rubbish are you talking about?' he placed a greasy hand on my cheek and stared at me, as if he were trying to use his eyes to draw out of my soul whatever it had been poisoned with. 'Three things. One: the *kabuki* – to be entertained. Two: the brothel, to be … but I suppose you have never known a woman before?'

I stammered out something about my mother, and my aunt who sometimes came to stay.

'Seen one naked?'

My mind clutched at an image I had coveted for years; the time I saw, through a gap in the wooden slats in the side of the village bathhouse, one of the girls my age, Jaewon, as she washed herself.

'I have,' I replied.

'But you didn't touch, did you?'

I confessed that I had not.

'But I suppose like all boys you touch yourself, am I right? *Koko*?' To my shock, Yamato clamped a hand over my private parts and squeezed. He was right of course, except that since that day in the teahouse garden, I had resisted the urge to do so under the covers at night, using a rag to absorb the spurt of my juices. All while God watched, totting up another sin, and my Chinese roommates snored or passed the hours playing *Go*. 'Some youngsters use drawings to help them. Or you can get dirty photos for a pretty penny. But far better the real thing. If you want I'll show you the ropes. How about it? The day after tomorrow we'll see the *kabuki*, then go to the Persimmon together, you and I?'

Dimly understanding what he might mean, I indicated my willingness, sputtering out the words like the rusty tap in the lodging house washroom. He was pleased, and for the rest of that shift he allowed me to handle the eels in the batter, only mildly critiquing my work while he did the chopping himself.

'What's the third thing?' I remembered as we cleaned up.

'We'll round the night off the way I always do, with a visit to the temple to pray to the Dragon King, Ryuo'. He smiled as if this was the very treat any boy in my position would have dreamed of.

Walking back to the lodging house through streets bedecked with lanterns in preparation for the *Obon* festival, I imagined my future under Yamato's guidance: a life spent preparing eels to be cooked, the urges of my body sated by visits to this mysterious Persimmon, those of my spirit by worshipping a mythical sea dragon. It was a far cry from my conversations with Nith, and the pages of my evening reading, featuring the rational deductions of my new favourite hero, Sherlock Holmes.

Talking of Sherlock, I understand that certain readers – if any there are – may be growing frustrated with the form in which I have constructed this tale, and which I fear it is now too late to change. I am well aware that I have wilfully set up the expectation of a narrative about an artist who disappeared and a young woman who was drowned. Since doing so, I have talked almost entirely about myself, recounting events which have no bearing on what happened to Archie Nith or Tsubaki. For this, please imagine me offering a deep bow of apology. And now, allow me to make some promises. Firstly, that my voice is soon to be replaced for a while, by that of Archie Nith himself. Secondly, that the events still to be recounted by me in this section of the narrative do bear a direct relation to the case. They tell of the final night on which Tsubaki was breathing on this earth.

Ten

It was that time the painters love when the light softens and all the edges sharpen in readiness for evening. We had made good business, and Yamato, who I had once thought only a boss and a mean one at that, had treated me to a bonus bag of dried squid from a rival vendor. He pulled the cart while I chewed the fibrous lengths through busy streets to where he lived in the fishing port of Noge, at the mouth of the Tsurumi River. I had never seen so many Japanese people thronging the streets; there was hardly a white face or a letter of the European alphabet in sight.

Yamato rented the second floor of a wooden building on a street behind the main road leading away from the harbour. We left the cart in the space under the steps that led up to his door, and I helped him carry the things inside. It was dark at first, then my boss flicked on a gas lamp and I could see the palace of solitude to which he came home each day. A screen divided the single room into two parts: the half that I could see was used for cooking, eating, storing food and equipment; the other was hidden by the folding screen, behind which Yamato disappeared after he had lit the fire and put some water onto boil, telling me to wait while he washed and changed. I sat cross legged on the worn *tatami* matting, next to the square cooking pit. The pot with boiling water hung on a hook embedded in the ceiling. The air was heavy with woodsmoke, sweat, fermented soybeans and eel: the exact combination of scents which added up to the essence of Yamato.

Peering around one side of the screen, I could see, through the shadows, a roughly made altar against the wall.

63

A shelf divided it into two levels; on the lower was a block of wood inscribed with Japanese writing, surely a prayer. But it was the items resting on top of the shelf that surprised me: there was a hair ornament made of shimmering mother of pearl, and a carefully folded piece of patterned silk – one of the *obi* belts a Japanese woman would wear. Why would Yamato possess these women's items, I wondered? I slid on my backside nearer the screen to see better, but just as I was doing so, Yamato returned from the other side of the room, having changed out of his work clothes and into a dark blue, loose-sleeved *yukata*. I feared he would notice that I had been prying. He was more concerned, however, that the water was boiling and the rice had not been added. Correcting this, he then flung me another *yukata*, pointing to a basin of water and a bar of soap which I could use to wash myself.

'Have you heard of the *Chushingura*?' he growled when I had finished changing. We were kneeling on either side of the bubbling pot, and he had poured us each a cupful of clear sake. I sipped the alcohol warily at first, but it was far smoother than the whisky, stoking a pleasant warmth in my chest and a loosening of my tension.

'I haven't, *sensei*.'

'No good!' he snorted. 'You can't live in Japan and not know *Chushingura*. You'll always be a foreigner. You don't want that, do you?'

'No.'

'Course it won't happen overnight. Not like your first time with a woman. *Bushido*, boy. That's what *Chushingura* is about, but you'll see for yourself tonight.'

'What's *bushido*?'

A bark of laughter. 'Always the difficult questions from you. *Ja*, it's like this. Imagine you're a samurai. I'm your lord. You'll never leave me. You'll fight to the death for me.

And if someone kills me, what will you do?'

'Who would kill a man as kind as you, Yamato-san?'

'Lords always have enemies, even kind ones. But if you follow *bushido* you'll kill them for revenge, then kill yourself because you can no longer serve me.' He tapped my chest. '*Wakatta*?'

I told Yamato that I understood, privately thinking that this seemed to stretch the concept of loyalty beyond the bounds of reason.

We had two tickets for the evening performance at the theatre on Isezakicho Street. I had walked past it before, assuming it was some kind of temple: a two-storey structure of unpainted wood, with tiers of blue-tiled roof, the lower jutting out over steps that led up from the street. Hawkers clustered round them, thrusting and shouting: 'Tickets!', 'Fans!', 'Prints of the actors'. Yamato sliced a path through them and up into the building. We showed our pre-bought tickets and were given pairs of slippers, placing our own footwear in a latticework of alcoves. Then we walked into the buzzing auditorium, already crowded with spectators sitting in rows on the *tatami* mats, some buying food or drinks from a counter on one side. At the front was a raised stage with a painted backdrop showing a forest and a night sky with a full moon. As we took our seats behind some girls in bright summer *yukatas*, I could sense the anticipation for the performance that was about to begin.

The lights went down, an old man shuffled onto the stage, carrying a bag of money. He made a short speech which I could only half understand, then in the shadows to the side, a lantern illuminated an evil-looking fellow whose eyes were outlined in red make-up. This fiend forced the audience into silent complicity as he crept up behind the old man and swished his sword through the air. The old man fell with a thin death cry, then the murderer relieved him of his money, making a speech glorying in his crime. My attention was drawn to the group of young women in front of us, most of them waving white handkerchiefs, keening out squeals of appreciation for the charismatic actor who played the villain. He had come to the very front of the stage, almost within their reach, and was saying that with this money he might go on the straight and narrow, all he needed was to find an honest woman to cook and keep house for him. Casting his eyes over the fluttering handkerchiefs, he then looked up at the rest of the audience and said with exaggerated wickedness, 'Looks as if I won't find any like that here!' Yamato, and most of the audience, howled; the women screeched in mock indignation; except for one girl I noticed, whose hair was pulled into a bundle, held in place by a pin decorated with a red flower. It was not her costume, however, that drew me to her, but her expression: she seemed to radiate a smouldering bitterness; her eyes remained locked on the murderer as in a mournful voice, he declaimed: 'No, some people, like me, are not meant to settle down. We are born with evil ways and we must live with them. Mine is a life of robbing and killing, and that's it.'

At this point many things happened at once that I only understood when Yamato explained them later: a wild boar thundered, snorting across the stage, its speed enough to make you miss the actor's legs; at the same time another actor appeared in a pool of light on the far side of the stage, raised a weapon and fired. The murderer's hands flew to his chest, but a red stain was already spreading across his robe. His mouth opened and closed like a fish as he searched in vain for some final words. With an imploring look at the audience, he fell to the boards with a groan. I checked for the reaction of the girl. She was smiling – what a change in her face! – and I noticed that on her bare neck she had two freckles just below the ear.

At the interval, I went out to empty my bladder. Off a

corridor that ran beside the auditorium, a row of men stood against a wooden wall with a trough running at its foot. As I added to the communal stream of piss, my mind kept returning to the girl. I sensed that she was closer to me, both in age and status, than the vision in the teahouse, who I was beginning to doubt even existed outside my imagination. Picking my passage through the audience back to our place, I watched Yamato in conversation with the man next to him. My boss was sitting cross-legged in the glow of the ceiling lanterns, hands flat on his knees, sweat glistening on his grinning face. When I sat down again, he enquired how I was enjoying my first *kabuki*. He was pleased that I had many questions about the plot, which made more sense when he explained that the first four acts had been performed earlier in the day. At a certain point, noting that my attention was distracted, he followed the direction of my gaze. When he saw the girl I was looking at, I was sure that for a second his expression changed. Something akin to pain passed across his features, but he quickly disguised it as a laugh.

'Aha! I see what you're looking at. Never mind the *Chushingura*, Han's spotted a pretty piece that he likes. Can't wait, can you! But you might be in luck.' Before I could reply he had levered himself up and was walking towards the girl, who was sitting quite still, apparently oblivious to the chatter around her. I looked on in despair as Yamato squatted next to her, and with a wink back to me addressed her loudly enough for everyone around to hear. 'Oi, Tsubaki! My young friend over there is wondering if you are working later this evening?' I longed for the lights to go down and the actors to reappear. But it was as if Yamato had said nothing. The girl didn't even turn to face him, and he repeated himself, leaning closer to her, then when she still didn't answer he became rude. 'What's wrong with you, Tsubaki? Anyone would think you were the Empress, not just a Persimmon girl.'

At that point she did turn around, and I was surprised to see her face was composed; it seemed lit from within by a mysterious energy, like the electric lightbulbs in the lampposts on Bashamichi Street. Her voice, when she spoke, was husky, as if, like the Reverend Hare, she frequently inhaled smoke into her lungs.

'And you're just an old man who's going to be worm food while we're still painting our faces.'

She spoke loudly enough for everyone in the vicinity to hear, provoking a flurry of laughter.

Yamato rose to his feet, humiliated. He said something to her, I guessed an insult which I did not know. Sitting back down next to me he muttered darkly:

'Forget her. She'll get what's coming to her one day.'

When the play resumed, the backdrop had switched to a fashionable teahouse in Kyoto. The hero, Yuranosuke, had forgotten his loyalty to avenging his master. He was spending his days in dissolute fashion, drinking, gambling and going to the theatre. My mind began to wander ahead to the Persimmon, where Yamato was taking me after this, where this Tsubaki worked. Yamato was right. She did seem to carry herself like royalty, scorning the idea that Yamato was her equal. That must have hurt his pride! When I glanced sideways, he looked as engrossed as ever, his face creasing into laughter as the actors strutted and postured across the stage. Covertly, I checked for Tsubaki's reactions too. Her intense focus on the action never dropped. She seemed to take an especial pleasure in the scene where Yuranosuke and his band put his master's enemies to the sword, then at the bloody climax, where they disembowelled themselves before their trial, she wept.

I lost sight of the red flower on the back of her head as the crowds poured down the steps outside. Back out on the street, feeling almost Japanese in my *yukata* borrowed

68

from Yamato, I promised myself that I would speak to her at this Persimmon and see if I could win her over without his interference. It was a relief to be on our feet after sitting for so long with cramped limbs. The street thronged with people in bright *yukatas* walking under lanterns. We queued at a stall where Yamato bought us balls of grilled octopus.

'Now we give the orders, we are the masters,' he laughed, as we walked down the centre of the street, heading away from the sea. The octopus slipped down easily, even Yamato complimenting its flavour. The air was soft, the sky now dark, accentuating the lanterns glowing orange and yellow. Yamato's commentaries on the play were like the trilling of crickets, background noise. I was intensely aware of everything: the fine particles of dust floating up from the street, catching between my toes; the mingled odours of soy, horse dung, and the salty tang of the sea.

The Persimmon was set back from the road, with a small garden containing several of the fruit trees that gave the place its name. A row of red lanterns hung from the eaves at the front of the building. We accessed through a gate flanked by two guards, former samurai, Yamato warned me. 'Don't make them angry or they'll slice your belly open.' One of them scanned me head to toe, but grunted and let me through. We crossed the threshold, beside which a *tanuki* statue squatted - the Japanese raccoon, always depicted with swollen testicles. A thickly made-up woman wearing an expensive-looking *yukata* of black and embroidered gold emerged from the shadows and bowed deeply to us. Yamato spoke to her briefly, handed over money, then we were directed under a high beam, into the main room with its clamour of music and conversation.

My first thought was that it was another theatre. My eye was drawn to a raised stage in the centre, on which four girls performed, two of them plucking the strings of *samisens*, conjuring an eerie melody while the other two danced with sinuous, circular movements. Yamato requested a table in front of them. It was wise to admire the dancers, he remarked, as it would raise my anticipation of what was to come. While he ordered a vase of sake, I tore my eyes off them long enough to survey the rest of the room. It was an open, high-ceilinged space, with a gallery running around the sides half way up. This provided cover for partitioned niches on each side of the room, in which various groups of men, most of them Europeans, sat around low tables drinking and talking. The atmosphere was raucous, lubricated by alcohol. I had already sampled the delicate properties of sake before the *kabuki*, but now Yamato encouraged me to down the cup in a single gulp then slam it on the table as if I were severing an eel's head. I could not help but notice that from the moment he entered the Persimmon, Yamato acted with an exaggerated vigour, as if he, as well as the guards on the entrance, were a samurai. I think he wanted to remind the white men that he had as much right to use the place as they did; that they were the foreigners in his country and not the other way around. He talked continually in praise of Japanese culture and Japanese women in particular, although, he said, glaring at the group of sailors beside us, in recent years this had been diluted by foreign influence. 'Take the one playing the *samisen* there,' he indicated one of the girls plucking strings on the stage. 'She's no good. She can hardly play. But it doesn't matter to the foreigners. They don't even know what proper playing sounds like.'

This was unlike the terse back and forth Yamato and I would exchange at the eel cart. It was also unlike my conversations with Nith, in that the space for me to answer was limited, although even if it had been offered my mind was preoccupied. Now that we were in a place where the pleasures of the flesh could be obtained, all my interest in them had dissipated. I felt only a vague terror at the thought that I would shortly be expected to act my role in an unknown performance. Like millions before and after me, I diluted my fear in alcohol to the point where Yamato warned me to go easy, otherwise I would be at risk of 'putting my son to sleep before bedtime'.

A girl in a persimmon-patterned *yukata* appeared at our table. I thought she was there to offer us more sake, but then realised she was asking me to follow her. Yamato was grinning more like a devil than ever, urging me on. I hauled myself up. The room was swaying like the deck of a ship in a high swell. Reminding myself of Jim Hawkins' example, I steered a course between the tables, following the lighthouse beams of the fruits on the girl's *yukata* to the stairs leading up to the gallery. Ascending them, a memory came to me of Yoona when she was very young, perhaps only four or five, and the Reverend Hare had made her a necklace from persimmon pips. This delighted my sister, and as she was showing it off to Mother he turned to me and said with a wink: 'After the Devil tempted Eve to eat the forbidden fruit, the next thing he told her to do was make hurrrself a necklace from the pips.' Angered by the recollection, I resolved to put him out of my mind and concentrate on the experience.

Up in the gallery, the noise from below was muted, as if I had somehow become submerged in water. The girl looked behind her and caught my eye, beckoning me onwards. I followed her past sliding doors covered by rice-paper decorated with various flowers. I did not realise at the time, but these were the flowers represented by each girl's name, names which they took on when they entered the Persimmon's service. Out of one door just ahead, a white paw emerged and a cat slipped into the passageway, entangling itself in the girl's legs. While she bent to stroke it, I stopped next to the room from which it had come. I could not help glancing in through the gap, and what, or rather *who* I saw made me certain I was dreaming. But it was only for an instant, then the girl reached out for my hand and pulled

71

me after her. She slid open the next door, decorated with a purple azalea, and led me into the room.

It was no more than six *tatami* mats, and contained only a large futon and a small dressing table with a bowl of persimmons. If she had not ordered me to lie down, I don't think I would have been capable of moving. I did exactly as she asked, letting my head sink back onto the pillow. Without wasting time, she slid the *yukata* back off her shoulders. I watched, transfixed, as it cascaded to the floor like the petals falling off a flower. My mouth had dried up; I gaped at the pale bulbs of her breasts and the dark hairs between her thighs. She knelt over me with a leg either side and undid my belt. My 'son' had taken on a life of his own and pressed against my underwear. She patted him playfully, telling me to wait as she caressed my bare chest. Suddenly she pressed her teeth around my nipple, sending a spasm of pain shooting through me. Laughing, she lifted the dead weight of my hand, sucked my fingers and pressed them to her breast. With the same swift sureness that I had learned to fillet eels, her other hand glided across my ribs down to where my son was now wholly dominating his father's thoughts. At a sign from her, I arched my back and wriggled out of my pants. She asked me in Japanese if it was my first time, and I nodded. She positioned herself carefully and began to move, while I lay still and enjoyed the delicious sensation of pleasure. All too soon, of course, it was over.

Suddenly remembering the girl with the red flower, I asked her what her name was.

'Tsutsumi.'

I told her my own name and she repeated it, probably amused, as a lot of Japanese people are, by its single-syllabled bluntness. I heard a rattling noise. Tsutsumi sprang to her feet and undid the latch on the window. The head of another cat poked in, this one black with a blotch of white across half of its face. It slipped into the room, arching its body against Tsutsumi's strokes while I retrieved my clothes and put them back on.

'I must go?' I said, meaning it half in the form of a question. I had no idea if I had used up all of the allotted time or not. Tsutsumi nodded, but seeing my downcast expression, she bent forward and kissed me lightly on the cheek. I turned back to meet her smile one last time before sliding the door shut, with no conception of the ritual she would now perform to purge herself of my seed. Later, when we grew to know each other a little, she would tell me what a pared slice of persimmon skin could be used for. But this was the last thing on my mind as I walked to the end of the gallery and down the stairs, back into the brightness and bustle of the main room. Yamato saw me and waved me over. Either he had been faster than me upstairs, or, more likely, he had decided to satisfy himself with the sake and the dancing. Perhaps he could not get his own son up any more, which was why he was so pleased that mine had seen some action.

He clapped me on the back as I sat down.

'You're a man now! How does it feel? You enjoyed it?'

I nodded, thinking again of the red flower girl in the theatre, and how, for the time I had been with Tsutsumi, she had disappeared entirely from my mind.

'Good. You're not human if you don't. I remember my first,' Yamato sighed, pouring more sake into my cup. 'I was about your age. Not long come to the capital. Skittish as a kitten I was, thought I might get eaten alive. Much better to have an old hand like me to show you the ropes.'

I said nothing, then decided to voice the thought that had begun to form when I had seen the items in Yamato's shrine.

'Did you never want to marry, Yamato-san?'

His face turned stony for a second, then he downed his glass of sake and gave a bitter laugh, wiping his mouth with the back of his hand. He narrowed his eyes, and I realised this was a question I should not have asked.

'Who do you think would want to marry me?'

'I don't know.'

'Think.'

Despite the sake, my tongue was tied. The twanging of the *samisen* continued over the buzz of chatter, but the air between us beat a silence that I didn't know how to fill.

'You're meant to say that every beauty in the city should be queuing up to walk to the temple with your esteemed master.'

'I didn't mean ...' I began, then stopped. Whether Yamato had really been angry with me, he chose to release me from my quandary by bursting into laughter and pinching the skin of my cheek.

'Don't look like that, boy. You've just dipped your bloody eel in the soy sauce! It takes more than that to offend me. But you're not fooling anyone. I see you're thinking about yourself. Was that it, you're thinking. Was that what I dreamt about for so long? Now, it's over, what now? Marriage? Not so fast!' He leaned towards me, wafting sake breath into my face. 'The Dragon King, lad. Now, we go to pay our respects to Ryuo, without whose favours none of this would be possible. It's thanks to him the eels return to their rivers to breed, while out in the open ocean the fish and the octopus spawn. Without him we have no living, and one day he'll welcome us all. Better pay your respects first!'

Was I still a Christian, I asked myself as we walked along Motomachi Street, past the paper signs flapping in the breeze. We turned up the Hundred Steps to the temple on the hill, our sandals slapping a rhythm up the worn stone steps. Did I still believe in God, though I now had reason to doubt everything the Reverend Hare had said? We reached the top, passed under the red temple gate and crossed the flat courtyard to the dragon king's statue. Yamato instructed me to bow before Ryuo's bulbous eyes and gaping jaws. He pressed a coin into my palm and watched me toss it between the slats of the prayer box. We stepped forward, clapped twice, and palms pressed together, we prayed. But between the bearded, crucified figure on a hill, and the bewhiskered master of a palace on the ocean floor I found myself in the void, unable to believe in either. My prayer was a hollow one.

Yamato and I parted at the foot of the steps and I wound an unsteady path back to my bed in the lodging house. I slept instantly, and the following morning surfaced from uneven dreams, with yellow sunlight filtering through a gap in the gauze curtains. From the backyard came the screech of crickets and Chinese voices shouting. I twisted my neck and saw my *yukata* borrowed from Yamato lying beside my futon. Bells began pealing from the church on the bluff, reminding me that it was a Sunday. I did not have to work today, and so I drifted back to sleep. I dreamt I was listening to one of the Reverend Hare's sermons, but instead of the tiny church in our village, it was in a vast cathedral. Behind him Christ on the cross looked as small as a child. The Reverend Hare was telling of His 40 days and nights in the desert and various events that befell Him, how He was bitten by a snake and about to die when He found a woman to suck the poison out. 'Why did she do it?' I stood up and asked. 'Would you not do it,' he said, 'For our Lord? It was a privilege, He was giving her a privilege. She died for Him and then He died for us!' Then the cathedral started to shake violently, and I awoke and found that the shaking was real. There was hardly any furniture to fall in that room, but a couple of dressing tables toppled, sending possessions tumbling onto the floor. From the street outside I heard shouts, a loud crash from somewhere – then just as suddenly as it had begun, the shaking stopped. I asked my Chinese neighbour in the bed across from me what had happened. He laughed. 'Don't worry. The earth moves often here.'

I remembered the geological phenomenon of the earth convulsing with destructive force caused by Satan stoking his fires down in the basement of Hell. As if the Reverend Hare were patting me on the back for recalling his teachings, there was one further tremor, then stillness.

Part Two - The Artist

Eleven

Some things are truly universal, among them the price to pay for a night on the ran-dan. Small wonder Hardie's teetotal: no one ever had a decent socialist thought feeling as if a dozen Lanarkshire miners were seaming out the inside of their skull. So why did you booze then, you daft eejit? Usual reason of course: because Horney and KG cajoled you into it, and you persuaded yourself the Japanese sake might be a case apart. That the clearness of the liquor might translate into an untainted head this morning. Isn't that how the Russians in those Dostoyevsky novels can drink vodka like water and still fight pistol duels to the death the next day?

An idiot's reasoning and you know it. Archibald Francis Nith, laid bare on the Scotsman's crucifix of intemperance crossed with regret, nailed together with a Calvinist's guilty conscience. Not the merest vestige of a chance do I have of accomplishing any work today. Pristine Japan outside, and me wasting all morning in these sticky sheets, assailed by visions of Alec Reid's red-bearded face glowering down at me like one of Dante's infernal imps asking if I know what the wages of sin are, then cackling the answer: 'Fuck all, pal, fuck all.' Despite the heat, I feel shivers of fear for my future, and think: truly, after today, I will work. I will produce precisely the kind of art the descendants of slave traders desire to have hanging on their walls to show off. If for no other reason than much like a crushing hangover, the absence of a roof over my head may imperil my already limited ability to act on my socialist principles. There. Promise made. Let the rest of today be hereby written off. Permit me now to step down from the cross and drill into the seam of memory, to extract the black ore of last night's adventures.

Like most of our Sauchiehall Street jaunts, it's prompted by the Horned One reaching the limits of his restraint:

'Auld Horney needs to let off steam tonight, boys. Otherwise he's going to blow.'

KG's sardonic response: 'Uh-oh. Moby Dick sighted off the port bow.'

Horney's eyes flash. 'Well, you know how that one ended,' Henry winks at me. 'Someone has to survive to tell the tale.'

'Call me Ishmael,' I quip.

Oh, what gallus, arty Boys we are. Such banter as this carries us all the way to a table at Yokohama's finest bordello, the Persimmon Number Nine, and its special offer of a one *yen* all you can drink sake: surely never the wisest thing to offer three Scots abroad. The Mama-san, her age inscrutable behind expertly applied maquillage, explains the system to us in her best English. One can make a request for a certain girl for four *yen* or take pot luck for two. Like a sommelier showing off the wine menu, she proudly unfolds a group portrait showing two rows of girls on the steps outside the establishment. It's shocking to say, but what the composition put me in mind of is a school photo taken on some excursion, the only absentee the stern-faced dominie marshalling the back row. The Mama-san points to each in turn, informing us of their names. We can have any of these fair Japanese flowers, except one in the front row whose face strikes me as bolder than the rest. This one, the Mama-san says in a disapproving tone, is not here tonight.

KG and I both shrug. Horney turns on his most charming smile.

'They are all very beautiful, Madam. We shall venture our fortune at pot luck.' She bows, relieves us of a ten *yen* note, and shows us through to the main salon, installing us in a booth at the side opposite three French naval officers who are finishing off a round of cards.

'*Bonsoir, mes amis,*' KG begins to show off his French. '*Nous sommes peintres Ecossais.*'

With roars of '*les Ecossais!*' they hail us like reinforcements on some foreign field. The Auld Alliance is back in vogue. We toast our sake cups to Mary Stuart, Voltaire, Hume, Dumas, Bastien Lepage, Queen's Park Football Club, and the beauties of Japan. The French sailors are stationed in Yokohama for a month on a tour of the Far East. In a bastard melange of French and English they tell us of the wild old days soon after Japan was opened to the West: how two young officers were murdered by samurai after a visit to the brothel; their bodies now lie buried in the graveyard behind our house.

'Just as well we're not in those times,' Horney remarks.

'Let's hope they've not gone completely,' says KG. 'The old romantic Japan is the one they want back home.'

'And the one we want tonight,' Horney winks.

'And you, my friend?' the Frenchman opposite asks me in English, causing all eyes to turn my way. 'What do you want? *Juste un petit baise*?' I can't help but smile under the barrage of laughter.

'Don't worry about him, he's just a socialist revolutionary,' Horney cuts in. 'He thinks the working man is a single species regardless of creed or colour.' As usual, the Horned One succeeds in riling me out of my reticence. I correct the misconception and explain that the exact form of socialism will depend on the country in which it takes root. The Frenchmen listen to me with an air of concentration that indicates either respect for my logic or incomprehension of my words.

'*Mais, vous n'est pas peintre*?' the one who addressed

me first says when I finish. He's staring intently at me, in a way that makes me wonder why I didn't take note earlier of his dark, tight curls and aura of intensity that puts me in mind of Caravaggio's *Bacchus*. The others may have stopped listening as I talk about how an artist's subject matter can indicate sympathy for the working man, hence no contradiction between socialism and art. The curly-haired one listens and then, to my surprise, replies in immaculate English: 'A century after the revolution and France is more unequal than ever. The only way for a young man from a shithole country town to make his way is to join the military. *Et voila*,' he indicates himself.

'I too, am from a shithole country town,' I add, causing a wave of memories to crash in my mind: of sand-dunes, rockpools and all the other joys the seaside affords regardless of affluence. For several long seconds our eyes meet across the table, and it seems, to me at least, that an understanding passes between us of all that cannot be said. The fellow reaches forward, extracts another two cigars from the box in the centre of the table, offers me one and lights it, then does the same for himself. The ends glow like fireflies as we inhale. I feel the exultancy of the tobacco entering my lungs and some lines of Baudelaire enter my mind. I recite them aloud. Assuming I did not commit some hideous error of pronunciation, I think I can scarcely have come closer to admitting my predilections. But the Frenchman, as if toying with me, only raises an eyebrow.

'*Impressionant*. So, tell me, *mon ami*, how you became the great artist?'

Just as I'm about to launch into the more picaresque version of the tale where I arrived in Glasgow penniless, on the run from my father's violence, I feel a featherlight touch brush my shoulder. I turn to find a courtesan beckoning me to follow her. I shrug an apology at the Frenchman and, handing the freshly lit cigar to KG, rise and follow the navy kimono, patterned with orange persimmons, past the tables in the centre of the room. She's the tallest one from the photo and as her rapid pigeon shuffle carries her up a flight of low wooden steps, I try in vain to recall her name. The buzz of chatter fades as we reach the top of the steps, and she turns right onto a wooden panelled corridor. On the left side are several sliding doors. She slides open the third or fourth of these and waits for me to enter, shutting it again behind us with a soft clatter. She unclips her hair from its lacquered clasp, and I watch it cascade down her back in a black waterfall. While she adjusts the gas lamp, I look at the prints on the walls depicting ancient Japanese engaged in amorous contortions. The room itself is sparsely furnished apart from a wooden dressing table beside the futon mattress. On top of it there's a bowl of the same fruit that gives the house its name and adorns the girls' uniforms. The girl kneels on one side of the futon and slips her robe off her shoulders to reveal a body as smooth and slim as a lacquered vase. Informing me that her name is Bara, meaning Rose, she motions me to lie down next to her. I give her 'Archie' to try to get her tongue around, but half my mind is still on the conversation downstairs. I was hoping to try out my language skills but I'm struck by a sudden shyness. Happily, Bara does not seem perturbed by my silence. After placing the comb down, she begins to remove my clothes as patiently as if she were peeling an awkward fruit.

I try out a line from the phrasebook. Presumably I succeed in communicating my admiration of her beauty, for she thanks me in her own language. Encouraged, I try to follow up with 'I am from Scotland,' but this is less successful, judging by the way she smiles politely then turns her attention to a less confusing part of my anatomy. Remembering my experience at the eel stall I repeat the phrase more slowly, working on the separation between consonants. Sadly, the result of our respective efforts is still negative. I try the word the newsman, Murchison, suggested as a shortcut to cultural understanding, 'whisky,' miming the act of drinking and pronouncing it as if I were asking 'Who is key?' Whether she understands this or not, the tension between us lessens. Soon, thanks to her skill and persistence, we're riding merrily away, almost as if it's the thing we both want to be doing, at least until I'm distracted by the clatter of the door sliding back. I look round Bara's bare shoulder, prepared to defend myself against a band of vengeful samurai, but there's no one there. Have we been so ardent that we disturbed some spectre of the house? Then my gaze is drawn down by a flicker of movement: a black and white cat ambling across the lamplit floor, its whiskers bristling, white-tipped tail aquiver. It pauses at the end of the futon, looking at us with that defiant mockery of human activity that all cats possess. On seeing it, Bara gives a venomous shriek and leaps off me, making a grab for the cat, which does what any sensible mog would do and, quick as a flash, squeezes itself between the nearest gap, in this case under the cloth blind covering the window. Then something truly bizarre happens. Through the opening in the door that the cat has created, I see a face looking in at me. I am unsure if I can trust the evidence of my eyes, but they definitely perceive young Han. I am of course still with my full glory on show, at which his attention could hardly not be focused. I raise a hand and offering my most paternalistic smile, give him a friendly wave. Then his face disappears and Bara is racing over to pull the door shut, raving in Japanese out of which the only word I can catch is *neko* which I know to mean cat. I'm so shaken by the apparition of Han that I haven't the slightest chance of returning to my stroke. In any case her reaction has filled me with a new linguistic inspiration, even as my mind races over the strangeness of what has just transpired. Remembering both the word for 'funny' and the particle which equates to the verb 'to be', I construct, on the spur of the moment, a perfect grammatical sentence:

'*Neko wa omoshiroi.*'

She's crouched beside the futon, looking less than pleased at the prospect of having to recommence from the zero I'm evidently back to; but at my words, she smiles. After pausing a moment to consider, she turns and opens one of the drawers, pulling out some rolled sheets of paper which she smooths out onto the bed. What I see soon makes me smile; they are cartoon drawings of the cat who just disturbed us. He's depicted in fine black ink lines, walking on his hind legs, wearing a fish-patterned kimono and engaged in various human pursuits. The scenes are extraordinarily detailed: in one he's buying fish at a market; in another painting calligraphy. In each of the drawings are men on all fours, Western and Japanese, lapping milk from a bowl or chasing mice.

'You drew these?' I ask her, lamentably having to return to my native tongue.

'*Watashi,*' she says, laughing and jabbing a finger at her breast with obvious pride. I lift the next sheet and find one which makes me laugh out loud. A European man poking his head through a curtain is scandalised to see two cats embroiled in the act of lovemaking.

'My work,' she says, pointing at the cats.

'These are very good,' I say. 'I will give you money for one.' I make a gesture signifying the act of payment, realising as I do so that I've slipped into capitalism's trap. How will a few extra *yen* help Bara? For this talent she deserves far better: the opportunity to make a regular income that will allow her to leave this place.

But what else can I do? She allows me to purchase one of the sketches, which will be needed if I'm to think of a way of helping her further. I return downstairs and find only KG at the table. Horney is upstairs with his girl and the Frenchmen,

85

KG explains, have all gone on to a sailor's bar, to which we're invited to follow. When Horney comes down, we leave the Persimmon and head along the main street towards the harbour. Despite Henry's certainty of the directions he was given, the bar does not materialise and we're soon stumbling along alleys lit only by the occasional lantern. A group of Chinese men pass and KG accosts them with the name of the bar which the Frenchmen told him. The Chinese men react to his words first with incomprehension, and then, when he repeats them, hilarity. They walk away laughing, leaving the three of us standing on the street corner. Just at that moment, from up on the bluff, fireworks begin whizzing up into the night sky, exploding over the settlement with reports like artillery.

I have only hazy memories of what happens after this. I believe we visit one or two of the port's less salubrious drinking establishments. Do KG and I lose Horney at one point? I think so. I can only remember the two of us making our way back home, me with just enough consciousness to undress before collapsing and plunging into oblivion the instant my head hits the pillow.

Twelve

Perhaps thanks to the violent earth tremor, by the afternoon my hangover has cleared. I cram in a good four or five hours fixing the picture of the children into a much better state. Two Japanese cherubs in vivid kimonos, one red, one gold, kneeling on *tatami* matting, at play with a wooden toy. Behind them, the steaming cookpot hanging on its chain from the ceiling; on the table, a pair of lacquered bowls waiting to be filled with rice. All in all, a delightful image of Japanese domestic life, cosy yet exotic. The fact that the whole scene was not in a real house but a studio at the Japan Photographic Society won't matter a bean. Nor will it matter that the children were the son and daughter of the society President, and only changed out of their Western clothes and into kimonos to create the sort of image he correctly imagined we'd be looking for. Quite as if he knew what Reid told us in that final pep talk before we left. 'Three words boys: Simplicity, Innocence, Restraint. That's the essence of Japan the public want, and that's what you're going to bring back with you. How you interpret it will be up to you, and I know you'll produce your own versions. But before you start working on something, ask yourself: does it fit the rule? What were the words now?' And he made us repeat back, like a trio of schoolboys, Simplicity, Innocence, Restraint, which I was first to notice forms the acronym SIR.

The relationship between artist and dealer is a strange one indeed. Only a fool would believe everything their dealer tells them. Reid told me once that I had more potential than Henry and Hornel combined. But Horney, in a moment of indiscreet bragging, claimed that Reid once told him that he was the only one of us with a truly innovative style, while KG confessed to me in a bout of insecurity that Reid told him he could hold a line better than any other artist in Scotland. KG being KG, what he took from that was only that his use of colour is prosaic and conventional. I suppose this is artist management, in the form one hears about in business. As a socialist I should despise Reid for playing us against each other with half an eye on the profits we can generate. Also, for his inherited wealth, which allowed him to spend years on the scene in Paris, amassing contacts and canvases for next-to-nothing from desperate artists. And yet, he loves art and artists, and when I think now about how I can help my poor Japanese courtesan with artistic talent to burn, it's to Reid, not Hardie, that I consider writing. What would I say? 'Bearing in mind your main condition that Japanese works must display Simplicity, Innocence, and Restraint, I have acquired a delightful picture which I think may interest you: it depicts two Japanese cats at it in the French style while in the corner of the frame a European gentleman in a suit laps milk from a bowl.'

How would he respond? Probably in his usual laconic style: 'Scene good. Ensure Mount Fuji visible through window.'

Let's imagine then that he believes he'd not be short of buyers for Bara's little vignettes. Then to more practical considerations? How would she go about mailing the drawings to Europe and receiving payment for them in return? Well, the money could be wired if she could open an account with a Japanese bank, but what if the drawings were ruined or lost in the shipping? The risk would be all on her side. No, the more one thinks, the more impossible it is for an individual, never mind one in such a weak position as Bara, to sell their works on the international market. Then what? Then obviously I must help her find a domestic buyer. I'm sure the rules of Japanese society prevent a courtesan from being an artist at the same time, but what if there were a foreign dealer locally situated? Such a person might be amenable to acquiring works of the curiosity value presented by Bara's. Perhaps the newsman Murchison would know if one exists.

Thirteen

Murchison may be a Dundonian, but he has a gob worthy of any Glaswegian. The first time we met him he recounted his life story in between pointing out the landmarks. He went to sea as a young man, did ten years on the trade routes, then on shore leave in Yokohama ten years ago he met a man called J.R. Black. Black runs the finest English newspaper in the Far East and he offered Murchison a job on the strength of him being from Dundee. Murchison has since taken a Japanese wife and is probably set for life here.

He said anything he could help us with, anything at all, we know where to find him. Okay, sir, I am coming. I have your business card and a rough idea of where your newspaper's office is located, but I make the mistake of trying to approach from the Motomachi side, thinking from there I'll be able to recall which of the bisecting streets to turn up. Of course, I take the wrong one and only after a spell of walking in circles do I finally locate the building on the corner, its Grecian pillars either side of the entrance, every bit as grand as the mock temples of our own Merchant City.

The offices of the *Japan Mail* occupy the floor above a bank. After passing through a marble entrance lobby I climb the stairs to a landing. There's a sanded glass door inscribed with the emblem of the newspaper. I give a couple of brisk raps and wait. When, after a minute or so, nobody's answered, I lift my knuckles to knock harder. Suddenly, the door swings inwards. The figure, not quite fitting the frame, towers over me by a good five inches: heavyset, black-bearded, a gold watch chain hanging across a paisley-patterned waistcoat.

The voice booms at me in an unmistakably Fife accent.

'John Reddie Black, founder and editor of the *Japan Mail* and what can I do for you, sir?' As he pronounces these words, he extends his hand and I find my own being shaken vigorously by this titan's grip. It's the directness of his manner coupled with his full beard that makes me recall my first encounter with Hardie. Just as on that occasion, I feel an instinctive discomfort at announcing myself as an artist and stress instead my Scottish provenance, which as I hoped he fastens onto immediately, expressing his admiration for what he calls 'the intrepid spirit of the Glasgow man'.

'We're delighted to have you and your fellow Glasgow artists here, Mister Nith! Fantastic news for Japan it is. You'll be our missionaries. You'll return with the good news. But even better for Scotland, because the eyes of her people will be opened to the East. And just as Japan is learning the best of the rest at a galloping clip, so the Scots can learn from the ways of the Japanese, of which you, I am sure, are already cognisant. Bridges, that's what we are, Mister Nith, bridges, just as vital as the one that spans the Tay!'

Whether Black delivers a similar editorial address to all who knock on the office door, I don't know. I feel a great desire to engage with his enthusiasm, but remembering the original purpose of my visit, I check myself and enquire after Murchison's presence.

'I hope you've not come to confess to something,' Black says darkly.

Evidently, my face betrays my confusion, for he apologises for his 'wee joke'. 'Only Murchison is our crime specialist, you see. And a bloody good one too. Has all these contacts in the police and speaks the lingo like a local. A real diamond of a reporter, one of my top men. Don't you go persuading him he should be an artist, you hear me!'

After satisfying himself that I will not corrupt his staff

with artistic ambitions, Black then seems to take serious appraisal of me for the first time. I must somehow pass the test of his scrutiny, for he motions me forward into the office. Several heads swivel in my direction, before quickly turning back to typing machines or sheets of print. The editor is telling me that if I truly wish to speak to Murchison, I will have to hasten to the Osanbashi pier, where he has just gone to report on the discovery of a body pulled from the harbour. Alternately, Black concludes, I could leave a message for him, or if I prefer, return later in the afternoon. 'Though if you come then there's a fair chance you'll find him manacled to his desk sweating blood to meet his deadline.'

Not wishing to interrupt such an eventuality, I tell Black that I will try to locate Murchison on the quayside. I withstand the editor's vice grip a second time and take my leave from that industrious factory of words.

Outside again, I have barely commenced the walk up the street to the waterfront, when I bump into Murchison coming the opposite direction. We exchange warm greetings as rickshaw pullers carry on past. 'How are you enjoying your stay in Japan?' the newsman enquires, and as I fill him in with the broadest of brushstrokes I cannot help wondering that a man who has just reported on the discovery of a drowned body can produce a display of such heartiness. 'And where are you en-route to this fine afternoon?' Murchison smiles, as if he himself has just come from a cocktail party.

'That, you see, is the thing, Mr Murchison,' I reply. 'It's yourself I have been looking for.'

Throwing his deadline, and perhaps Black's wrath to the wind, Murchison proves true to his word. Soon, he and I are sitting opposite one another across a low table in a traditional Japanese hostelry. The newsman decants green tea into each of our cups and invites me to tell him the matter on which I seek his assistance. The question of how to introduce my request without embarrassment has already occurred to me, and the tale of how I met Han trips off my tongue more readily for being entirely true. Murchison smiles at my description of the boy and his master working like Trojans to keep the waterfront fed on battered eel.

'I know exactly the pair you mean. And a very decent *unagi tenpura* it is too. So how did your gift of a sketch sit with the boss? Impressed, was he?'

Murchison's amusement grows when I recall the older man's disdainful reaction. 'And that, I thought, was the end of it,' I say, as a tray of raw fish garnished with pickled radish is laid on the table.

'I must confess, I'm fascinated as to how your story will proceed,' Murchison chuckles, manipulating his chopsticks to transfer a piece onto my plate. I explain how, on the next occasion I went to buy lunch at the stall, Han covertly presented me with something in return. I lay my chopsticks down and reach into my haversack to produce Bara's drawing of the cats at the *kabuki* theatre. A glistening chunk of tuna pauses an inch or two before Murchison's mouth. An incredulous smile spreads across his features.

'You are telling me that a waterfront stall boy did this?'

'Quite remarkable, is it not?'

By the time we have polished off every succulent morsel, leaving only a few slivers of garnish on the tray, I have obtained from Murchison a promise that he will contact a couple of significant figures in the settlement who are known to purchase Japanese art.

'And what's in it for you, my friend?' he asks me as the waitress removes our empty plates. 'When you have once been a struggling artist,' I say, 'you tend to look out for other young talents.'

'Regardless of their nationality?'

'Of course.'

'A noble commitment. Perhaps when you get back to Glasgow you will open a school for young Scottish artists?'

How strange it is that such ideas can come to people who have only just met us. I am struck, on the instant, by acute shock that the idea has never crossed my mind. It's in this state that Murchison catches me out and pays the bill himself, leaving me rather awkwardly, doubly in his debt.

'Not a bit of it, man,' he reassures me, patting my shoulder as we move back out into the brightness of the street. The sun is directly overhead, leaving us almost entirely devoid of shade, but Murchison shows me the Japanese trick of tying a handkerchief around one's head. As we walk back to the offices of the *Mail*, I ask him about the matter he was called out to report on. His face clouds, as if he's belatedly reacting to the presence of death.

'Tragic case. A native girl, around twenty, almost certainly drowned herself.' He looks at me sharply and asks if I can be relied upon for discretion. I assure him that I can, and his next words send a chill running through my bones despite the torpid heat. 'The girl worked at a certain establishment popular with Western gents. You'll be familiar with the Persimmon Number Nine?'

I nod, and Murchison does not appear to register my discomfort as he continues. 'This makes it a rather sensitive matter. There's a danger you see, that such events could fan the flames of Japanese nationalism.'

We part company at the front of the steps leading into the bank. Even after the building swallows him up, I continue to stare at the entrance framed by Corinthian columns and topped by a frieze depicting what I now see to be Athena offering to Perseus the shield with which he'll defeat Medusa. Realising that the second-floor windows overlooking the street are those of the newsroom, I turn and hurry away. I know the Persimmon employs at least a dozen girls, but even the slim odds that Bara is the victim and I am trying to sell the art of a drowned woman is enough to fill me with nausea. And then - shameful though it is to report – I'm struck by fear that if Bara has drowned herself due to my momentary raising of her artistic hopes, then I might bear some part of the responsibility. At least I was wise enough not to tell Murchison the truth of where I obtained the picture.

I return home to find H and H at their most irritatingly endeavourous. Both have all but completed the paintings they are working on. Horney's brace of infants is undeniably good. He has transplanted them from the shady interior to a sun-drenched garden, overlooking an ornamental pond complete with carp nuzzling the surface. Horney's signature mastery of colour is in evidence; with those thick brushstrokes he makes the figures blend with their surroundings so his Japanese babes exist in a shimmering harmony with their perfected natural world.

KG, in his own way, has also tried to marry his style to the fantasy of exotic Japan. But with his fine lines capturing the contours of their faces, he makes it too apparent that they are merely on display as artefacts. Horney's excesses might provoke the ire of the odd critic, but they are more in keeping with the mystic *zeitgeist*. Looking at his canvas gives me an idea for my own. I'll paint Han in a glade of thick bamboo, and in the spaces between the stems conceal the outlines of modern buildings, the steel hulls of warships and mechanised paraphernalia of industry.

Whether this will pass SIR's censorship as readily as mosquitoes through the mesh of our bedroom window, I can't be sure. But the idea of it allows me to forget what Murchison told me, and carries me through a productive evening of preparatory sketching alone in the house, while H and H attend a reception at the villa of one of the head honchos from Matheson Jardine. If what I have heard is correct, that long-established firm of traders has its roots in the smuggling of opium into China. An empire built on such rotten foundations surely cannot last.

Fourteen

I keep taking out Bara's drawing in the night, unable to shake the thought that its maker might be on a slab in some local mortuary. In the morning I go out early to purchase the *Mail*, stopping to read it on the first bench I can find. At first it seems Murchison must have aroused Black's wrath and missed his deadline: a scan of the main stories on each page reveals nothing. Only on my second read-through, several pages deep, do I find the few short sentences near the foot of a side column.

The body of a young native woman was retrieved from the harbour on Monday morning. The matter is being looked into by local police, however present indications are of another tragic case of self-murder, of which we cannot help but be aware of the disturbing frequency among the Japanese community.

There is no mention at all of the Persimmon, never mind the identity of the poor girl. I remember what Murchison said about the potential sensitivity of the case and wonder whether the reticence of a Dundonian newsman is capable of quelling local outrage. Surely there are native sources of news which will pick up the story and include the details missing here. Not that it would help me. Even if such a journal were in my hands it would make as much sense as the hieroglyphs on an Egyptian sarcophagus.

I roam Chinatown for a while, comforted by its incomprehensible babble of street vendors. I'm forced to admit that in my concern for Bara I've been neglecting my

97

first protégé. In truth I've been avoiding Han ever since that bizarre sighting of him in the Persimmon, which has taken on the quality of a hallucination of the type to which I understand opium addicts fall prey. I'm almost sent into a fresh panic at the notion that I might not be able to trust my own memories of what transpired that night. What if I was the last human contact of a young woman who has taken her own life? Did I say or do things in my encounter with Bara that I now don't recall?

By the time I approach Han's stall I've rediscovered my self-possession. I take out my sketchbook and from a discreet distance commit to paper an impression of the bustle of the quayside with those two at its centre busting a gut to meet the demand. So absorbed do I become that I don't notice Yamato must have declared the lunch rush to have ended. When I look up from my depiction, the pair are busy tidying up the stall and I've missed the chance to buy my own lunch.

Knowing it won't do to interrupt now, I watch as Han carries the heavy skillet down to the harbour's edge, his legs threatening to buckle as he descends the steps out of my view to rinse the grease in the ocean. The master meanwhile places the uneaten lengths of eel in a box and covers them. No doubt he'll slip them in the pan tomorrow and sell them as 'fresh' to the less discerning customers.

'*Konnichiwa*,' I announce my approach. Remembering the words for 'two please,' I make my request for servings for Han and myself. He eyes me suspiciously, scratching an itch on his forehead as if to make clear he's in no mood to be hurried now the official work shift is over. His glare moves from my face to the sketchbook I carry under my arm. I recall what Han told me about his response to my earlier offering: 'he prefers Japanese art.' The boy was no doubt being diplomatic. It's obvious that Yamato loathed my depiction of him just as much as a Scottish navvy, my father say, might turn up his nose if a Japanese artist came and produced a cartoon of him at work. Still, he takes my money grudgingly and hands me two portions of battered eel with rice just as Han appears beside us. I greet him warmly, but he only mumbles and stares at his feet. Realising he's embarrassed to display our familiarity in front of Yamato, I retreat to the sanctuary of my sketching vantage, the step beside one of the customs buildings. As I hoped, Han comes to find me after his boss leaves with the cart, though he hovers a few feet away, seemingly hesitant to come closer.

'I didn't expect to see you the other night,' I venture, attempting a breeziness I don't feel.

From his awkwardness, at least I know that part wasn't a hallucination. It was Han's face I saw in the corridor at the Persimmon, not some figment of my fevered imagination. In the time it takes him to accept an extra lunch and a seat beside me, I've decided how to address the situation. Yet it's him who pre-empts me. 'A girl from that place is dead,' he hisses.

I'm taken aback. 'How do you know?'

'I saw her.'

'Who is it?' My appetite for lunch is destroyed, the delicious eel now holding as much appeal as a decomposing finger. Words begin to spill from Han, a rambling account that at first makes no sense. I tell him to stop and suggest we walk, that the act of moving will clear his head and allow him to control the current of what he wants to say.

It emerges that the previous day he was at the stall, working as usual, when there was a commotion down at the water's edge. He and Yamato went to see what was provoking the shouts and gasps of horror. It was a young woman, floating face down in the water. Someone ran to the police building at the end of the pier, while another dived in and pulled the girl out. Han recognised the pattern on her *yukata*, and when she was placed on the quayside he saw her

99

face and it too was familiar to him. Horror fills his eyes as he recalls this, and I assume it's the girl he was with that night, but he shakes his head. It's a different Persimmon girl, who he says he saw at the *kabuki* theatre earlier in the evening.

'Are you sure?' I ask.

He nods, describing a red flower in her hair and two freckles under her ear. I feel a wave of relief that it's not Bara.

'And you only saw this girl at the theatre?'

It strikes me that Han must have paid very close attention to notice these features, and for a terrible few seconds I wonder if he's about to confess that in the derangement of one whose passions have been thwarted, he was somehow involved in her death. But as if he has read my mind he looks me straight in the eye and makes the following accusation:

'It was Yamato. Yamato killed Tsubaki.'

'Yamato?' I repeat. 'Why would he have killed her?'

Han begins to tell me some story about a hair clip and a silk belt in his boss's house, and an argument between Yamato and this girl, Tsubaki. The facts seem disconnected, or at least I'm struggling to make any link between them. I'm also conscious that Han is avoiding any reference to his sighting of me in Bara's room. It hangs in the air unspoken between us, although I can already detect a change in his attitude towards me, as if he now sees me on an equal footing. I suppose, by one definition, he has become a man, and he thinks I am a man by that same definition as well. I feel a sudden emptiness, a great gaping void opening within me. Meanwhile I keep talking, playing Yamato's advocate. A mere argument is hardly motive for murder, I suggest. Han tells me that Yamato warned Tsubaki that she would pay for her insolence. He appears to be waiting for me to draw a conclusion, so perhaps I still occupy a position of some seniority and respect in his eyes. I duly consider, and conclude the following: if Han has concrete proof that his boss is guilty, then he should go to the police. But judging from what he has told me there is no such evidence. By going to the police, he would risk placing himself under suspicion and losing his job into the bargain.

We've reached the end of the promenade and are walking along a grassy path between the rocky shoreline and the Russian consular building. We stand before each other in front of the pole flying that nation's flag, not a soul observing us unless there are any Tsarist officials looking out. At that moment the emotion which has been bubbling inside Han comes to the surface, and he begins sobbing uncontrollably. I take him in my arms, and let him bury his face in my chest, all the while keeping my own feelings tightly under control.

Finally, he has cried as much as he can and faces me again.

'We must investigate,' he says in a voice still thick with tears. 'We have to be like Holmes and Watson, and find Tsubaki's murderer.'

I inform him as gently as I can that the newspaper report indicates her death was most likely a suicide, not expecting him to react as venomously as he does.

'I've been told enough lies,' he shouts. 'I want to find out the truth about this.'

How could anyone pour salt on a conviction that entering manhood means beginning a quest for the truth? Against my better judgement I've agreed to help him with what he terms his 'investigation' into Tsubaki's death.

Fifteen

I spend all afternoon at work, making fine progress on the bamboo glade aided by sketches and cuttings of the plant I took from the grove up the hill opposite the church. KG, approving of my attention to realistic detail, has learned the *kanji* for bamboo.

竹

He has already reproduced these strokes dozens of times and attempts to compare his efforts for their aesthetic virtue. He and Horney are going through one of their periodic bouts of animosity. Refusing to address one another, they communicate only with me. Strangely, both have asked how Han is doing, but I respond brusquely that I need to concentrate on my work. With my silence adding to the general toxic brew, the thin Japanese walls are close to collapse under the weight of repressed Scottish rancour. Horney's announcement that he's going out for a walk is like the release of a pressure valve. KG takes the opportunity to vent his spleen against the Horned One. While I was out this morning, it seems they argued. Horney snapped and told KG that their famous *Druids* painting of '91 would have been superior had he done the whole canvas himself. I assure KG that this is untrue; the delicacy of the composition could never have been achieved by Horney in a million years; without this the painting would lose all its tension and collapse into absurdity. KG's gratitude for my analysis is more extreme than I bargained for.

'You've got it', he says, 'You've hit the nail on the head. That man has no sense of refinement. He's a bloody bull in a china shop.' We're laughing now, sitting in the immaculate and peaceful back garden, sharing a pot of green tea.

'You know what we've done, Nithy?' KG lowers his voice as if there might be spies stationed behind the bamboo fence, pressed up against the graveyard wall, intent on discovering the precise nature of a quarrel between two artists from a small country ten thousand miles away. 'We've created this monster: Auld Horney, the Borders Bacchus. He'll never let it go now. Even in Japan.'

'It's who he is, isn't it,' I suggest.

'Oh, come on, Arch, he wasn't always so cocksure. I knew him when he didn't know a soul outside that damned village of his. You wouldn't believe how needy he was. Practically begging me to introduce him to the right people. And he wasn't always such a hit with the lassies either. Not until he got his act right. He was as dumb as a tattiebogle. If it wasn't for the booze –

I've heard it before, I know they'll make up, and, cruel though it is, I take some pleasure in pulling the rug from under KG's feet.

'Talking of lassies, did you hear they fished one of the girls from the Persimmon out of the harbour on Monday morning?'

The uncharacteristic rancour that has taken hold of him dissipates in an instant. He's horrified. Like me, it occurs to him that the victim may have been the girl he was with that night. He can't remember her name but proclaims her 'as sweet a flower as ever he met.' I explain that the police are working on an assumption of suicide. KG shakes his head: 'Who knows what goes on in their minds behind those smiles,' he remarks.

I can't help suggesting that if he wants to know he could ask them.

'We're not all adept linguists like yourself, Nithy,' he

replies.

It occurs to me that Bara's drawing might expand his perspective. I go inside to retrieve it, and when I place it on the table between us, his reaction, like Murchison's, is one of amusement and incredulity. He goes so far as to ask me whether I drew the picture myself. To assure him that it really is Bara's creation, I tell him in some detail about the circumstances of her showing it and the other pictures to me. I even describe the appearance of the cat who distracted us; in fact, my only departure from the truth is to substitute Han's appearance in the doorway for that of an unknown Japanese gentleman.

'Good God, Nithy,' KG says through tears of laughter. 'I hope it wasn't the fellow from the Photographic Society. The one who carries his camera with him at all times! What was it he said? He's always ready to capture that elusive moment of beauty!'

I've made George Henry fall about laughing, which is no easy feat, but remembering my intention to raise his awareness of Bara's powerless state, I tell him of my idea of helping her sell her pictures. He listens while I describe my contact with Murchison in pursuit of a domestic buyer. KG seems to find it difficult to deal with what I'm saying, judging by the number of times he shakes his head and mutters some fresh expression of amazement.

'How could I call myself a socialist and not try to help a struggling artist?' I say. He does not look me in the eye, but stares across the lawn at the graveyard wall.

'Sometimes you make me feel bad, Nithy. Here am I struggling to get my head around this place enough just to paint a few pictures. Meanwhile you're out there learning the lingo, helping eel sellers and geishas turn into artists.'

Protesting that all I've done is eat fish at the expense of a Dundonian newsman, I describe Murchison's assurance that he'll try to arrange a meeting with a dealer.

'Perhaps you're more of a businessman than you think,' he chuckles, his usual ironic equilibrium seemingly restored. Indeed, after Horney returns, it's KG who makes the first move towards their reconciliation. Soon enough, the pair are thick as thieves again.

Sixteen

It's the middle of the night but the heat and my head will not allow me to sleep. Careful not to wake H and H, I step out into the garden to look up at the half moon painted on the heavens. I sniff the fragrant air and train my lumpen Scottish lugs to the love song of a Japanese toad, croaking somewhere in the darkness of the graveyard. 'When sleep won't come, Nithy, the worst you can do is fight it,' KG told me once, and the toad it seems already knows this. If I were a Japanese court poet, I would form a *tanka* verse from these insights. Maybe something like this:

In a house of sleep, called by moonlight

and a toad's swarthy song,

I soften my waking with this thought.

But can a toad's song be swarthy? I don't think this verse would qualify me to enter the list of a hundred glorious poems. What a curiosity that was earlier! Who but the Japanese would conceive of a game invoking poetry like a form of ritual combat?

To the best of my understanding the game goes something like this. The cards spread out on the floor between the two competitors contain the last lines of a hundred great poems. When the referee starts to intone the opening line, that's the cue for them to search their memory and slap their palm down on the matching ending. Yet to describe it thus does no justice to the speed and aggression of the geishas we witnessed in the demonstration. If the cards were mice they would have been savaged in a second. And how often did they both seem to land on the right one at exactly the same instant, so the referee had to step in and arbitrate – though how he did this without a tape measure I couldn't fathom. Karuta they call the game. What a spectacle! And what a way to appreciate literature. As we walked home the three of us talked of adapting it on our return to Glasgow.

'Why stop at poems?' said Henry, 'we could have a version for novels too.'

'Starting with Walter Bloody Scott,' Horney said, and we all agreed, though I remembered how I took Scott's romances with me when I first moved to Glasgow.

*

I retreat back to my futon, still replaying the images of *karuta*, which bleed into an unusually vivid dream. I am one of three players, the other two being KG and Horney. We are outside on the lawn in front of Stirling-Maxwell's house in Pollok on a summer's day. Spread out before us are all the cards covered in *kanji*. We have an audience of all the Boys, Reid and his family, and a host of curators and critics. I'm trying to explain to them how the game works but they're not listening. Instead they're carrying on conversations between themselves, laughing and joking. I realise we lack a referee to call out the opening lines and arbitrate. I look to H and H for help but they've melted back into the crowd. Suddenly, everyone's looking at me, and I realise to my horror that I'm not wearing a stitch of clothing. I wake up at this point. The whole thing is too ridiculous to take seriously, but didn't Shakespeare compare life itself to the fabric of a dream? Maybe that dream is as real in my life as anything else. Oh, enough, Nithy. Stop these useless speculations and try to sleep again!

Seventeen

Is it possible that my thoughts have some form of generative effect on future events? This afternoon my throwaway allusion to life as theatre comes to pass. The three of us have gone for a stroll up the hill onto the bluff. It's baking hot, and even with our shirts unbuttoned and sticking to the shade, we're pouring with sweat. At KG's suggestion we go into the Jollity Theatre to see if we can acquire some tickets for the upcoming Hallowe'en performance of *Frankenstein*. Barely have we entered the blissful cool of the foyer when a lady pirate in a headscarf, eye-patch, red lace-ruffed shirt and billowing black pantaloons comes cannonballing out of a side door towards us. She thrusts her arms wide in impressario style, and addresses us in a voice of almost masculine pitch that would carry to the back of the grand circle.

'So, the Glasgow Boys have arrived! How positively splendid!'

It turns out that this Yokohama Bernhardt has already made the acquaintance of KG, and claims to know Horney and I by reputation.

'All bad, I hope,' growls Horney.

'The worst,' she laughs, gesturing us through the door from which she emerged. She spirits us through a warren of backstage corridors, sweeps aside a dark curtain, and we emerge onto the boards of the stage.

Miss Arabella Hawk, for this is the pirate's name, leads us to a sturdy metal table into which rings are embedded in places corresponding to the neck, wrists and ankles of a giant.

'Our monster will be manacled here, you see. You have read the novel?' Assured of our literary credentials she expounds at length on the greatness of Shelley, before swooping back to the technical complications. 'How do you convince an audience that a current of electricity is animating a grotesque assemblage of dead limbs?'

'It sounds like giving an after-dinner speech at the Royal Academy,' I remark. Miss Hawk looks at me quizzically for a second then laughs. 'Our audience will have its share of old fossils too. But they will expect sparks to fly. Like in the demonstrations by Tesla. We want to blow them away. You too, I hope!' Her utterances are like the members of some esoteric club, loosely connected by a current of Tesla-like alternations. Horney's horn is up and he offers his services, in that deadpan drawl of his, as an experienced player of monsters. In a minute or so he's on the table, his head placed in the neck strap and his joints as near the manacles as his stature will permit. Miss Hawk, thrilled by this Byronic display, disappears into the shadows backstage, returning with a metal box boasting a lever and trailing a multi-hued entanglement of wires.

'I'm afraid this is the best our props man could do,' she says, handing it to me. 'Would you be my Victor?'

'I'll try,' I say, and thrust the lever forward. With admirable timing, Horney converts his carcass into a spasming conduit of electricity. He raises his torso, lurches off the table and takes a few steps befitting a monstrous birth. I summon the full range of my Thespian capacities to express the horror of Victor Frankenstein on seeing the fiend he has created. Miss Hawk applauds, and I feel for an instant a glimmer of the thrill of performance, which a painter may never enjoy.

'My goodness, I wish my leading men were as good as this!' she gushes.

'Electrifying. Simply electrifying. These men are quite wasted as painters.' Henry satirises the role of critic with dry aplomb.

As we continue to talk, two other members of the Players appear on stage. A married couple from Liverpool, they're young and amusing, and we hit it off. In the midst of the conversation Arabella Hawk announces she's had a thought. Several of the Players are going tomorrow to Enoshima, a small island just off the coast. They'll visit the renowned shrines and spend the night at the villa of a wealthy, theatre-loving merchant who has bought much of the island. He's got plenty of free sleeping space and a well-stocked wine cellar. Why don't we join them? The three of us exchange glances, a collective spark: we've found a group whose idea of fun might tally with our own. But I realise that being alone this weekend will solve the thorny problem of when to visit the Persimmon again with Han, as we have agreed we must do to pursue his investigation. There can be few more persuasive people than Arabella Hawk. However, H and H know the truth of my argument: I've hit a hot streak of painting and I can't risk abandoning the muse. Eventually even Miss Hawk accepts that only two of the Glasgow Boys will be accompanying the Jollity Players' jaunt to Enoshima this weekend.

We walk back down the hill and I leave H and H at the entrance to the bakery, explaining that I prefer a light snack of battered eel and rice. The walk to the waterfront is a chance to be alone and gather my thoughts. At the stall I sense a tension between Han and Yamato. Has the lad been digging further into his suspicions about Tsubaki's death? Resisting Yamato's glower, I tell Han that tomorrow we can pursue our investigation as planned; we'll meet at the foot of the Hundred Steps at six. I don't mention the Persimmon by name in case Yamato's ears should catch that familiar word amidst the general incomprehensibility of our tongue.

Eighteen

After breakfast, when Horney has cleared out of the room, KG wants to chat.

'Is everything tickety-boo up here?' He taps his forehead meaningfully. 'I know you've got your principles, old soul, but don't let the work and everything else get on top of you.'

I assure him that everything is right as rain, I'm just focused on the work. I tell him that he's been working hard himself and he deserves to relax. He's reassured by the levity of my caution to be wary of the talons of Miss Hawk.

'Ah, but the thing is, Nithy,' he laughs. 'I might just enjoy a spot of gouging from those talons.'

KG's love affair with the *kanji* seems to have begun and ended with bamboo. Is he aware, I wonder, that his artistic flaw is his inability to pursue a certain course and stick to it, come hell or high water?

Now the house is mine alone. Except for Tsuki of course, who sits watching me, sphynx-like, on the divan. H and H will by now be looking out onto the glittering Pacific. A shame, in a way, not to be going, but I shall work on the painting until the evening and then, time to play Sherlock. The more I've thought about Han's desire to investigate, the more it seems correct. It cannot be right that a young woman was drowned in the harbour only five days ago, and this international society based around the pursuit of capital and leisure ploughs on without a thought. It is possible, I suppose, that somewhere, professional police officers are furiously at work on the case. Somehow, though, I doubt it. I think it may well fall to an eel-stall boy and an artist to confirm the truth of what happened to this Tsubaki, the theatre-going girl of the red flower, the quick riposte and the two freckles behind the ear.

The work goes well through the afternoon and I almost lose track of time as my canvas takes shape. When I notice the hands of the clock, I have to hurry to wash the paint off my hands, change, and go out. Thankfully the temperature is cooler now, so I don't sweat through my new shirt. Han is waiting for me at the foot of the Hundred Steps, wearing his one good suit of clothes. We shake hands. He looks clean and smells only slightly fishy; fresh, he tells me, from a visit to the baths. If he is nervous he does not show it. As we begin our walk to the Persimmon I start to tell him about H and H's trip, and about *Frankenstein*, but he interrupts me. This morning he broached the subject of Tsubaki with Yamato, asking his boss why they did not tell the police they saw her at the *kabuki*. I ask him how Yamato reacted.

'He was angry. He asked me if I was *baka* – stupid. What does it help to tell the police, he says.'

'And what did you say?' I probe, thinking that I can see where Yamato is coming from.

'I said I thought it was better to be honest. Then I asked him how he knew Tsubaki.'

'That was brave of you.' He shoots me a warning look: this is not a remark Watson would make to Holmes. It emerges that Yamato, predictably enough, was annoyed by Han's question. It was none of his chopping boy's business who he knew. He reminded Han there are lots of boys who would kill to be chopping eel for pennies on the waterfront. But then, perhaps realising that he liked the one he had, he admitted to Han that he knew Tsubaki from the Persimmon. Yes, he had been angry at her behaviour in the theatre, but Tsubaki was *muzukashi*, she made enemies easily. If Han thought he, Yamato, had anything to do with her death then

112

he was mistaken.

'How did he seem when he was telling you this?'

Han considers: 'Not like himself.'

'And do you believe him?'

'I don't know.'

One more thing: Yamato told Han he knew Tsubaki was fond of alcohol; as he saw it, she had drunk too much and fell in the harbour by accident. I think, sadly, it could be true. Hasn't the Clyde welcomed many a poor, staggering victim into its chill embrace?

We've made our way through the summer evening crowds along Theatre Street, and arrive at the Persimmon. I'm worried about the guards, but they only watch us walk between them, their faces revealing nothing. We pass under the red lanterns and over the threshold. The Mama-san, a spider in black and gold, emerges from the web of shadows behind her desk. It's a repetition of the same routine as when I was here with H and H, except selection comes at an added cost. Bara for me; Tsutsumi for Han. Eight *yen* for the house, out of Alec Reid's pocket. So much for SIR, but what he doesn't know won't hurt him.

When Bara and Tsutsumi appear at our table together, if they are surprised to find a white man and a young Asian in each other's company, they are much too refined to show it. It occurred to neither of us that for the extra cost, they might sit with us at the table rather than leading us straight up to their rooms in the gallery. We get to our feet just as they kneel down, but the misunderstanding serves to relieve the tension. We all laugh. Tsutsumi, who looks younger than Bara and is certainly shorter, manoeuvres herself down next to Han. Bara does the same with me. I believe she looks pleased to see me again, and I wish I were bringing her good news about a purchaser, although I have brought something. Both girls begin to amuse us with their comically limited

113

English, in what seems like a practised skit. Just as I'm asking Han why he doesn't quiz them about Tsubaki now, when we have them together, they tell us it's time to go upstairs. I look at Han and he nods. I suppose it's only to be expected that this is the way he wants to do things.

With my limited Japanese, my part in the investigation is always going to be the weaker one. Indeed, for most of the half hour I end up neglecting it entirely. It is delightful to have Bara curled up at my side, purring her approval of the sketches I've brought to show her. Shyly at first, then with growing confidence, she shows me more of her own. As I unleash my repertoire of Japanese praise words, of which I have two, I sense that she is building up to something. Still, I'm not prepared for the final sheet; and when it's unveiled, I have no words and am reduced to grinning like a fool. It's a picture of the human-sized feline I now know represents Bara, sitting on the lap of a naked man, an affectionate caricature of me. As if she has heard my speculation as to Reid's response, the view through the window behind us looks across the plain to the hills behind which rise Mount Fuji's majestic cone.

'For you. *pu-re-zen-to*,' she says.

Finding my tongue, I thank her for the gift, and from my semi-reclined position, perform what must be one of the most ludicrous bows ever attempted. I'm glad to say this does not alter her delight. Then it's her who moves to the topic I should be at already. She grows suddenly serious, and casting her eyes downwards, stroking the real *neko* which has appeared again, she says: 'In Persimmon last week, 12 girls. Now 11.'

'I know. Tsubaki is gone.'

She looks sharply at me, no doubt surprised that I know about Tsubaki. I retrieve from memory the word I learned and had Han test me on until it was ingrained. What I didn't bargain for was the effect of me knowing the word for suicide: *jisatsu*. Eventually, I quell her fear that I am from the police.

But this is only the start of my problems. For taking my utterance of one item of advanced vocabulary as proof that I must in reality understand Japanese very well, she launches into an extended monologue. From the stream of her speech, the word *shashin* leaps up repeatedly, like a salmon trying to jump the falls of my incomprehension. I say it back, and thanks to Bara's gift for mime, reach the point of understanding it means photograph. I am still none the wiser though, and she has grown impatient with me. We've breached the allotted time limit despite not even removing our clothes. I kiss her an apology, and make certain promises, which she may or may not understand, to do better next time, before taking my leave.

Downstairs, I find Han already seated at our table wearing an expression of what I can only describe as satisfied cogitation. Wondering how much of his time with Tsutsumi was spent interviewing her about Tsubaki's death, I attract the attention of another girl and order some sake.

My *shashin* glimmer is greatly enlightened by Han's discoveries. It seems Tsutsumi poured cold water on his suspicion of Yamato's involvement. Instead, she told him what many of the girls think, and what Bara, presumably, was trying to impart to me. They believe that Tsubaki sold her spirit to the camera, or rather a devil that lurks inside it. As with most superstitious notions, there is some basis to this: apparently some of the Persimmon girls were in the habit of having themselves photographed at a professional studio. Tsubaki, it seems, was one of the most active in pursuing this extra source of income. It made her absent from work on several occasions, arousing the ire of the Mama-san and some of the girls who had to cover for her.

'That fits!' I cry, recalling for Han the picture the Mama-

115

san showed us, and the disapproval in her tone when she highlighted the girl who was absent. 'That must have been Tsubaki. Perhaps after you saw her at the *kabuki* she went to this studio when she should have been working here. But where is it?'

Han tells me that the studio is on Motomachi Street, and again I come in useful as Watson. It must be the same place, I tell him, where I was taken with H and H early during our stay in Yokohama. The owner is a Japanese man named Sakemoto. I do not add that he is the very man about whom KG and I laughed as I recounted the story of the cat.

'Then Sakemoto may be the murderer,' Han announces with conviction, downing his sake cup and smacking it down on the tabletop, a gesture I am sure he must have learned from Yamato.

'What about Yamato's theory, that Tsubaki was drunk and fell in the water?' I remind him.

His face clouds momentarily. 'Tsutsumi told me that once Tsubaki was drunk at work, and the others had to carry her to bed.'

That will be us tonight if Han carries on drinking like this, I think. I suggest it's time we were getting home, and to my relief, he agrees.

There is one more thing Han tells me as we walk out into the balmy night, alive with the chirruping of cicadas. Tsutsumi told him she saw Tsubaki talking to a foreigner on the street outside the Persimmon a few days before her death. Unfortunately, she could not recall anything about this figure beyond his white skin, so even assuming it was a corporeal entity and not an evil spirit, we have little to go on.

With the house to myself, it would be strange not to offer Han a more comfortable bed than he is used to for the night. He takes my futon while I borrow KG's. As I bid him goodnight, he's still playing with the electric switch,

116

throwing us into alternate light and darkness. He wants to know how electric current works and I promise I will try to explain it to him tomorrow. Before I fall asleep, it occurs to me that this must be something akin to how it feels to be a father. For a while at least, even as you prove unreliable, your child is still inclined to regard you as the source of all knowledge.

Nineteen

I forgot that Han has his day off today. Luckily, he has forgotten about electricity. I make us fried eggs on toast and he watches me paint for a while in the garden, then goes in to lie on the divan reading the *Japan Mail*. Towards the middle of the day he leaves, saying he is going back to the lodging house to write up some notes on what we have learned. I work on. When KG and Horney return, as the sun begins to dip below the hills to the West, and the last strip of sunlight in the garden turns to shade, they find me still at my easel. In truth, I heard them as they entered the house from the front, conversing loudly, as if they were playing to an audience. They've been with actors, of course they're now actors themselves. I purposely wait for them to come out to the garden, as I want them to see how my canvas has developed.

'Well I should be frigged, the Nith is still in full spate,' the Horned One stumbles from the veranda onto the grass. I can't yet tell whether he's still playing the monster, or if it's the effects of the drink, but a sign from KG tells me it's the latter.

'Let's see the masterpiece then,' Horney steers a course towards my easel, a punch-drunk pugilist trying to fasten on his opponent. Henry follows behind him, no less eager to see what I've produced, and I'll not deny I'm anxious as I wait for their verdict. After a series of theatrical squints, Horney beams and claps me on the back. 'I like it, man. I like it. You're learning from me at last.'

KG wraps me in a hug: 'Don't listen to a word he says. You're onto something all your own here.'

Moving forward, leaning even closer to my easel, Horney starts laughing.

'What is it?' I ask, irritated.

'Your eel, Nithy, your eel!' He's doubled up now, rocking with laughter.

'What about it?' I demand angrily.

He turns and lurches towards me, opening his arms to grip me in a hug that might be as much about him having adopted the role of Frankenstein's monster, as wanting someone to hold onto to stay upright. Either way, we hold onto each other, and I can smell the drink on him. With his face up close to mine, I see the fine web of veins already pushing at the surface of the skin on his cheeks and nose, and have a vision of what he might look like in ten years' time: even more rubicund, the scowl he wears for sport starting to settle into permanence.

'What's wrong with my eel, Horney?' I ask him again, gently. He's tired and he needs his bed, I realise. He might not remember this in the morning, but I will, and I want an answer.

'Sorry, Nithy,' he croaks mirthfully. 'It's just that it's smiling. I've never seen an eel smiling before. But it's good.'

KG leads him back inside while I pack up my paints. Before I lift my canvas off the easel, I look at it again. I've painted Han holding an *unagi* by the neck. To convey the ceaseless flicking of its body there are in fact multiple eels, each a tiny distance away from the last. I've applied rapid horizontal strokes to link them and create a blurring effect. The entire foreground of my canvas is given to this whip-cracking eel, water droplets flying off its scales. Behind it is Han's face, which I worked from the earlier sketches and one I made while he was sleeping this morning. It's an Asian homage to Lepage, showing the dignity and pity of the boy at work. In the background, fencing Han in, are ranks

119

of bamboo. I've done the leaves as a frenzy of dabs with the brush angled sideways, in the style of Horney himself. Horney is right. My eel's bewhiskered mouth is turned up at the corners in what seems the subtlest of smiles. This was not intentional, but I don't see any reason to change it. Nature jokes at our expense all the time, so why should my canvas not reflect this?

Back in the house, over a tea while Horney snores, I ask KG about their trip to Enoshima. He shows me pictures of steps up to shrines and gardens; views between trees out onto the ocean; fishermen carrying nets and women mending baskets. It looks like a postcard paradise, perfect for SIR. He sips his tea thoughtfully: 'We weren't exactly restrained. But yes, it's tranquil. Beautiful. If I had the money and I didn't think Reid would send someone to kill me, I'd be tempted to live there and ignore the rest of the world for ever.'

'But did those talons gouge you?'

He smiles, rueful, 'Miss Hawk turns out to have a marital glove calling her back to earth.'

Twenty

A few days later, and Han and I have found a chance to investigate our lead. Sakemoto's studio is next to an English bakery on Motomachi Street, the one where Han directed me in search of pies. As we approach, the scent of bread and pastry fills my nostrils. I can't help wondering why Europeans and Americans come to Japan to eat what they could consume in their own backyard. I suppose plenty of them want home comforts, and the local 'colour' only within limits, in safe packages. The studio has a shop window full of souvenir prints and guidebooks catering to exactly these tastes. A doorbell tinkles as we enter the shop, which is cramped and surprisingly dark. A few steps take us up to the counter, behind which a slim, neat figure rises from a stool. Just as he was when we were introduced before, Sakemoto-san is wearing a well-tailored suit, his pencil-thin moustache trimmed more carefully than many a lady's eyebrow. I remember the fleeting impression he gave me of assurance and self-control, though I put it down then only to his vocation as a camera man. Perhaps recognising me, he smiles and bows. On the counter, I notice, is the latest edition of the *Japan Mail*. It occurs to me that Han may have a rival for his mastery of English as a second tongue.

'Good afternoon. You are the Scottish artist, am I correct?'

After congratulating Sakemoto on his memory, and introducing Han as my assistant, I explain that I have a special commission for a painting. I tell him that I need photographs of young women sporting the very latest fashions. He listens, nodding, then motions for us to follow him behind the counter and up a steep wooden staircase.

121

We emerge through the ceiling into a room with a table in the centre. Around all four sides are cabinets of dark wood with more shelves and drawers than you would find in a medieval apothecary. Sakemoto goes to one of these and opens a drawer. His fingers move with delicate efficiency as he retrieves a small box. He locates a further three such boxes and brings them to the table, where he entreats us to sit down.

'The pictures in these are all from this year. In them you will find ...' he pauses, as if recalling the phrase from a textbook, 'the flower of Japanese womanhood. Each box contains 50 postcard-size prints. One print costs two *yen*, or you can buy six for ten *yen*. Please look through them at your leisure and select any that you want. There is one more thing.'

He moves to another drawer and returns with a magnifying glass, which he hands to me, 'in case you need to see more closely.'

Apologising that he must 'return to his post,' he bows again before turning and disappearing down the stairs. Han and I look at one another, thinking this is hardly the behaviour one would expect of someone who has a guilty conscience.

We settle to the task of looking through the boxes. Not knowing the fashions of previous years, I can only speculate as to how the images I begin sifting through represent the latest trends. Presumably a modern twist lies in the hairstyles and the dress patterns, for there seems little else to indicate modernity. I cannot help but contrast them with portraits of women fighting for the equality of their sex, who face the camera squarely as if to challenge its authority. These young women, whether by instinct or instruction, look downwards as if embarrassed by its technological gaze.

Half way through the first box of charming but tedious

domestic portraits, perfect for SIR, I come upon a familiar face. From the photo, one would not know Bara is capable of laughter, far less that she could be the creator of those wickedly vengeful felines. Here she is, the ideal obedient housewife, kneeling on the *tatami* matting, all her concentration on the needlework spread across her lap. The plate has been tinted, and her kimono matches the pale pink of the cherry blossom on the wall hanging behind her. The next picture is Bara again, this time pouring tea. On the third one, I stop, as nonplussed as I used to be in my school days, faced with Mr J. McKenzie's terrifyingly complex division sums. The print shows Bara kneeling in profile, lovingly combing the hair of an infant who is in turn absorbed in playing with his wooden toy. I pass the magnifying glass over the image, enlarging her cheeks and nose to a liquid shimmer. Only then, looking through the warping lens, does it occur to me that Bara and the child had probably never laid eyes on each other until they were brought together in the studio. I place the print to one side and continue, though in fact, I think, there is hardly any point in me doing this. Han is the one who would recognise Tsubaki, if she is here. I only have his description and the haziest of memories of a scowling face in the group photo that the Mama-san showed us. Han is flicking through the cards far more quickly than me; he's already nearly finished two boxes. I am about to replace another card when something makes my hand stop. I show Han the picture I am holding and I know instantly that I was right. Tsubaki's untameable aura is so strong that even a dissembling photographer has concluded she could not possibly fit a domestic setting. She's pictured alone, in the doorway of what looks like a teahouse, glaring at the camera over the rim of a fan as challengingly as any suffragette.

We return downstairs bearing four prints, as I think it best to include others to divert suspicion that we are on the trail of Tsubaki. Sakemoto is engaged serving another customer.

While we wait, I observe him covertly, trying to read his face for clues. Nothing evil or saintly jumps out. All I can conclude is that he takes great care over his appearance.

'How do you find the girls in these photographs?' I ask him as casually as I can when he is ready to serve us.

'It is … how should I say. Not difficult. I am sure it is the same in your country. Beautiful girls want to have their pictures taken. Especially when I pay them.'

'And do you take a note of their names, the girls who come?'

'Of course.' Smiling still, he retrieves our pictures from the paper bag he has placed them in, turns the top one over, and shows us a series of tiny Japanese characters written on the back, where any half-decent investigators would have looked. 'Is there any girl in particular that you are interested in?'

Han, who until then has been silent, spreads the prints out on the counter. He places his finger on the picture of Tsubaki. 'This girl.' he says, looking Sakemoto in the eye.

There is no doubt that this produces an effect. The photographer looks sharply at Han, then back to me, as if he can't quite work out what we add up to. Then he calmly turns the picture over. 'This one is called Tsubaki.' He pronounces her name syllable by syllable, moving his finger over the pictograms. 'It means camellia. In Japan we often give women the names of flowers. I believe you do the same in England.'

'Did you take this picture?' Han presses him.

'Naturally I took it. I am a photographer,' Sakemoto says evenly. 'I remember this Tsubaki. She made an interesting subject. I think not, but I will check to see if I have any more pictures of her.' From under the counter he retrieves a bound ledger. After turning to the back and running his finger down a list, he shakes his head. 'I'm afraid the others have all been

124

sold.'

'Thank you for checking,' I say quickly, keen to end the encounter before Han commits us any further.

'You are most welcome, Mister Nith.'

He nods and bows one final time to us as we exit the shop.

Outside, when I suggest to Han that we have no reason to suspect Sakemoto merely because he took some photographs of Tsubaki, he shakes his head.

'Didn't you see the way he looked when I pointed at her? I'm sure he knows that she is dead.'

I concede that Han may be right, but knowing that Tsubaki is dead does not mean he had anything to do with her death. Han is forced to accept the logic of this, but is unsatisfied. He is convinced Sakemoto is hiding something and wants to investigate him further. I cannot help feeling that the photographer is not someone to trifle with. I try to dissuade him, and before parting at the entrance to Chinatown we agree at least that we should consider before deciding on our next move.

Twenty-one

The following evening, I am out with H and H, the three of us dressed to impress in our dandiest threads: paisley waistcoats and fancy cravats. The British Consulate is an imposing two-storey villa, like one of the big merchant's houses in Glasgow, only cream and white, and flying a Union Jack. We go through a gate, across a lawn, past rose bushes, and enter a high-ceilinged, marble-floored hallway. Now we're in Japan, but we're not in Japan. We've come 'home', but we haven't travelled anywhere. A terribly polite chap checks our names and finds them on his list. We are guests of Arabella Hawk, whose 'marital glove', it turns out, is the consul himself.

Drink, of course, is necessary. We arm ourselves with champagne flutes in a reception room lined with enough naval scenes to bore an admiral, then step out some French doors into a courtyard. A hum of chatter rises from groups clustered round a broad cinnamon tree. From under its lantern-lit branches, the effervescent Mrs Hawk sees us and shouts across. She's wearing a turquoise satin dress with puffed sleeves and a lace collar. Her gloved arms dance arabesques as she calls over a tall, whiskery figure in top hat and tails. She introduces us to him with our collective noun, and I sense she enjoys its emphasis on our youthfulness and place of origin. The chap with the whiskers seems less impressed.

'Leonard Hawk. British Consul.' He shakes hands with each of us, then his wife begins to pitch an idea to him: we should be given an exhibition in the consulate, since we are 'major modern artists.' He replies with non-committal politeness and Arabella Hawk sighs.

'He thinks artists are just a bunch of layabouts. But I know that Archie for one has been working furiously on a painting for the past week.' She looks at me and I feel exposed by her gaze.

'It's true.'

'You see. He's been working so hard he's almost forgotten how to talk. And we're going to lose them soon enough. Their dealer's calling them back to Glasgow next spring.'

'Well, I'm sure they'll have their exhibition there, my dear. I'm just not sure the consulate is appropriate. Nothing against you gentlemen.' Whiskers turns a diplomatic smile on the three of us. Horney assures him that we quite understand, our style may be too experimental for some tastes. Arabella gives a theatrical sigh, tosses her dark curls, and places her hand at a jaunty angle on her hip.

'Experimental is exactly what we need. I'm sorry Leonard's being such a stiff old Britannic bore. Do you know he was picked for this post because he's one of the few people who can out-formalise the Japanese?'

Whiskers then reveals that he does possess a sense of humour, by bowing to his wife so deeply that his nose almost touches the ground.

We laugh. 'I suppose Arabella has approached you to play a part in *Frankenstein*,' KG remarks. For a second, I wonder if he has gone too far, but the Britannic bore responds in spirit.

'She has indeed. She wanted me to be the monster.'

'Rubbish! The monster is too full of human emotion. I'm afraid my husband is expert at learning lines, but lacks the spontaneity to emote them on stage. George and Edward, on the other hand, have proven themselves to have a great deal of acting promise.'

'I'm sorry gentlemen. My wife has obviously been distracting you from your art.'

I begin to suspect that Arabella rather enjoys these disputatious theatrics with her husband. They are like a music hall double act. She, I realise, is someone who wants to live as though she is permanently on stage. As Leonard Hawk resorts to the much-beloved topic of how we have 'found Japan', she sees some other people she knows and leaves us to talk to them. Aided by the champagne, I find myself describing the poetic jousting match we witnessed last week. The consul listens politely, then suggests there are some people we might like to meet. As we follow him, KG looks over his shoulder at me.

'Enjoying being back in society, Nithy?' When I indicate ambivalence, he leans in to me and whispers, 'She's a fine woman, don't you think. Wonder what she's doing with that old vulture.' There's no time to reply, as the vulture has led us to a new set of carcasses, who he introduces with their own collective noun: 'The Old Japan Hands.' Declaring that we are 'all ears for tales of the real Japan,' he abandons us in their company.

A few awkward moments pass: this trio could hardly make it more obvious that they would rather have been left to themselves. Finally, their centreman, a shaven-headed fellow, speaks up. His accent is heavy with the dropped 'h' and crushed vowels of the north of England.

'Ow long you lot planning on staying then?'

When KG replies that we'll be returning next March, the fellow snorts, as if it confirms his worst fears. 'Sort of artistic smash and grab raid are you?'

'Aye. We're just burglars with brushes,' Horney drawls.

'And on what basis are you selecting the Japanese culture you use to create your art?' The one diagonally opposite me enquires. He is squat, powerfully built, with a neck squashed into his body and bulbous eyes, rather reminiscent of a toad. His coppery hair is pulled into a knot on top of his head and he's wearing a Japanese robe in expensive-looking silk. His accent has a hint of something that I can't quite pin down. KG decides to follow Horney's lead, replying with exaggerated earnestness.

'Well, Sir. The pair of us just paint whatever's sat in front of us, which tends to be geishas. Nithy here's the exception. He goes for eels, preferably battered.'

For all their cultural know-how, the other two seem to be encountering facetiousness for the first time. But the coppery toad eyes me with a shrewd glint.

'Eels. Is that so?' He seems about to ask another question when the consul claps for the crowd's attention. The violinist is ready to play. We are ushered inside, filling up rows of chairs which have been assembled. At the front is a dark-haired young woman, holding a violin and bow. Her arms are so slender they look as if a strong breeze might snap them. Next to her, behind a piano, sits a male pianist of similar tender years and elegant appearance. The consul takes to the stage and introduces them as the Miscovic twins from Zagreb, brought to Yokohama 'by the endeavours of that indefatigable agent of culture, Augustus Dowd.' Hawk indicates the toad, who dismisses the applause with a regal wave.

As the pianist begins to play, images of joint exhibitions with Bara in the salons of Europe are flying through my mind. Then the violin's opening bars come in and I'm soon lost in admiration of the fingers dancing from string to string. As if to compensate for her slenderness, she uses her upper body as an extension of the bow, wielding it almost like a sabre. The piece is a sonata by Cesar Franck, and it mesmerises the audience for the duration of the four movements. I'm not the only one whose spinal cord is galvanised into a veritable Tesla coil. When the final bar is over and the twins take their bows, KG leans over to me as we join in the applause. 'What's a few splodges on a canvas compared to that?'

'We might as well be burglars with brushes,' I agree.

Restoring our bruised painterly pride with champagne, we follow the shuffling feet back out into the courtyard. Darkness has fallen quickly, as it does in Japan. Suddenly I feel a hand clamp onto my shoulder. I spin round to find the heavy-lidded eyes of the toad, otherwise known as Augustus Dowd, boring into mine.

'I believe you wanted to see me, Mister Nith?'

I stammer some incoherent response. Did I make my fascination with his appearance so obvious?

'A certain newshound told me you have some Japanese art I may be interested in.' My relief is double: my failure to make any progress in helping Bara has been playing on my mind. Finding my tongue, I praise the pictures while remaining vague on their content and provenance. The strategy seems to work. Dowd is intrigued and makes what is effectively a pitch for himself as the buyer of choice. He explains that while he is originally a silk merchant, he has built up expertise in recent years in the local art market, selling pictures by Western artists to wealthy Japanese clients, and vice versa.

Dowd is not a man to waste time once he is set on a course of action. When can I come to his house to show him the pictures, he wants to know. At the first hour I propose he gives his approval, pressing a card into my hand, with his address printed both in English and Japanese. One more thing that makes me think I like him: he is not a man for small talk. As soon as our meeting is confirmed, he apologises and says he must go to thank the performers. To conclude our interview, he offers me a small bow. I suppose he has been here so long that Japanese formalities now seem natural to him.

Later in the evening, I find myself in conversation with a young Japanese man, Soseki-san, who is not only a student of English but a translator of literature. I'm describing my own attempts to learn Japanese, and trying out some phrases on him. We hit a stumbling block and as usual, it happens suddenly: one minute I'm fine, the next I'm overwhelmed by the enormous effort required to sustain social interaction. Making some feeble excuse, I leave the poor fellow and make my way inside, through the reception-room. I walk out into the hallway and up a staircase, emerging into an empty corridor on the second floor of the building. On the wall is a series of framed maps showing the growth of the settlement of Yokohama. As I move along the corridor looking at them, I travel backwards in time to 1859, and a small fishing village that happened to be the place where the Japanese received an American gunboat captain who would not take no for an answer. Just as I'm feeling calmed by the grand sweep of history, a voice right behind me growls. 'Open yourself to trade or I'll blow you to bits.'

It's Arabella Hawk. She's highly amused at the success of her gag, but my face must betray a degree of shock, for she apologises and expresses concern about the state of my nerves. I manage to play down my reaction and ask her about the progress of *Frankenstein*.

'That's exactly what I wanted to talk to you about,' she says huskily, drawing me further along the corridor.

'I'm really not the acting talent you think I am,' I protest.

'Oh, it's not that. I –' she breaks off. 'This is rather embarrassing. Shouldn't be, but is. The thing is I wanted to tell you –' she stops again, lowering her chin and jutting out her lower lip in a parody of childish guilt.

'What?'

She lifts her eyes to mine, '*Frankenstein*. It's mine. I wrote it.'

131

For a second or two I'm struck dumb, thinking that she is claiming to be Mary Shelley. Finally, it dawns on me what her meaning might be. 'You have written the play script?'

She nods, exhilarated, then a rush of words begins spilling out of her that leaves me little to do other than make brief interjections. None of them prepare me for the sudden revelation that she's expecting her first child, information I must keep absolutely secret – 'not even Leonard knows yet.' I make the appropriate noises of congratulation, wondering why on earth she has chosen to tell me, practically a stranger.

'You know, Archie, the urge to make a child springs from the same well as the urge to make art. You'll sacrifice everything for it. I knew you understood this when you turned down the trip to Enoshima.'

Unsure of what I ought to reply, I promise to go to see her play. This pleases her, and I offer my arm as we walk back down the stairs together.

Twenty-two

It's late morning and I'm putting the finishing touches to the picture when KG pokes his head round the doorframe to tell me that 'a certain young adventurer' has come to call. I catch the whiff of the eel stall as I come into the entrance porch and find Han standing there in his vest and baggy work pants. He has to show me something, he declares, not as discreetly as I would like, though fortunately Horney is out at yet another temple visit and KG's on his way to the garden to work on his latest geisha. Han, himself, should be on the waterfront working, but he explains that Yamato is ill, 'shitting his guts out.' Smiling at his phrasing – learned, I remember, from my description of our unfortunate reaction to the food in Cairo – I invite him into our living room. His eyes light upon the sheets of sketching paper I've spread out over the table. He asks me if he can use one and I watch while he sketches, with an impressive accuracy, the outline of the settlement reduced to the points which relate to the case: from the perpendicular angles of the waterfront, with the warehouses as squashed oblongs, to the long thread of Isezakicho Street, on which he marks the *Kabuki* theatre, and the Persimmon further along. Leaving a space for Chinatown, he adds Motomachi Street running along the foot of the bluff, which he represents with the flat of his pencil as dark shading. Finally, he places a cross at the location of Sakemoto's studio and then turns to me, pointing the pencil almost in the manner of a teacher addressing his student.

'Let's suppose Tsubaki went to Sakemoto's after I saw her in the theatre. Or to the Persimmon. From either, it's a 20-minute walk to the sea. But what if she didn't walk?

What if she was murdered somewhere else and her body was taken to the sea?'

'But how would somebody take her to the harbour without being noticed?'

'Easily. Carts are always coming and going from the warehouses. All you see on them are the shapes of crates or sacks. They're often covered in cloth, like when Yamato and I went for charcoal. The murderer could have waited for darkness, then driven his cart near the edge, and dumped Tsubaki in over the side.'

It's a horrifying image, a young woman being disposed of in this way, as if she were no more than unwanted goods; But Han's reasoning is undeniable. Tsubaki could have been murdered in a way that left no mark, and as soon as the water received her, as long as there were no witnesses, the assumption would be that she had drowned. No sooner have I accepted this sequence of events in my mind than Han, with a few quick flourishes of his pencil, explains that it's also possible Tsubaki made her own way to the waterfront, that she met someone there who was responsible for her death and disposed of her in the same way; or, as Yamato suggested, that she had been stumbling in a drunken state, fallen in, and drowned accidentally. It's left to me to add the hypothesis the *Mail* is promoting – that she deliberately drowned herself. That means we have four possible scenarios to examine. Suggesting that this would even tax the resources of professional policemen, I ask Han what he proposes to do. He begins to list examples from Conan Doyle's stories to argue that the murderer must have left some evidence of a connection to Tsubaki. 'All we have to do is find the connection,' he concludes, with an emphatic stab of his pencil.

'And where do we look for that?' I ask, aiming to lead him gently to conclude that our pursuit is impossible. 'We already have three suspects.'

Thinking of who he can mean, I produce Yamato and Sakemoto, both of whom, it seems to me, can only tenuously merit the term 'suspect'. The third, he reminds me, is the mysterious foreigner who Tsutsumi saw talking to Tsubaki outside the Persimmon.

'And what if we're investigating a murder where none took place?'

He considers my point for a few moments and then responds: 'Is it not better to investigate a murder that didn't happen than fail to investigate one that did?'

Again, this prodigy confounds me with his youthful ideals.

And so, to the nub of it: inspired by *The Red-Headed League*, I agree to work on creating a pretext to lure Sakemoto out of his shop, allowing Han to break in and search the premises for incriminating evidence. Meanwhile, he will try to find a way to do the same in Yamato's house. As for the mystery man, the only option we can think of is to ask other Persimmon girls if they ever saw Tsubaki with this foreigner.

After Han leaves, I cannot help thinking it's all funk and bunkum. That for all his undoubted talents, the boy is too naïve and the official version is probably right, after all. Though no one asks the question why; what could provoke suicidal mania in a young woman whose sole asset is her body in its unblemished form? I can think of one reason, which for the sake of delicacy might be kept out of the press, even if it were known to those investigating. And yet, if Tsubaki were carrying a baby, would that really eliminate the possibility she was murdered? On the contrary, in bringing a definite, though unknown male into play, it may even make it more likely. Remember the terrible case of Jack the Ripper, just a few years ago in London. Wasn't it speculated that the killer was a religious madman, hellbent on punishing women for aborting nature's path to creation? But this is Japan: warped interpretations of the Bible should not hold sway here. Anyway, such speculations are useless. I must get back to my painting, and not entirely neglect the kind that Reid is after: Simplicity, Innocence, Restraint!

I lose myself working late from one of Sakemoto's prints – a lowered gaze, kimono folds and the stippled surface of a teapot. Finally I am satisfied, and think that even Reid, were he looking over my shoulder, would approve. My entry to sleep's realm comes easily, and no doubt it knits my ravelled sleeve, but only for the rips to reappear with a vengeance before I'm allowed to emerge. Black is blocking me at his office door, telling me that he knows me for an impostor: I am not one of the Glasgow Boys, but I can meet Murchison on the condition that I give up painting and become his apprentice correspondent. Then, I'm with Bara in her room at the Persimmon, and we're showing each other our pictures. From behind a screen, Arabella Hawk materialises, wearing the *yukata* of a Persimmon girl. I seek to cover my nakedness, but she only laughs as Bara becomes a cat and slips out the window. Now, I'm in a teahouse confessing to KG that I'm laying down my brush and becoming a journalist. A sliding door opens and Han appears, holding his knife. I look down at my body and see my limbs have shrunk to stumps, and my torso has become black and sinuous. At last, I awake, drenched in sweat. A blade of early morning sunlight is slicing through a gap in the shutters and across my body. For von Hartmann and his theories of the unconscious, all this must have meaning. I could try to decipher it further; or I could channel my energies on the day ahead.

Electing the second course, I make myself a pot of tea – black, not green – and sit down with the *Mail*, which I have not read properly yet, apart from the snippet about Tsubaki's death. Among other things, I learn that seven foreign vessels of war are at anchorage in Yokohama harbour; *Eczema,* a book on skin troubles, may be sent free for one *yen* and a stamp by Messrs North and Rae Ltd; and a meet of Yokohama cyclists will take place this Saturday at 2pm at the boathouse – there will be a dismount at Kawasaki bridge at 3pm to meet the Tokyo men. I still cannot cycle, but I am a different, worldlier man by the time Horney stumbles into the room in his dressing gown, complaining that KG is now trying out some Japanese brand of callisthenics, which he believes will keep his body supple into middle age. The early rise has served a purpose. I feel fortified in my sense of my own negotiating prowess. My dream has lost its power and become a foolish parody of Poe. One sees the attraction for these journalists who elide their insecurities and write about the world, rather than their messy interior selves.

Twenty-three

At times, during Augustus Dowd's tour of his house, I feel as if I really am a journalist given a glimpse of some of the finest examples of *ukiyo-e* by masters including Hokusai and Kuniyoshi. Certainly, I could write a dozen articles about the works I see on his walls, masterpieces of elegant line and colour, full of references to Japanese culture, some of which Dowd explains to this uninformed correspondent.

From the gallery room, he leads me back out into a corridor, which opens onto a veranda supported by cedar columns. This veranda runs the length of the back of the house. At the far end of it are two wicker chairs either side of a table. I expect we will sit down here and talk, but Dowd wants to show me his garden first. This, he confides, is his true pride and joy. As we begin to meander along the intricately twisting paths formed of flat stones, he imparts botanical information about the native flora he has expended great effort to collect. Of maple alone, he has 19 different varieties. I enquire about the moss-covered statuettes nestled among the vegetation. They are Japanese nature spirits, he says. I ask if they don't belong in Shinto shrines, but he tells me this is a Judaeo-Christian misconception; in Japan, any natural place can become a shrine.

It takes some time for us to complete the circuit, which allows me to comprehend the full extent of the garden. It must be three acres or more, walled in by mature bamboo on two sides, while at the back the cliff-face of the bluff provides an impenetrable natural wall. Returning to the house, we cross the hump-backed wooden bridge over the stream, pausing to admire the jostling carp; flickers of lemon yellow, green and gold. Then back up onto the veranda, where the table is positioned to have the brightness and heat of the afternoon sun filtered through a screen of maple leaves. On the table is yet more proof that nothing in Dowd's domain is left to chance. While we've been walking, a carafe of sake and two cups have appeared. 'From Kanazawa, the home of lacquerware,' he pours, adding, 'And Niigata sake, the finest in all Japan.' We touch cups before drinking, then he turns the conversation to the crux of my visit.

'So, Mister Nith. These pictures of yours?'

I reach into the satchel I've brought and unroll them on the table. I've chosen their order carefully, positioning at the top the one I think is the best of all Bara's efforts. It shows a pair of kimono-clad cat courtesans applying maquillage to each other with their forepaws. One of them is using a hind paw to trap the tail of a diminutive Westerner, who struggles in vain to escape. He's wearing a shirt and tailcoat, but on his lower half only socks. His undershorts and trousers have been hidden by the curving tail of the second cat. The whole scene is beautifully rendered in flowing lines of black, by necessity, as Bara told me she can't afford coloured ink. Like the classical works of *ukiyo-e*, the picture bears a title in *kanji*, from top to bottom:

猫
の
手
も
借
り
た
い

Dowd's laughter, when it comes, is long and appreciative.

'May I?' I motion for him to go ahead and look through the other pictures. He does so, pausing on two or three longer than the others, his expression conveying amusement bordering on wonder. Returning to the first picture, he tops up our cups and leans back in his chair, staring hard at me. 'Do you have any idea what the writing signifies here?'

I admit my ignorance, and he leans forward again, pointing at the elegant strokes on the first picture. 'The literal translation is: 'I would even borrow the hand of a cat.' A Japanese idiom. You say it when you are extremely busy, it means you'll take any help you can get.'

'A visual pun.'

'Exactly. All but unknown in European art, but Japanese art is full of them. Kuniyoshi, for instance, is a master of the genre. You remember the examples of his work I showed you earlier?'

I nod, though the impact of the wordplay at the time passed me by.

'So, who did these?'

'Will you tell me first if you're interested in buying them?'

'Ha! Out comes the hard-nosed Scot. But I'm afraid it's impossible to say without knowing the artist.'

'Why?'

'You know why. You give me any old doodle with Rembrandt's name on it, and I'll give you 5000 *yen*. Give me the same by some unknown Johan Van Loon, and you'll be lucky to get 20.'

'This is different. We're not talking about Old Masters. This is modern art. Reputations can be built overnight if the work is fresh and has something to say.'

'Does that explain why you and your friends are in Japan copying ten-for-a-*yen* postcard photos with oil paints?'

I choose not to respond to this provocation. Dowd shifts forward in his seat and scrutinises some of the pictures again.

'No European copyist did these.'

'Correct,' I concede.

'Murchison mentioned an eel stall boy, but I don't believe that for a second.'

'I assume you're familiar with the Persimmon Number Nine?'

My change of tack seems to wrong-foot him for a second, before he adopts his usual knowing air.

'A few years ago, there was a humorous tongue twister doing the rounds among those of us old hands who've bothered to learn the language: *kare kekkon katta kedo kaki o kau*. Loosely it translates as, "the chap bought a wife but still buys persimmons."'

I laugh in appreciation of what's obviously considered great wit among the 'old hands', and then tell him:

'The artist who did these, she works at the Persimmon.'

Dowd's eyes almost pop out. 'Works ... in that way?'

'In that way, yes.'

He bows his head and mutters something in Japanese, which of course I don't understand. Then, he resumes in English. 'Let me tell you a bit about myself, Mister Nith. I'm no natural businessman any more than you. I fell into it almost by accident. But whichever way you come in, commerce is a stressful game. You have your money and you lay it down, in my case, on the ability of little white worms to produce silk in sufficient quantity and quality. There are many variables which could go wrong – just this year, a late spring frost came close to obliterating my yield. Now, I'm secure enough to survive a bad year. I have as much money in art as I do in silk, but it wasn't always that way. For a while I could only dream of dealing in art; my

141

days were spent inspecting crops and fibres, figuring out which farmers I could trust and which ones were giving me the dross. What it does to you, living like this, is it gives you a great desire to … how shall I put this? Expend your seed. To fuck, Mister Nith. I must have fucked a lot of women in that place over the years. And not once, not once, was I ever shown an artistic masterpiece as an encore. So how is it that you, fresh off the boat, can already have struck gold?'

Deciding that his openness deserves mine in return, I sketch out as rapidly as I can the incident with the cat, my astonishment at seeing the pictures, Bara's reluctance to sell to me, and my desire to help her by finding a buyer.

'So, at no point did she ask you to become her agent. Am I to understand you've taken it upon yourself to act on her behalf out of a spirit of pure charity? Or do you see a profit for yourself in this?'

Just as with Murchison, I explain my motives, and in doing so let slip Bara's name, which Dowd seizes on.

'So let's consider this talented rose. As I'm sure you can imagine, all these young women have their own troubled pasts. We can presume that before she was indentured into prostitution, this one had some artistic training. You agree that no one could produce these without it. Also, materials. One doesn't tend to find them lying around a brothel, even a Japanese one.' Dowd allows his large head to loll back as he thinks, the loose wattle of his neck reminding me again of a swollen toad.

'My guess is she comes from an artistic family. The father is a painter. A struggling one, but determined. Something happens, I don't know, perhaps he displeases his patron. Debts are piling up. One way out is to indenture his daughter for ten years as a courtesan. A perfectly legal arrangement. Possibly he even chooses the Persimmon, knowing the shame of giving her to foreign men will be balanced by the

142

benefits of learning some English and French.'

I'm appalled at the idea of an artist who would do this, but I have to admit it's convincing as an explanation for Bara's talents.

'I would buy these pictures, certainly. But my pockets aren't deep enough to offer Bara permanent patronage out of charity. I would need to be sure that I could sell some of them on.'

Dowd leans forward and examines the topmost picture again, the tip of his tongue curling out between his teeth. I take a sip of sake, trying to quell the feeling that I'm out of my depth.

'There is something, I think, in this picture and a few of the others, that might sell.'

This is what dealers do: they see audiences and commercial possibilities where artists only see form and meaning.

'Do you know anything about the political climate, Mister Nith? As the new Japan gains strength, she grows ever more resentful of being patronised by Western powers. Some of these pictures fit a certain narrative. The Westerner appears weak, ridiculous, undone by his own decadence. The cats fight back.'

'You mean the cats represent Japan?'

Dowd makes claws of his hands: 'Indeed. Japan, armed and dangerous.'

'But what about the pictures with Japanese men?'

'Those would be a harder sell.'

'So you would make Bara a propagandist for Japanese militarism?'

'I would keep Bara in a tidy income.'

This hypothetical compromise hovers in the air between us.

'And you think you could?'

'I'm not a bad negotiator. Of course, you would need to let me have these first,' he gestures at the pile of sketches. 'For a respectable sum, of course.' In the silence that follows this, a sudden catch of breeze sends the corners of the papers fluttering. I place my hand on them and keep it there, even though the breeze dies as soon as it came. Do I have Bara's authority to do this? How would she feel if she knew her art could serve a nationalist goal? Is Dowd right? Surely it's obvious the cats represent the workers, not a rival set of future imperialists? But she might not even care. Having the chance to make money from art and buy out her contract at the Persimmon is probably more important. But I can't make the decision on her behalf.

'Very well,' I say to Dowd. 'I'll sell you these, give the money to her, and hope you can find a buyer to make the arrangement permanent. But I insist that you meet Bara and lay it all out straight to her. She must receive a proper cut. Something in writing.'

Dowd initially winces at the idea, but then relents. 'On Friday I am hosting a party here, an evening of intercultural entertainment. I was going to invite you anyway, but why don't you ask Bara to attend and I'll talk things through with her?'

I agree to do this, and Dowd accedes to my request to bring two extra guests as well.

I leave his house with a handsome wad of *yen* to give to Bara, feeling that the encounter has undoubtedly been a success. Friday evening may set her on the path to the artistic career she deserves. Han will have a chance to make inroads into society, and both will benefit from the company of Tsutsumi. I'm intrigued myself by this event; from what Dowd says, it sounds like a real cultural mixing as opposed to the staid exchanges promoted by officials.

Twenty-four

The three of us take a rickshaw up to Negishi racecourse, on the other side of the bluff. From the grandstand, we walk through rolling parkland until we find a spot with views south over the ocean. We set up our easels, just as if we were in the Trossachs. The heat is relentless as ever, but a slight sea breeze is coming in, and it's refreshing to think about nothing but the age-old problems of transferring nature to canvas.

On the way back in the afternoon, telling KG and Horney that I need to pick up supplies, I get out early and drop by Han's lodgings to tell him about the invitation to Dowd's. The old lady who runs the place has no English, but she understands his name and manages to communicate to me that he's out. She tugs me over to the doorway and points over the rooftops towards the sea.

'*Shigoto*?' I ask, remembering the word for work.

She beams in surprise at my linguistic prowess. However, as in my conversation with Bara, this only serves to give her a false confidence in my ability. She launches into a monologue which, despite my best efforts, does not resolve into meaning. Suddenly, she sinks to her knees, clutching her stomach, spasming and moaning in the most pitiable fashion. Alarmed, I bend and place my hand on her shoulder, feeling her sharp, brittle bone through the robe. It makes me think, for the first time in months, of my mother. I push away that thought, and when the old lady springs to her feet, laughing, I eventually understand that she was merely miming Yamato's illness.

145

As I approach our house, I see Han waiting at the gate. He comes hurrying down the hill towards me and I can see from his expression that he has something to tell me. I ask him to wait while I go inside to leave the coffee and biscuits I've bought, then we walk up the hill and a story tumbles from his mouth. It seems that, while caring for Yamato, who remains feverish, unable to hold down food, Han asked his boss about the feminine items he possessed. Yamato confessed that he had not told Han everything about his relationship to Tsubaki. He had loved her once, and asked her to marry him when her period of indenture to the Persimmon ended. The items were gifts, proof of his serious intentions, but she had refused him, leaving him with a silk belt and pearl comb. He was keeping them for whenever a more receptive candidate for the title of Mrs Yamato should emerge.

Han tells a tale well, and it touches me, hearing him describe these affairs of the heart, as if his grizzled boss were a character in a Jane Austen novel, set among the workers of Japan. During our talk, we've cut along the graveyard path, past the memorials of foreigners who never left this land. I stop when Han reaches the end of his story. After some thought, I suggest that now we have a more concrete motive for Yamato wishing harm to Tsubaki. Does Han still think it possible that his boss was involved in her death? I'm not expecting him to reject this idea as vehemently as he does. He has concluded, on such evidence as the look in Yamato's eyes and the way he spoke, that he was telling the truth. Is this a case of loyalty blinding logic, I wonder? We walk back the way we came, and I'm reminded of another matter weighing on poor Han's mind. As long as Yamato's illness continues, his wages have dried up, and he must soon find another source of income to sustain himself.

Later, we go out as a trio again, and have a few too many in a sailor's bar. I sleep dreamlessly this time, and lie in bed late next to KG and the snoring Horney. A languorous

Sunday morning unfolds, like the ones in KG's flat on St Vincent Street after a night in the Cabaret Bar. We sit drinking coffee, talking about the night before and what might be happening back home. Tsuki, too, is satisfied and at peace with the world. She drags her unfortunate victim, a mouse, thankfully, not a Western gent, into the living room. After receiving a scolding and then some fish scraps from KG, she darts from my lap to Horney's, purring and nuzzling against us promiscuously.

'Why do those two get all the thanks when I'm the one who fed you?' KG complains.

I'm making more coffee when I hear a knock on the door. I'm bracing myself for Han with more news, but when I come back into the living room, KG is opening a letter addressed to the three of us. His eyes light up when he identifies the sender.

'It's from Walton!'

'Entertain us then,' Horney growls.

KG clears his throat and reads: 'My Dear Boys, Glasgow is a safer but more tedious city with three of its most notorious rogues temporarily sent to a penal colony in the Far East End for corrective treatment. I dread to think what nefarious practices this previously unblemished region has been introduced to.'

It continues in this vein for a few paragraphs, before Walton embarks on his main narrative: 'For your amusement, Boys, I have a vintage Colquhoun story. This one concerns a commission our favourite artist recently received to paint a ceiling. Your man with the money is an ex-sailor who's been out living in Greece. He's made himself a fortune in the import trade – wines, olives, dates; you name it, he's traded it. The lad's a regular Phoenician. Not long after you lot headed off down the Clyde, he comes up it. And no sooner does he hop down onto the Broomielaw than he's splashed out on one of those big new villas south of the river for him and his lovely new Greek bride. It looks a treat from the outside – big garden, turrets on the roof, but inside it's as bare as a monk's cell. He needs to stop his girl from getting homesick, and she's the artistic type, so he thinks what better way than a nice Greek fresco on the dining room ceiling. And somehow or other – maybe since you boys are off the scene – the man who gets the job is Colquhoun. Yes, you can imagine his joy. Finally, he's the chosen one! And boy does he take it seriously. He comes up with his designs: shiteloads of nymphs and centaurs; a drunken Bacchus with cups overflowing; a bare-breasted Aphrodite on a wagon loaded with wine, grapes, olives, wheels of cheese; all pulled along by a fine pair of oxen. He takes them round to show your man. He's nervous – so nervous he feels like he's moving through a kind of fog up in that fancy southside street – but it turns out the lad's not the hardest to please. 'Smashin', ah love it,' he slaps Colquhoun on the back with a big meaty paw. Did I mention he's got the build of a heavyweight boxer? 'The morra me and Daphne set sail for Greece, but you just let yourself in and start paintin. Dinnae skimp on colours, ah'll pick up the bill, just make sure you're finished by the time we get back cuz the next day we're gonna hae a big weddin feast, and ah want the ceiling ready to show the in-laws, ye ken.'

Colquhoun's getting two hundred for this, and he's going to give it everything. He turns up at the house the next morning, and finds the front door locked but the back one open, so in he goes and sets to work. And boy does he work, like a bloody Trojan. He even takes to sleeping in that house. The weeks whizz by and he feels like bloody Michelangelo, he's spending so long lying on his back. But he gets there, and he's just putting the final touches on the last nymph when he hears a key turning in the front door. Shite! Surely the Big Man can't have come back a day early. He wanted it to be all ready and perfect. Phew! It's not the Big Man, just a couple of removal fellas heaving in a bookcase. That makes sense, it's about time your man got some furniture in. 'Surprised I've no seen you lads earlier,' Colquhoun calls down from his ladder. The pair look up and seem a wee bit surprised, but they don't say much, just go back out and come in again with more bookcases and boxes that they leave on the floor. They disappear and Colquhoun gets curious. He climbs down and opens one of the boxes, expecting maybe a Grecian vase, but what he finds is a stack of posters. They all show the same cartoon of men and women steaming in the gutter under the slogan: 'ALCOHOL DOES THE DEVIL'S WORK!' Colquhoun's confused now. He checks the address label. *Christian Temperance League. Number 23.* Ah! Now he sees. It's a simple case of mis-delivery. He's at number 25, and these were supposed to be delivered to the next house. You can hardly blame the fellas, Colquhoun thinks, all these new villas look the same. He'll do them a favour and explain what's happened. So he carries the box out the back door, round onto the street, up the next driveway. He sets it down and rings the bell. The door opens and Colquhoun just about shites himself. It's the Big Man.

'You – you're in the wrong house, Sir,' Colquhoun stammers. Big Hercules grabs him by the collar and hoists him up about a foot into the air. 'Naw pal, ah'm in my ain hoose, but ah dinnae see ma fuckin painted ceiling.'

To which Colquhoun replies: 'I've done your ceiling, Sir. It's in the house next door.'

After the laughter, we grow peckish, but the cupboards are bare again. We head out, but as it's Sunday, the bakery on Motomachi is closed. We walk on in pursuit of victuals, and I have an idea, which I outline to H and H. If we employ a housekeeper, we could avoid this and save money for more entertaining pursuits. Once the plan has caught their interest, I inform them of Han's present predicament and suggest that he could fill the role on a temporary basis. I'm expecting some opposition, but both KG and Horney are enthusiastic.

'I was wondering when we'd get to meet young Han again,' KG remarks.

Horney agrees. 'Tell him we want the next instalment of his life story.'

Twenty-five

The weather is a little fresher, a hint of autumn in the air, and we've joined an organised outing, a convoy of three carriages going to Kamakura, a dozen miles down the coast. In our carriage, a pleasant white-haired gentleman with excellent English tells us that at one point in Japan's past, Kamakura was the main seat of power. Still today, its temples are unparalleled in their importance to Buddhism, whose difference from Shintoism he tries to explain. In return, Horney tells him all about the pre-Christian legends of Galloway, and by the time we arrive, I think the old boy is as glad of the break as we are.

The temple complex is nestled at the foot of forested hills, a few hundred yards back from the ocean. We walk under great red *torii* gates into wide courtyards, around which the temple buildings are arranged. The harmony of the architecture is marvellous. The gates look like one of the simplest of *kanji* characters, with four strokes, two upright and two on top. The slight curvature of the beams really does give these structures the feel of something written by a human hand. From the courtyard, steps lead up to the main temple building. There's a low wall with donation boxes behind it. You toss a coin in and watch it roll through a gap between the slats, disappearing into a gleaming sea of currency. Our snowy-haired friend shows us how you then step back, clap your hands twice, and keeping your palms pressed, you close your eyes to pray. I can't help but compare the experience to the dark interior of a Catholic church: the bloody crucified Christs, the pitiable Virgins, the uncomfortable pews jammed together. Here in the open

151

air, I feel tremendously light. As I address a concept of God that I don't really understand without the slightest concern whether He, She or It exists or not. I raise my eyes to the intricate latticework of the overhanging roof and pray for Mother's health, for Han and Bara, for the success of my canvases, and for the international socialist revolution.

Our devotions complete, we stroll into one of the other buildings along the side of the courtyard. It's set up rather like the ticket office at a station, with a series of windows where pilgrims queue to talk to one of four or five priests, who listen and scribe a prayer suited to their wishes. This does not come for free, our friend explains, but the knowledge doesn't alter my sense of a place filled with harmonious devotion. KG and Horney seem similarly affected, and the three of us separate to wander and sketch until the agreed meeting time for our departure. As I'm mapping out the lines of a priest at work on his inscriptions, I spot a familiar figure taking photographs in the courtyard. Recognising Sakemoto gives me a jolt of shock, though it shouldn't be surprising he's here, as the trip is organised by the Photographic Society.

I manage to avoid him until the tour's final stop, the great bronze Buddha statue several miles from the temple complex. Horney approaches Sakemoto and asks him to take a photograph of the three of us. Inscrutably polite as ever, he makes no acknowledgement of my visit to his studio in Han's company. As we pose against the pedestal on which the great cross-legged figure sits, facing the cape-covered photographer, I'm struck suddenly by the camera as a potentially sinister force. With one click, it's pinning us here for ever, with these fixed smiles in this single moment in time. Perhaps, I think, we should take more seriously the women's belief that Tsubaki bargained her soul with some devil of the celluloid.

Twenty-six

'What happened to you?' I gasp.

Han appeared at our door, as I told him to, in the late morning. His smell of fish is stronger even than usual, but what's shocked me is the state of his left eye, a livid mess swollen half-shut.

'I can still work for you.' He seems to be stating it, not asking. I draw him into the porch, where he shows me a bagful of portions of fresh fish, their juices seeping through the thin paper wrapping.

'I got them at the market, the one Yamato goes to. Cheap. They think I'm Japanese.'

I remember I gave him extra money to buy shopping before he came here to prepare our lunch.

'Is that why they punched you in the face?'

'I'll tell you after,' he promises me. Accepting this compromise, I show him into our kitchen and equip him with a knife and chopping board. I watch as he fillets the fish, his hands moving with a professional's skill and precision.

'How is Yamato?' I enquire.

'Still sick. I'm worried about him.'

'Has he been to the doctor?'

'He says he doesn't like doctors.'

'Does he say why?'

'He says they take your money and give you fake medicine.'

Announcing his presence with a song, Horney enters the

kitchen, followed by KG. They are pleased to find Han here, especially pleased that he's at work making our lunch. He explains his black eye to them as the result of an altercation in a sailor's bar. A Japanese man insulted Korea and he responded. The other fellow came off worse as Han tells it, full of bravado. I sense, even though he's convincing, that the truth must be different. As we eat the fish, grilled in a tasty soy glaze and served over rice – much praised by all of us – it strikes me that I need to encourage Han to cultivate his literary instincts more. Sometimes, I have to remind myself that if he had been born somewhere else, he would be in school, preparing to go to university. Instead, he is working for us, though KG and I both help him wash up and put the things away, while Horney gets back to his Kamakura canvas and Tsuki enjoys a plateful of scraps.

I tell KG I'll show Han the laundry where we take our dirty clothes. As soon as we are out on the street he blurts out: 'I broke into Sakemoto's.'

'You did what?'

'I had to. It was the only way to find out.'

As the act has already been done and is too late to alter, all I can do is listen to his account. It seems that yesterday afternoon, while we were in Kamakura, Han walked past the shop on Motomachi. Seeing it locked and the photographer obviously away, he thought this was a chance. He found an alley to the back of the building and was able to climb through an upstairs window into the room containing all the boxes of photos. Remembering how Sakemoto had taken the ledger with Tsubaki's name out of a drawer under the counter, he went down the stairs. The drawer was locked but he managed to force it open. I don't ask how. The ledger was written almost entirely in Japanese characters that he couldn't decipher. He examined the rest of the contents but found nothing of note, until he checked on the bottom of the drawer – this he was particularly proud of – and found a key dangling from a string.

I remember the door behind the counter, to the left of the steps, which had been closed on our visit. The key opened it, and Han found himself in what he calls 'the secret room'. I understand, from his description, that it must be the darkroom where Sakemoto develops his photos. But I can relate to Han's sense of supernatural horror – even to me, these darkrooms carry a frisson of alchemy or magic. Undaunted, he unscrewed the lids from jars of chemicals and examined images in their spectral, negative forms. He could find nothing that linked Sakemoto to Tsubaki, but in his mind, the very existence of this room was evidence of criminality. With admirable, albeit misguided bravery, he decided to wait for the photographer's return and confront him.

I can picture the scene: Sakemoto, with those precise, controlled movements, letting himself back in on his return from Kamakura, and finding Han sat fearlessly on his own stool at the counter.

'What did he do?'

'He was calm until he saw that I had opened his secret room. Then he became angry. I told him I thought he'd killed Tsubaki, then kept her in this room and taken her to the sea at night.'

'Let me guess. Then he punched you in the eye?'

'No. I did that climbing in the window. I hit my head on the roof. He told me it was an insulting accusation. Then he asked me if I was working for the British government.'

'Why the hell should he think that?'

Han shrugs and looks guiltily at me, as if only now he thinks he might have done something wrong.

'I said that I was. I thought it might be useful.'

'Useful? To spy for Britain?'

'For him to think this. And it worked. He said it meant there was no point calling the police.'

'He let you go?'

Han nods. 'He said: tell the people who sent you that what they're looking for is in a much safer place than here.'

'What the devil could that mean?'

'What is your country looking for?'

'I don't know. Anything it can get, probably.'

By this time, we've reached the laundry, and who should be coming out but Arabella Hawk. She explains that she has been dropping off costumes which are to be used for the performance of *Frankenstein*. As soon as she utters this word, Han steps towards her, and asks if she remembers him.

Mrs Hawk, never one to be flummoxed for long, throws back her curls and laughs.

'Why, I remember you! Your English is even better than I recall.' She gazes from one to the other of us. 'And what, I wonder, could be your connection to Archie?'

My mouth opens but I'm unable to offer a coherent answer. Han steps into the breach. 'I work for him, and Mister KG and Mister Horney now. I'm their housekeeper.'

She offers her approval, smiling at me with a look which I'm not quite able to decipher, then demands to meet with me; there are some 'literary matters' she wants to discuss. We arrange to rendezvous outside the French Consulate tomorrow afternoon.

After dropping off the laundry, I spend the walk back with Han trying to quell his increasingly wild theories. And yet I'm forced to admit they are not without basis. Presumably, Sakemoto is embroiled in the shady game of espionage, one assumes as an agent for Japan. In this game, Britain seems to be at some obscure disadvantage, but whether this has any connection to Tsubaki's death, we are none the wiser.

Twenty-seven

Arabella Hawk is waiting for me with her bicycle when I arrive outside the French consulate. It rained heavily this morning, but the sun has come out fighting and the ground is visibly steaming. I've put on a clean, white cotton shirt, and Arabella is wearing a loose, white blouse and skirt.

'We look like we're dressed for tennis,' she laughs.

'I'm glad we're not, in this heat.'

'Do you cycle? It's cooler, you know, when you pick up a little speed, to feel the breeze on your face. I know a *monsieur* in there,' she indicates the consulate behind us – 'he won't mind you borrowing his wheels. I'd just have to ask.'

I apologise and explain that I've held a phobia of two-wheeled transport since the time I accidentally rode into the Forth and Clyde Canal. She is sympathetic as well as amused, and doesn't try to force me into the saddle. As we begin to stroll along the seafront path, her wheeling the bicycle, I tell her about the trip to Kamakura. She listens for a while, and then, in typical fashion, abruptly turns the conversation.

'You must have thought me very strange the other night.'

'Not at all. I'm sure I behaved strangely myself.'

'Sometimes I talk such nonsense. I'm sorry. I just thought you were the person I wanted to tell. You don't think badly of me, do you?'

'Of course not.'

'Shall we sit?' she draws me to a bench overlooking the bay, propping her bike against it.

'Leonard isn't the father. I'm pretty sure of it.'

'That's …' I try to think of the right word. 'Awkward.'

'Do you think badly of me now?'

'Why should I?'

We look out at the sails and funnels flecking the bay. She lets her head rest on my shoulder.

'Do you ever wonder about the future, Archie?'

'In what way?'

'You know, do you ever ask yourself what the world will be like in the next century?'

'I do, aye. I think that workers around the world will take control of their own destiny.' Hearing myself, I can't help measuring up against a Hardie speech and thinking how much conviction I lack. But she looks up at me, with what seems like admiration.

'You're a radical!'

'I'm a socialist. Have you heard of Keir Hardie? I believe one day he'll be our Prime Minister.'

'And will he give women equal rights?' A sharpness has entered her voice.

'Yes, I'm sure that will come. Why should half of humanity be denied basic rights on the basis of biological differences?'

'Quite. And what about our empire? What do you think of that?'

'Well, obviously it's rotten – it's based on violence and racism and exploitation of resources.'

'It pays for my dresses, though.'

I consider this point. 'I think we would still need consulates, even without an empire.'

She turns her head to look round, as if checking for the husband, who's unmentioned, but on both of our minds.

The bench is isolated, at the end of a natural promontory, hidden from the main promenade by purple azalea bushes. Unless someone is hiding behind them, or watching through eyeglasses from a boat out at sea, no one can see us.

'What do you think the future holds?' I ask her.

She turns back to look at me: 'That depends on what kind of mood I'm in. Sometimes I think there will be flying machines, and we'll go to the moon, and be able to read each other's minds and cure horrible illnesses. Other times I think we'll just make new ways of killing each other and that new diseases will spring up that we didn't even know before, and when we read each other's minds, we'll end up wishing we hadn't.' She laughs. 'I'm not talking about yours, of course.'

'And what about the moon? Will that disappoint us too?'

'That depends on what kind of cheese it's made from.'

'If it's Camembert?'

'Too sticky.'

'Parmesan?'

'Too crumbly.'

This proceeds for as long as I can keep thinking of different cheeses, each of which she parries. Suddenly, apropos of cheddar (too British), she asks me if I mind putting my arm round her. Cautiously, I deploy my right arm back over her shoulder, but manage to almost knock over the bicycle in doing so. Had this happened, no doubt it would have prevented what follows. But fate dictates a mere wobble, which has the effect of relaxing any tension between us. She takes my right hand and, as if it were a fur stole, adjusts it so that my fingers are brushing the back of her neck. Then she takes my left hand and lifts it so the palm is laid flat to her cheek, using it like a cloth to absorb some of the drops of perspiration on her skin. 'Now, I want you to look closely at me,' she dictates, 'as if you were going to paint me, and tell

159

me about all my wrinkles and imperfections.'

I do as she asks, and assure her that she does not have many of those, indeed she reminds me of Renoir's portrait of a French actress, whose name I've forgotten. A new and still more outlandish request follows, which could be classed as a form of gunboat diplomacy. First contact established, Arabella presses forward, extending her territories inland until I'm forced to put up some form of resistance.

Twenty-eight

Another afternoon, another assignation, but this time I am its instigator. Han and I are waiting for Bara and Tsutsumi on the street across from the *kabuki* theatre. It was Han, resourceful as ever, who solved the problem of how to contact them without the Mama-san as an intermediary. Having discovered the Persimmon girls are in the habit of going out for a walk in the morning, before he came to make our lunch he waited until he saw Tsutsumi come out. He asked her to bring Bara to meet us here, before they have to be back for work this evening. Just as I'm thinking that maybe the message didn't get through, or maybe the Mama-san wouldn't let them out, Han nudges me: 'Look, here they come,' and I see them, in the wake of a rickshaw, tottering towards us in their sandals. They make an unmistakable pair: Bara, tall in a red *yukata*, Tsutsumi in a yellow one beside her. I'm glad they're not in the Persimmon's uniform. At least they're able to dress how they like when they're off duty. They must have chosen to match the colours of the leaves that are just starting to turn towards autumn.

I tell Bara, in my best Japanese, that she looks *utsukushii*, beautiful, and offer her my arm. Han does the same with Tsutsumi, and as a foursome we join the flow of the crowds walking along Theatre Street, in the direction of the sea.

Han has even scouted out some places to take them to eat. We go up a side street, into a small but busy café, which seems cut out for a theatre crowd, the walls festooned with prints of *kabuki* actors. Han orders for us, and I cut straight to the chase, giving up on Japanese and letting him interpret. Would the girls like to join us next Friday evening for a party? They can't, Bara says via Han, they have to be at work. But what if we pay the Mama-san for their company outside? Han translates and they consult one another again. This is possible, but it will be expensive. *Dai joubu*, I use a phrase Bara taught me: don't worry. I get Han to translate more details: the fellow who's invited them is a renowned art dealer, he's well-connected, with deep pockets. I presume Han translates this accurately, as Bara catches my subtle smile and returns it with a nod. With Tsutsumi's agreement, she says that they will be glad to come.

The beers arrive, and we clink glasses. Does Tsutsumi know about Bara's art, I wonder? Surely such talent could not be kept a secret in the confines of a bordello. But I don't bring it up. Who knows what jealousies might exist between the girls, amplified by their cramped confines, and maybe even a sense of competition the Mama-san creates between them.

When the food comes – small, delicious pancakes filled with cabbage and other savouries – I steer the conversation onto the harmless ground of Scottish food and habits of dress. We move onto Korean customs, and soon the three of them are encouraging me to try the language of the majority. Despairing of my efforts, Bara attempts to give me a Japanese lesson, while Han – my model of fluency – converses with Tsutsumi. All in all, we have fun, and it only ends when Bara says they have to be getting back: *shigoto* calls. I settle the bill, taking care not to use any of the money which is Bara's due. On the walk back, I allow Han and Tsutsumi to gain ground on us before slipping the five crisp, ten *yen* notes into her hand. Her eyes widen in astonishment and wonder as she stares at them, hardly believing that all this money is hers. It's a moment that I remember well; the first serious payment for a picture. Proof that there's a living from this game, waiting to be made.

But not yet. The Mama-san, still the ruler of her minutes

and hours, is waiting at the Persimmon's entrance, like a spider at her web. I follow Dowd's instructions and request the girls' company for the following Friday. Suspicious, she quotes me a figure that seems excessive, but no matter: I have the extra notes from Dowd to pay for it. More *yen* changes hands, and without the spider knowing it, the threads of her web are loosened. Everything is set for Bara's cats to start earning her the money to break free.

As we walk back onto the bustle of Isezakicho Street, Han is exultant for different reasons. It seems he managed to tap Tsutsumi's memory for more information about Tsubaki.

'Apparently, she came back to the Persimmon that evening. It must have been after the *kabuki*. She went upstairs. They thought she was going to come down to work, but instead she ran back out, past the Mama-san. One of the girls heard her shout that she was never coming back. And what do you think the Mama-san said? She said "I hope you die on the streets."'

'Good god, does that mean we have yet another suspect?'

But Han ignores me: 'There's something else. Tsubaki met with her sister the day before she disappeared. Tsutsumi thinks she wanted to go back to her family.'

At this point we're passing the steps of the theatre again, now crowded with patrons arriving for the evening performance. Han reminds me that this is the last place where he saw Tsubaki alive.

'And where are they from, her family?'

His tone of excitement switches to one of despondency. 'That's the problem. They're country people, like me and you.'

It touches me, Han remembering in this moment that I told him I also grew up in a small town, before I made my way to Glasgow. And now, I think, there is a connection between all three of us: me, Han, and this poor dead Tsubaki, who I never met or even once laid eyes on.

'Is it a long way from here, the place she grew up?'

Han shrugs: 'I don't know. It's a village called Hakone.'

On hearing this word, I realise fate must truly have decreed a part for me to play in Han's investigation. Just this morning, KG, and Horney and I booked a two-night stay in the famed Hotel Hokusai, next to this very same village of Hakone. For a few seconds, as we walk on, I contemplate not mentioning this to Han. It would make everything so much easier. The three of us could just go and come back, and Han need never know. By then, Yamato will surely be better and he will be working on the stall again, anyway. What use can it possibly be for him to track down Tsubaki's family? All these things are going through my head and yet, in spite of them, I am not surprised when I hear myself telling him.

'We are going to Hakone. Soon.'

From there, it is, of course, a short step to agreeing that I will do my best to persuade H and H to allow him to accompany us as our man-servant. Han's gratitude and excitement are ample rewards for the headache this will bring me.

He then confides that he has been feeling guilty for suspecting Yamato, who is very ill. He wants to go to a temple to offer prayers for his recovery. I agree to accompany him, and after bridging the creek onto Motomachi Street, we make the climb up the Hundred Steps. At the top, we pass between two monstrous stone dogs, furred with moss, then up the steps to the front of the shrine. It's a much simpler affair than the ones at Kamakura: almost bare, the matting on the floor worn smooth, the paper scrolls hanging from the walls, fraying, their *kanji* characters faded. Yet, how extraordinary is the statue against the back wall. While Han prays, I take the opportunity to sketch the ferocious figure with bulging eyes and flowing beard.

As we make our descent, the rooftops, sea and sky spread before us like a woodcut print, Han tells me about a dragon king who presides over a palace at the bottom of the sea. A boy was taken there on the back of a turtle, and returned home to find fifty years had passed in a single day. He was told this tale by Yamato, he says, and by the time we reach his lodgings and part ways, he has translated and passed it on to me.

Twenty-nine

There. It's always so hard to know when a canvas is finished, but I think that's it. I step back for one more look. Yes, I really don't think there's anything more I can add. *Boy Working at an Eel Stall* is complete. I think it is the best thing I've done. If the only paintings by Archie Nith that anyone ever remembers are *The Matchstick Girls' Strike* and this one, then I'll be happy. Is it arrogance, I wonder, to think I'm giving Han his place in history, like Renoir did for that actress whose name I can't remember. Probably. Meanwhile, he's making us something far more tangible: our lunch. Today, we're being treated to Yamato's famous battered eel with rice. I go through to the kitchen to wash the brushes and find that it's ready; he's already dishing the rice into bowls.

'Can you get them to come?' Han says.

I go out to the garden to drag KG and Horney away from their Kamakura pictures.

'I've finished *Boy with Eel,* and Boy is finished with eels.' Boy with Eel is what Horney calls my canvas. He's reluctant to leave his Japanese wedding scene and I have to remind him that Han has gone to special efforts.

At the table, I wax lyrical about the contrast between the tender flesh of the eel and its crispy casing. I'm explaining how the soy sauce soaks into each rice grain, making it a tiny explosion of flavour, when Horney interrupts:

'Would you mind just shutting up and letting us eat, man?'

Han finds this very funny.

We wash the meal down with bottles of beer, and I

suggest a game of Whist. I fetch the cards and I'm almost finished dealing, as KG explains the rules to Han, when a firm bout of knocking sounds at the door. Horney goes to answer, and we hear a familiar cry. Arabella sweeps into the room, wearing a loose blue kimono. We exchange looks for a second. I wonder if she might already be having to avoid tight waists, and how long this strategy will work. But if she's worried, she certainly doesn't show it.

'I hope you don't mind me popping by. I fancied seeing what kind of decadence three artists live in. And now I know – cards and beer by two o'clock!'

'You can't have decadence without the presence of a woman!' Horney grins, bringing another chair from the bedroom. Arabella feigns outrage: 'Mr Hornel. How dare you associate me with your Scottish debaucheries.'

'It was you who made me into a monster, remember?'

'No, that was your choice,' she indicates the cards lying untouched on the table – 'You were about to play Whist, it appears.'

I suggest that we play Brag instead, so Arabella can join in. I go to the cupboard for the jar, upending it to send our painted rice grains cascading onto the table. We separate them out: white for ones, blue for fives, red for twenties. While Horney distributes the grains, I outline the rules to Han and Arabella. She knows Brag but thinks that some of our rules are unique to us. The wild jack of clubs is familiar, but she has never heard of the killer queen of the same suit, able to negate any card of a chosen opponent, or the king as the sole defence against her.

It's apparent from the start that the game is to be taken seriously. Arabella is the competitive type, and for one who has only just learned the rules, Han seems to have an instinctive knack. After a few hands, he catches us all in a terrific bluff, unveiling a hand of complete dross after KG drops out with a straight. The play ebbs and flows with the beer. Horney is first to fall after staking all his grains on a flush, only for me to produce a triple. KG, who's been doggedly guarding a diminishing pile, is next to go. They both decide to fetch their sketchbooks to caricature Han, Arabella and I as we play on. After losing a close hand to Arabella, it seems inevitable that I'll be the next man down, but on the following deal I receive the perfect hand of the jack and queen of clubs. Han unwisely matches my bet and is almost cleaned out, succumbing in the next round after Arabella calls his bluff. To soothe his disappointment, we all commend him on his showing as a first-time player. Arabella winks at me across the table: 'Just the two of us left, Archie. May the best man, or woman, win.'

Horney sets up a drumroll with his palms. 'How about some proper stakes?' he suggests. 'Something more than a few rice grains.'

Arabella is keen on the idea. 'Tell me, gentlemen. What does Archie hold dearest of all his possessions?'

'His eel,' Horney guffaws.

'How about his moustache?' suggests KG, who's been exaggerating its proportions in his caricatures of me. 'I don't think she would suit it,' Han says, proving his humour is catching up and earning a delighted clap from Arabella.

'Maybe I would. Though it tickles.'

Horney looks at her sharply. 'How would you know?'

She rolls her eyes: 'One imagines.'

He frowns: 'Ok, if Archie loses, he'll chop off his moustache. But what will you give him if he wins?'

Arabella considers. 'He won't win. But for the wager, I'll offer that.' She points to her parasol, leaning against the wall. It's an eggshell blue to match her dress, patterned with silhouettes of cranes in flight. Han picks up the role of dealer, and in the first hand I'm dealt the three and jack of diamonds. I put in five red grains and Arabella matches me. Han turns the first of the open cards, a four of clubs. Another two reds, why not? Han lays down the other two open cards. There's an ace of diamonds – I have a flush. I push in all my grains, hoping she doesn't have the killer queen.

She sighs. 'With most people, I can tell when they're bluffing; But you're a hard man to read, Archie.' Eventually, she throws down her cards, revealing an ace and a two. It's the right call – her pair would have lost to my flush.

On the next deal, it's her who goes all in, but once I've dropped out, she uncovers a hand of even greater dross than mine.

'The 'tache is feeling the pain of that one,' KG quips.

'It had a chance and it wasted it.' Horney's enjoying himself: I'm reduced to nothing but my moustache.

Han shuffles and deals again. I peel back the edges of my cards and find two kings. Even better, one of them is clubs, giving me insurance in case Arabella has the killer queen. I stake a hundred and she matches it. Han turns the first open card. The five of hearts. I put another forty in. She matches me. Han turns up the last two open cards. One is the three of hearts, the other the king of diamonds. Three kings! I can hardly believe my luck; my face may even twitch a fraction.

'All in,' I announce.

Arabella smiles: 'That makes two of us.' She pushes her grains in to join mine, so the whole multicoloured pile commingles on the table. Horney, KG and Han set up another drumroll.

'Can the moustache reveal its cards first, please?'

I turn them over, 'I'm not religious,' I say. 'But it seems three wise men have come bearing gifts for me.' Arabella shakes her head ruefully. 'Oh dear, does that mean I've just killed the Messiah?' turning her cards to reveal the wild jack of clubs. The other one doesn't matter. With the three and five of hearts already on the table, the wild jack becomes the four, giving her a straight flush. The room erupts into cheering, and Horney leads a chant of 'Shave it off'. He disappears to the bathroom and comes back with a bowl of water, soap and a razor. Arabella is given first dibs but says she doesn't trust her hand not to slip, so KG does the deed, tenderly, with a sure and steady hand. Not much of my moustache remains intact as a single entity, but Arabella is presented with what there is in a cloth bag to take away – surely the strangest souvenir she has ever had.

Part Three - The Dealer

Thirty

There's nothing like reading the diary of someone you've lost, to bring home what 'gone' actually means. Their voice on the page telling you that this person was here, seeing, hearing and feeling the world, but now they're not and you still are. I feel as if I know Archie better now than I did when he was alive. I'm amazed by how much he recorded, carrying on his diary right up until he disappeared. I hope he would not mind me using it as the base ingredient for the middle part of this account. Of course, I've filleted it, cooked it, and added various garnishes, but many of the words are still his. For a while, I wondered if he might have always intended them for a public audience, but they're too personal; there's too much about me and about our investigation. Though he seemed to believe in that only up to a point, and yet, he kept going with it. Why? Eventually, I understood, it must have been because he believed in me more than he believed in himself. He struggled to work out who he was and what he wanted. His paintings were where he could express himself best, but he wasn't convinced they were enough. Just as I'm not convinced that this account is enough, but now I'm too far on not to finish it. Even though our daughter was born two nights ago, and it feels like I should be looking ahead into the new century, rather than back into the last one.

I justify myself by saying that she is going to need stories. Perhaps, in the future, she'll even want one as strange and convoluted as this. But much sooner she'll need me to tell her the simple kind that will connect her with her Korean soul. Like this tale that mother used to tell Yoona and I:

173

Once upon a time, a tiger lived on a mountain. This tiger was a savage and terrible beast. One day, feeling hunger tickle his belly, he came padding down the mountainside. He emerged out of the forest and stopped outside the first house on the edge of the village, where he could hear the crying of a baby. 'That child will make the perfect meal for me,' the tiger thought. He went to the window, stood on his hind paws, and looked in. He saw a young mother lift her baby out of its cot and begin to rock it: 'Stop crying or you'll wake the dog,' she said.

But the baby continued to wail, and the tiger thought: how strange that a creature so small isn't afraid of a dog! Then the mother begged the baby, 'Stop crying or you'll wake the lion.' But the bawling only grew stronger still.

'Hmm,' thought the tiger. 'Either the lion has grown weak, or this baby is tougher than I thought.' The mother rocked her child some more, still to no effect. 'If you don't stop, I'll have to give you to the tiger who lives on the mountain.' There was silence for a second. Then the baby started crying again, louder than ever.

'What creature is this that is so small, and yet even unafraid of me?' fumed the tiger. 'But perhaps I should be wary of it. No, I am a tiger, I must prove my ferocity and so I'll eat it up right now.'

Just as the tiger was preparing to leap into the room, the young mother looked out. She looked right past the tiger who was peeping in at the edge of the window, and laughed despairingly: 'If you don't stop bawling I'll go outside and shake all the persimmons off that tree.'

Abruptly, the howling ceased, but this time it did not start again. The tiger looked over his shoulder and saw the tree. 'What are those orange balls? They must be more terrible,

even than me. They must be bombs that could explode any
moment and blow me to bits.' And the tiger, fearing for his
life, raced out of the garden and back up the mountainside.

*

I was six years old when the Reverend Hare entered our
lives. Mother often spoke in wonder at my rapid progress in
learning English, how I only needed to hear a word once to
remember it for ever, while she could hear the same word six
days in a row and forget it on the seventh. She told me once,
after she understood the story of Jesus, that my quickness
might be another miracle. But I remember that I laughed and
said: 'No, no, Mother. English is easy.' Even then, in some
part of my brain, I understood that the two languages were
governed by different rules. In Korean, like Japanese, the
object of an action comes before the action itself. By that I
mean that the sentences are ordered in a way that place the
verb at the end, while English is the opposite: the actor and
the action dominate the sentence from the start.

But I'm rambling, like an old man, about things that
Horney's 'bloodthirsty bastards' would never care about.
Somewhere out there, at the bottom of the ocean, the Dragon
King is growing impatient. Tsubaki's last moments on this
earth remain unaccounted for. I'm surprised Archie did not
ponder more deeply why I had become fixated on solving a
crime that no one else saw as one. He was content to attribute
my detective work to the influence of Sherlock Holmes, and
the fact that I was present when her poor body was hauled
out of the harbour. These were obviously factors, but there
was much that he did not know about my motivations.
How could he, coming from such a different world, and
only meeting me – at least until Yamato fell ill – for a few
hours every three or four days in the comfort of a teahouse?
While he painted, played and visited sites, I spent countless
hours butchering eels under the glare of the sun. Even after

Yamato fell ill and I became housekeeper to the painters, I continued to spend my evenings roaming the settlement, or in the logic-defying heat of the lodging house, guarding my two square metres of privacy in a room full of a language I could not understand.

I had begun to take my writing more seriously, and when I could immerse myself in the act of composition, the hours passed without my awareness of them and distractions ceased to matter. I could feel what it was like to be him or his countryman, Conan Doyle. Not that what I wrote had any of the discipline required for commercial success. While I told myself the growing sheaf of pages stuffed under my mattress could become my *Study in Scarlet*, it was really no more than a journal of the investigation. Of course, I was incapable of anything else. I needed to impose some logic on the random pattern of my life.

By then, experience had taught me that the most dangerous place to let my mind wander was home to Mother and Yoona, and so I pushed it away from that censored space towards Tsubaki, whose face I now saw when I remembered my encounter with Tsutsumi. Each night, I would lie on my thin mattress, one more foreign plant among many others, trying to settle in the native soil. The room was a jungle, alive with the smells of men, the screech of crickets and the scuttle of cockroaches. In the thrall of these hourless nights, when I wasn't writing, I would tease my stem until my juice spurted forth onto blankets already stained by fishy sweat. In its messy relief, my brain would mingle with the earth, conjuring the image of Tsubaki gasping a lungful of salty oblivion. My disembodied soul would rise up in pursuit, on nocturnal outings of the imagination, down to the harbour, up to the very edge. Sometimes, it would plunge into the dark depths, let itself be covered and create a future tense in which it didn't exist. Most nights though, it would avoid the edge and watch instead from a warehouse entrance, waiting for a fragile figure passing along the waterfront to be accosted by shadowy forms. Not even giving her time to scream before smothering her cries, they had their way with her, and dumped her over the side. I repeated these scenes until I learned by heart the sound of a body hitting the water. Then, somehow, my soul would flit back to me and I would sleep. When the yellow sunlight came spilling through the shutters to wake me for another day, I would be ready. Cheerful and determined as a young Peter, I would perform my morning ablutions, put on my fish-spattered pantaloons, eat my bowl of rice in the kitchen and head out into the early morning sunlight. I had defied the Reverend Hare, I was the chief disciple of the truth, and in all the world only I had the power to discover the answer to something which no one else even knew was a question.

*

On the morning of the party at Dowd's, Miura-san's face appeared in the doorway – a rare occurrence, as she always respected the privacy of her lodgers' sleeping quarters. I would have been writing furiously in my notebook, and she smiled as she called to me, trying to keep her voice low to avoid disturbing others who were asleep.

'Han. There's a boy here to see you.'

As I followed her down the stairs, my first thought was that maybe the Reverend Hare had sent word at last. In the village, children – myself included – had always been his preferred mode of dispatch. But as soon as I saw the Japanese lad, in a vest and short pants, barefoot with cropped hair, the absurdity of this notion struck me. He looked as if he wanted to run away, and Mrs Miura said to him, kindly: 'This is Han. You can give him your message.'

The boy was a full head shorter than me and must have been only around nine or ten. He stared at the floor and a jumble of words came spilling out.

'You have to come. To Yamato-san's house. You have to come. There's something for you.'

It was perhaps two days since I had been to see Yamato. After he told me about his past with Tsubaki, his belligerence had softened, though it might also have been the illness that caused this. He was very weak, only drinking water and eating the odd piece of fruit. Ironically, in this state, he had told me he was sorry and wanted me to accept some money while we couldn't work. I refused, telling him I had found other employment for the time being, but when he was better we could run the stall together again.

'Do you mean he's ready to go back to work?'

The boy raised his chin to look at me; his eyes widened. He muttered something and I had to ask him to repeat it before I understood.

Yamato had died in the night.

It had rained, and in the morning heat, moisture was steaming from the damp streets. We threaded our way towards the waterfront. Out at sea, a bank of retreating storm clouds towered along the horizon, as if the ocean and the sky were trying to merge. The boy told me that he lived in the house next to Yamato, with his mother and sisters. His mother had been helping to care for my boss. From the boy's confused account, I could not tell how quickly Yamato's condition had deteriorated. He had left his mother sitting with the body while his older sister went to fetch the priest. Why was he bringing me? His mother had only told him that Yamato wanted me to have some things, but he did not know what they were.

As we passed the fish market where Yamato used to buy his eels, I thought of Tsubaki's face when they had pulled her from the water, trying to imagine that same awful absence on Yamato's features. I thought of the two of them arguing in the theatre that night, when they were both so alive.

The interior of the house was lighter than I remembered, with morning sunlight falling through the doorway. The boy led me into the first of the partitioned sections, where the cooking pot still hung from the wooden beams. Water had recently been boiled in it, and there was some rice in a pan next to the fireplace. Had he felt as if he was recovering and tried to eat? A familiar smell still hung in the air, that mix of fish and charcoal and incense, making it seem impossible that Yamato could be dead. The boy had moved to the edge of the partition, and now gestured for me to follow.

Once my eyes had adjusted to the gloom, I made out a woman kneeling next to the futon, placing objects into a wicker basket. The boy announced that he had brought me, and his mother turned to look at me, saying something I did not fully understand. I moved closer to the side of the empty futon.

'Where is he?'

'He's gone.' The woman bowed her head.

An absurd parallel crossed my mind: a cave with a stone rolled back and a vanished body. But the woman began talking again, and though many of the words she used were new to me, I gathered that Yamato was not like Jesus. His body had been taken to the temple for funeral rites. She explained that all of Yamato's savings were needed to pay for the ceremony.

'There's no money left, but he wants you to have this.' From the basket, she took out the mother of pearl hair clip and *obi* belt that Yamato had intended for Tsubaki. She pressed them into my hands. Before I could begin to ask her why he had wanted me to have them, she got to her feet, and led me back out through the front room and down the wooden steps. She turned into the shadowy space beneath them, gesturing me to follow. I knew already what was there: the cart, loaded with the skillet, pan, basket, knives, pots and pans, stoppered containers; all the apparatus of the trade into which Yamato had initiated me with so much blood, sweat and soy.

'This is yours. He said you became a good *unagiya-san.*' A strip of sunlight arrowed through the gap between the steps, illuminating the lower part of her face. I saw her crooked teeth bared in a smile and a ridge of raised red skin running down the side of her cheek, as if someone had held a hot poker against her flesh. I bent over the cart, touching and lifting the items. She must have thought I was taking an inventory, but I was recalling my first, endless shift with Yamato, impaling those thrashing whipcords on the block. Suddenly, the woman fell into a deep bow. Apologising for her shamelessness, she begged me to take on her son as my apprentice. I felt awkward and had no idea what to say to her. Was she really only Yamato's neighbour, or had there been something more to their relationship? It seemed that there was no one else but us to take custody of Yamato's worldly goods. She had been on the scene first, and could have kept it all for herself and her son; in calling me she must have acted from a sense of obligation to my old master, faithfully carrying out his wishes after his death.

I took some time to compose the sentences in my head and then calmly told her I could not take on the eel stall, but that she and her son should take possession of it. I could see that the prospect was attractive to her, yet her protective instinct baulked at me passing up such a spectacular inheritance.

'What will you do?' she asked.

'I have other work.'

We had emerged from the shadows back out into the sun. The boy had joined us and his mother made him bow to me. They expressed their thanks and promised they would dedicate themselves to the art of eel cookery, striving to reach the standards Yamato would have wished. I bowed and thanked them in return, promising to visit to check that the eel was still as tasty as ever. Then I turned and walked away, wondering if I had been reckless, and if there was a shortcut I could take from there straight to the artists' house.

Thirty-one

Henry was slighter built than Hornel, and as I had broadened in the chest and shoulders, his dress suit only needed the legs turning up and the sleeves rolled to make it fit me. I looked at myself in their bedroom mirror, while Archie scrutinised me side-on. Noting a few bristles sprouting above my upper lip, and some longer, wispy hairs on my chin, he commented that it wouldn't do for me to have more facial hair than him. He led me to the bathroom and showed me how to lather my face with shaving soap and draw a razor over the contours. When we were done, he un-stoppered a bottle of *eau de cologne* and splashed some on both our hands, demonstrating the way to slap it on my face. Unprepared for the sting and tingle of it, I yelped and looked at him accusingly. He chuckled and put an arm around my shoulder.

'Trust me Han. The pain will be worthwhile. Smelling like oranges and lemons, Tsutsumi will find you even more irresistible than usual.'

I had told Nith about Yamato earlier that afternoon, after making the lunch. He was shocked at first, and then worried about me. I think there was already some discussion of the artists moving on from Yokohama, and he knew my employment with them might not last long. I did not mention that I had been offered the chance to take over Yamato's stall and turned it down.

Our toilette complete, Archie presented me to H and H, who were getting ready themselves for a night out with the Jollity Players. KG nodded approvingly, declaring that I had scrubbed up well in his suit. Horney gave Nith a curious look: 'With you moustache-less and him dressed up like that, I can hardly tell who's the senior partner in the firm.'

With a final touch of flowers in our buttonholes to match the names of our respective girls, we strolled down the bluff to meet Tsutsumi and Bara at the foot of the Hundred Steps. Here, I experienced for the first time, the pleasure of my appearance provoking a woman's admiration. Tsutsumi, wearing a dark green *yukata* decorated with crimson maple leaves, kissed me on the lips and hung onto my arm as if I were a prosperous gentleman. My nerves on the first night I had been with her, wearing Yamato's old *yukata*, seemed to belong to a different age. As the rickshaw pulled us through the streets in the warm September evening, I suppose most onlookers would have taken me for a young Japanese of the new internationalised elite.

Dowd's house loomed over us. With its white walls and layers of blue roof tiles, it looked more like a Japanese castle. Nith rang the bell, and while we waited, I wondered if our night would end here, in humiliating rejection. Then, a sliding door opened with a rattle, revealing Dowd's butler. The old man welcomed us with a deep bow, and in English so thickly accented as to be almost unintelligible, directed us to remove our shoes and put on a pair of house slippers. He placed our own footwear on a tray, taking such care to line up our black dress shoes next to Bara and Tsutsumi's *geta* sandals, that I imagined them being served up as a delicacy. We followed him along a hallway lined with Japanese art, turning several corners before we emerged onto a veranda at the back of the house.

As we put our shoes back on, I looked out at the garden. It was as if a curtain had been drawn back on a performance already in progress. It wasn't my first time out in society: I had already attended the *kabuki* and twice been to the Persimmon. But those were open to anyone, even commoners like Yamato and I, fresh from hard labour. There was an air of leisure and exclusivity here, of people removed from the daily grind. Everyone seemed to be wearing fine clothes, whether European or Japanese, of which there looked to be an equal mix. The lanterns hanging from the veranda and the trees around the lawn produced an effect that was almost supernatural, as if they marked the perimeter of a magical world.

While Tsutsumi and Bara exchanged impressions, I harvested Nith for knowledge and language. The pale-yellow liquid people were drinking out of long-stemmed glasses was champagne; it was French and expensive. The quality of it that made the corks pop and the drink froth up was fizz; this sounded like what it described, the little bubbles always rising, and there was a word for that, but Nith could not remember it. Something that looked like an item of furniture between a wardrobe and a table with teeth was called a piano. Had I really never seen one before? It could produce sublime music which I would surely soon hear. These exchanges did not go only one way. On the edges of the lawn were many of the little statues that you see in Japanese cemeteries. Archie didn't know what they were called and I taught him *Jizou-sama*, as Yamato had taught me.

I was beginning to wish Archie could bring us in from the fringes of the gathering, when a squat, powerful figure approached us. He was a Westerner, but his dress and hairstyle were Japanese. The rich silk of his *yukata* shimmered in the lantern light as he greeted Nith warmly and shook his hand. His voice was low and hoarse.

'I see you've brought your guests, but lost your moustache!'

Nith touched his upper lip. 'An unlucky wager, I'm afraid.'

Augustus Dowd laughed. 'Well, there are worse things to lose. But please, introductions.'

184

Apologising, Nith got around to introducing us: 'This is Miss Bara, whom you've already heard about.' Bara bowed and uttered the Japanese formality, to which Dowd responded in kind, adding that he was a great admirer of her work. With his guttural Japanese and masculine presence, I felt oddly, for a second, as if he were impersonating Yamato. The same performance was repeated for 'Miss Tsutsumi, Bara's friend', though Archie's tongue could never quite manage the syllables in her name. Tsutsumi seemed nervous, intimidated by Dowd. Even I was feeling a little of that as he turned to me.

'And who's this fine-looking young fellow?'

'This is Han. He's not an artist, but has numerous other talents. He speaks three languages and wants to become a writer.'

I looked Dowd in the eye and offered my hand. He shook it with a fierce grip, sizing me up.

'Do you, by any chance, know a thing or two about eel cookery, too?'

I nodded, wondering how he knew.

'An impressive range of skills.' Dowd looked back in Nith's direction. 'Maybe I could use a young man like him. We can bid against each other for his services.'

'I'm fairly sure you could outbid me,' Archie replied.

I thought my part in the conversation was over, but Dowd turned a shrewd gaze back to me and addressed me in Japanese: 'Do you think you would cope horse trading with silk farmers out in the sticks?'

Thanks to all those hours with Yamato, I could understand his words and the gruff masculine tone.

'I think so. I've practised at the fish market. If I can get prices down there, I can do it anywhere.'

Dowd smiled approvingly. 'I don't doubt it. The fish

market's a good training ground. But connections are everything. Maybe it would be better to make some higher-up ones.'

He led us towards a group in the centre of the lawn. My heart skipped a beat as I recognised a familiar figure in a well-tailored suit, smoking in a way that conveyed great poise and style. I watched Sakemoto offer one of his cigarettes to the fair-haired woman at his side. She bent her face towards him for him to light it. He flicked his thumb and a flame danced out. The tip of the cigarette glowed red.

'We Japanese are not the tallest, but our flames know how to find the mark.'

The group burst into laughter at his wit.

'Sakemoto-san,' Dowd interrupted. 'I have a young man you may like to meet. Han is from Korea. He speaks English as well as he does Japanese.'

Sakemoto's eyes flickered as he recognised me, but he recovered his poise in a second. As for me, passing Dowd's little test had pepped me up, and I was able to face him with a steady heart.

'Pleased to meet you. What was your name again?'

'Han.'

Blowing a puff of smoke over my head, he repeated the single, short syllable, which in Japanese sounds like a lazy version of 'yes'. 'I think we might have met somewhere before. But don't you have a surname?'

It was strange, I thought as I told him, that no one else I had met in Japan had ever asked me this. Sakemoto turned to Archie, switching to English: 'Mister Nith. We have certainly met, and now I remember where I saw Han before. He is your personal assistant, is that correct?'

'I'm afraid I'm not important enough to have a personal assistant. Han and I have a very ad hoc arrangement.'

186

'You mean sometimes he acts on his own initiative?'

'I should think so.'

'Interesting.'

Sakemoto gave the group his version of Nith's reputation: 'He's one of many foreign artists who take a great interest in my photography to assist their art.'

Archie was then forced to explain how artists used photographs as a source from which to paint.

'Isn't that cheating?' the fair-haired woman said, blowing a wreath of scented smoke into the air. Archie struggled to formulate an adequate defence, and it was left to me to back him up.

'They don't just copy them. I've seen their paintings. The photographs are only an inspiration.'

The woman was amused. 'Are they, indeed? And what are these inspiring photographs of?'

I looked from Archie to Sakemoto, but neither of them seemed inclined to answer. Others in the group were chuckling, and I felt a rush of anger as I thought of Tsubaki staring down the camera lens, her image fixed in time by those strange chemicals, but artificial, controlled by someone else who could go on selling her even after she was dead.

'Young women,' I said, 'like them.' I turned, expecting to find Tsutsumi and Bara. But they had disappeared, and when I scanned around, I couldn't see them.

'Invisible women?' Sakemoto said, provoking more laughter. 'I think we all remember those from our younger days.'

I don't know what act of intemperate violence I could have resorted to at that moment, had the host not clashed a pair of cymbals together, causing all chatter to cease and eyes to turn towards him. Dowd was standing on the veranda, between twin towers of flat, round cushions.

'Ladies and gentlemen. The night's performance is about to begin. Please take a cushion and sit down to enjoy it. You may kneel Japanese-style, or sprawl like a decadent Westerner, whichever suits you best.' He repeated this in Japanese for the benefit of some, including Tsutsumi and Bara, who had reappeared from wherever they had gone when I needed them. Sakemoto had melted away, and we joined an impromptu queue to collect the cushions. We sat down several rows back, me between the women, Archie on Bara's other side. Spotlights were shining on the veranda, and it now really did look like a stage set. The audience's murmuring slowly died as Dowd sent his bulbous-eyed gaze roving over us. Only when complete silence had fallen did he rip the air open with a powerful roar.

'Why do nations need heroes?'

He paused to let the question sink in, then said it again in Japanese. Like a true actor, he was talking with his hands and face as well as his voice. I was captivated, distracted from thoughts of Sakemoto. Dowd's question had never crossed my mind before.

'Perhaps,' he went on, 'we might learn the answer by comparing heroes from different nations. Japanese people here tonight, I am sure all of you are familiar with the warrior Yoshitsune?' He smiled as voices of agreement called out from the audience.

'For the benefit of the unenlightened, Yoshitsune was a legendary warrior from Japan's past. I will perform some of his story tonight. I will also perform that of a famous Irish warrior, so you may compare the two. A tall order for one man, but, fortunately, I will have the help of a friend.' The crowd gasped as a figure who had been waiting in the shadows of the house bounded onto the stage and adopted a warrior's crouched stance. The actor was wearing what looked like a *kabuki* mask, concealing his true identity.

188

Like every detail of that night, I can recall the performance as clearly as if it happened yesterday. It began with the tale of Yoshitsune, the legendary Japanese warrior. Orphaned young, he spent his childhood in a temple, until one evening he set out alone into the forest and encountered the King of the Tengu, a tribe of long-nosed goblins. I remember the laughter when Dowd produced an imitation nose, made, I think, from rubber, and strapped it around his face. The masked man feigned the action of a warrior, slashing his way through thick bamboo forest. Dowd, playing the Tengu King barred his path, growling in Japanese: 'Who dares pass through my forest in the night!'

What they did next was very clever. After a few exchanges set the scene for the Tengu King to train Yoshitsune, who would be eaten if he proved an inadequate pupil, Dowd removed the nose and stepped to the centre of the stage to address us as himself. Many thousands of miles to the east, he explained, a young Irish warrior called Cu Chulainn needed to find a way to defeat his enemies. And just like Yoshitsune – he gestured to the masked man frozen in a combat pose – Cu Chulainn had to go on a journey to perfect the art of battle. Across a short stretch of sea lay a desolate isle on which lived a woman called Scathach, the greatest fighter in the Western world, possessor of a deadly spear called the Gae Bulg. Behind Dowd, the masked man had donned a straggly red wig and retrieved a stick, which he was now brandishing in the manner of a spear. Dowd performed the actions of the warrior Cu Chulainn, squatting on his meaty haunches to imitate rowing a boat, then tying up and stepping ashore. He mimed a scramble up a rocky cliff and arrived at the foot of the masked man – now the Warrior Queen, Scathach, standing in front of her cave on the island.

The performance continued in this way, with the pair switching roles to tell the parallel stories, both of which ended in mock battles that produced no winner, but showed the pupil matching the teacher. Naturally, I could not help thinking of Yamato and myself, and the reality of his death hit me afresh. To my embarrassment, I found myself beginning to cry. Tsutsumi noticed and attempted to touch my face, but I shrugged her off angrily. On my other side, Bara was as riveted by Dowd and the masked warrior as Tsubaki had been at the *kabuki*.

'Our revels are not ended,' Dowd boomed after he and the masked man had taken a bow. 'In fact, they are only beginning. For too long we've been content to make the settlement a bubble of Western culture. Little wonder there are elements in Japan resistant to our integration when we live here like colonists, showing so few signs of wanting to change our ways in response. Small wonder Japan herself is seeing a rising tide of anti-foreign sentiment, a tide that not only opposes the opening of the country but wishes to abolish the foreign settlement as well. My friends, we must show why this must not happen! This is just the first in what I hope will become a regular fixture of Yokohama life. I will term them 'Intercultural Events'. Like this evening, they will celebrate the merging of the art forms of East and West, to create new and thrilling hybrids! Tonight, we had music and storytelling. The next time, I intend for there to be art on display – the artists are already known to me, and believe me, their art is most exciting and new. We also have literary talents who do not belong to any of the established categories. I have met one of them here this evening. It is my hope we will have poetry at the next event. And, if I can persuade my masked friend here, more from the stories of Cu Chulainn and Yoshitsune!'

The applause was even longer, the audience sensing as Dowd stepped off the veranda, that it was the signal for the party to resume. Could I be that literary talent, I wondered? Nith had mentioned to Dowd that I was interested in writing. I scanned the audience for someone else who looked like

190

they might be a writer, but they were all rising to their feet. Archie placed a hand on my shoulder and asked me what I had made of the performance. He had visited the island where the Warrior Queen lived and even climbed some of its mountains. Tsutsumi was speaking urgently to Bara and I tried to make out what they were saying, but Nith was intent on his story, oblivious to my distraction. A pianist had begun to play, and the music was indeed wonderful. I saw the ancient servant weaving his way through the crowd, carrying glasses on a tray. I told Archie I would go to fetch us drinks, but before I reached the servant, I came face to face with Sakemoto, smiling as he hissed at me in Japanese: 'Let's take a walk somewhere quiet, spy. I want some answers.'

Unsure what to do, I looked back at Archie, but he was talking to Dowd, his arm around Bara's shoulder.

'You're not afraid of facing me alone, are you?'

My pride at stake, I allowed Sakemoto to lead me beyond the lanterns, into the shadows of the garden. At the edge of the lawn, we crossed a bridge over a stream in which the moon's reflection danced. A narrow path threaded between shrubs and trees, sharp-edged leaves falling out of the darkness, brushing my face. The soothing sounds of piano and chatter faded, replaced by the urgent chirrup of crickets running out of time to mate before they died. Sakemoto had every reason to want answers, I thought. I had broken into his studio and lied to him. From Conan Doyle, I had a vague idea that spying for countries was a dangerous game. People who played it were liable to end up strangled, or with knives in their backs. But surely there would be witnesses who had seen Sakemoto lead me away. If there was one thing I knew about him, it was that he liked to produce a refined image, on the outside at least. Murdering me here would surely not be his style. We had reached a kind of clearing in the path, where moonlight shone through a gap in the trees onto a bench. We sat down and Sakemoto lit a cigarette, offering me one as well. I shook my head, then immediately regretted it, thinking this might be an attractive habit to cultivate. Sakemoto puffed out smoke before addressing me.

'The first time I met you, when you and the artist Nith came asking questions about the girl who died, I asked myself why. It troubled me, but not enough to do something about it. Then, that night I found you in my studio, I assumed I knew the reason: you were a spy, working for the British government. If you are a spy, you will know exactly why I thought so. If you are not, you will be confused. You did not correct my assumption, but perhaps you realised it was not in your interests to correct it. You do remember the message I asked you to convey before I let you go?'

I nodded and attempted to speak, but he silenced me and continued in his deliberate, perfect English.

'Had that message been conveyed, certain things would have been expected to happen. But they have not happened, and so I questioned myself if you really were a spy. I was beginning to think you were something else. And now I see you here tonight, and again I think, why would someone like you be in a place like this?' I opened my mouth and again he shushed me with a gesture.

'And then there is Mister Nith, who may or may not be an artist. So, what are you doing with him, or what is he doing with you?'

He paused, and I understood this time he was waiting for me to answer. There seemed to be nothing to gain from withholding the truth.

'I'm not a spy and neither is Nith. He lent me a book of Sherlock Holmes stories. Now he's helping me find Tsubaki's murderer.'

In the pale moonlight, I saw Sakemoto's forehead crease into a frown. He took another drag on his cigarette.

'So, you really are amateur detectives. I suppose that is

just about plausible. And you still think I killed Tsubaki?'

'Did you?'

I held my breath, wondering what I would do if he confessed. He must have been aware that I had tensed my body for action. Switching to Japanese, he spoke in a softer tone.

'Calm down, Sherlock. I haven't got a clue what happened to poor Tsubaki, but I promise you I had nothing to do with it. All I do is take photographs.'

As we made our way back slowly along the winding path towards the party, he explained what his photographs were used for, and why he had taken me for a spy. Before we came to the stream, he had made me his offer. The little bridge was too narrow to cross side by side, so I let Sakemoto go ahead. I was about to step onto it, when something came flying at me from the bushes with the force of a cannonball. I was thrown off balance, staggered, and fell in. My head went under and water rushed into my mouth and up my nose. I flailed about, feeling slippery things moving against my body. My head came up and I spluttered for air. Something had fastened itself round one of my fingers, and I thrashed it off before it decided I was worth a bite. I scraped back the hair plastered over my eyes, making out Sakemoto, crouched on the bank, offering his hand. I let him haul me up and pitched forward onto the grass, retching up a cocktail of pondwater and champagne.

By this time, a crowd had gathered around, and when Nith realised I was at the centre of it, he rushed to my side. I tried to explain to him how I had been attacked by someone hiding in the bushes, but he seemed more concerned about me catching a chill. Dowd called his servant and asked him to take me inside to find me some dry clothes. I followed the old footman, trailing drips along corridors and up a narrow flight of stairs, then into a room which was in darkness, until the servant flicked on a gas lamp. It must have been his bedroom. It was tiny and narrow, but at least, unlike mine, it provided him with a private space. From a shelf, the old man took down a towel, a folded black *yukata*, and a pair of undershorts, which he placed on a chair. Pointing to a wicker basket into which I could place KG's sodden dress suit, he bowed and told me he would be waiting outside.

Re-emerging onto the veranda, I found the crowd on the lawn noticeably thinner. Nith was standing by himself, his hands in his pockets.

'Nice costume change,' he remarked when he saw me. 'Are KG's togs drying off somewhere?'

Still smarting from the humiliation of my dipping, I changed the subject. 'I think it was Tsubaki's killer who attacked me.'

He raised an eyebrow. 'Then you are accusing the delicate Miss Tsutsumi of murder.' He pointed across the lawn to where Tsutsumi and Bara appeared to be arguing, their strident voices carrying across the convivial chatter. Nonplussed, I turned back to Nith for an explanation.

'She was annoyed with you, apparently, for ignoring her. Understandable, if you ask me, Han.'

I realised what he was saying. 'You mean, it was Tsutsumi who …'

'Pushed you in, yes. Bara is angry with her, thinks she's made a spectacle of us in front of her new patron. Maybe you should go and smooth the waters.'

I was incredulous – I had to apologise for her assaulting me? I began to tell him how Sakemoto had led me away and I had learned vital information, but Archie raised a hand to stop me: 'Tell me later.' Now I had to see things from Tsutsumi's point of view. The poor thing was a fish out of water here. After Dowd had taken him and Bara inside to lay out his proposals for Bara's art, Tsutsumi had looked to me

194

for company. Not finding me anywhere, and unable to talk to anyone else, she felt humiliated. She wandered off into the bushes near the stream, saw me with Sakemoto, and decided to take her revenge.

I still could not see how I was to blame, but since Archie insisted, I stalked over to them. Tsutsumi saw me first, and when she registered the servant's clothes I was wearing, a devilish amusement flashed across her face. So that was it, I thought, she enjoyed seeing me humiliated, my pretensions crushed. It was jealousy, pure and simple. And even as I pronounced the words of an apology, I felt my spine quiver with a horrific leap of logic. Nith had said it in jest, but it made sense. Everything fitted: the jealousy; the flash of rage, sparked by who knew what, a word or something else; the unexpected strength. And above all, the method: a body of water conveniently on hand, except in Tsubaki's case, no shallow stream and gentle bank, but the sea and a high harbour wall.

Tsutsumi accepted my apology and grudgingly offered her own, not knowing that I had pinned her for a far greater crime. Before I could accuse her then and there, Nith suggested that it was time we were going. My thoughts still fizzed with conjecture, and I was barely aware of taking our leave from Dowd and being led back through the house by the old retainer. He had wrapped KG's suit in a piece of cloth and tied it together for me to carry away. I thanked him and said I would return his *yukata*. '*Dai joubu*,' it doesn't matter, he replied, bowing as we walked away past the lamps on the front lawn.

We were obliged to walk some way along the shore road in search of a ride home. Moonlight glimmered off the waters of the bay, and Nith tried to lighten our moods with his attempts at Japanese. Mercifully, a rickshaw soon passed, and we hailed it down. This time, Archie and I sat opposite the women. Tsutsumi spent the journey avoiding my gaze, glaring sulkily out of the carriage. I was first to be dropped off, outside the lodging house. I would have to wait another day to tell Archie about my discoveries and conclusions. In any case, my brain and body felt utterly drained, and that night I could have slept through an earthquake.

Thirty-two

Perhaps Tsutsumi did me a favour. I needed the shock of being plunged into Dowd's ditch and nibbled by his carp. It reminded me that, though I could dress up and pretend otherwise, in reality, my position was precarious. Yamato had been my first guide on the long slog to a new life in Japan, like climbing Mount Fuji, a steady effort to the summit. Now, I had wandered off those sacred slopes and onto the rocky bluff of three Scotsmen who, for reasons I still could not fathom, were known as 'Boys', and who, in under six months, would sail back to their own country. It was true that one of them had singled me out to be his friend and seemed convinced that I should aim for some much grander purpose than frying seafood and surviving. Yet, his most concrete act of help was to provide me with temporary employment, where I did exactly that, as well as cleaning, washing dishes and paintbrushes, making beds and endless pots of tea.

I soon grew to realise that these tasks, performed usually while one or more of the artists were painting in the garden or in the room they called their studio, were less congenial to my nature than my work with Yamato had been. It was not so much while I was doing it that I felt this. I cannot really say that I enjoyed being at the stall as my arm muscles turned to lead, or the viscous mix of blood and scales crusted on my hands and wrists, or the gruff barking of Yamato: '*Isoide*! Hurry up!' when his stock of filleted eels was depleted and there were customers waiting. No, certainly not enjoyment, but there was urgency and its trick of speeding up time, which in the artists' house, for me at least, dragged minute by minute.

I never went to the temple to see Yamato's body. Possibly, even before Dowd's party, the priest had already performed the funeral rites and consigned my old boss to the flames. More likely, I think, it happened the next day. I could have gone early in the morning, up the steps to the temple, and asked for the chance to pay my respects before he became a puff of smoke from a chimney and a handful of ashes in a pot. I should have at least checked that the ashes were thrown into the sea, as Yamato would have wished. But it took me several days before I realised that I missed him more than I would have thought possible to miss a person whom I had, only a few months earlier, hated more than anyone else in the world. I missed how he rubbed my hair with a greasy hand after the lunch rush was over, when we would squat on our haunches like shitting monkeys. We'd look up the pier to see all the workers, going back to loading and unloading crates and chests from the never-ending to-and-fro of ships' launches and carts, trundling between quayside and warehouse. I missed the folk tales he told me and his constant supply of new words in Japanese: anything from the names of sea creatures to weird idioms and vulgar slang.

It was not that I hated my work during those few short weeks I was housekeeping for the artists. It was easy money and came with perks, like outings to teahouses and even writing advice. But I felt peripheral, and I resented the absent-minded way Henry and Hornel would sometimes pick at the food I prepared while reading a newspaper, or discussing the obscure details of the Scottish art world. Nith was different. He always used chopsticks, and respectfully chased every grain of rice out of the bowl. But even Archie, after a hand or two of cards, would be ready to pad back through in his stockinged feet to dab more paint onto his latest canvas. I started to form an understanding of the divide that exists between those whose labour demands physical endurance and those who need not break a sweat. Strangely, it was only when I could observe the lives of the artists at close quarters that I knew what Archie meant when he talked about the workers, with the intensity the topic always produced in him. But I did not make the insight into his character which, being older and having read his diary, I later could: that he suffered from the constant sorrow of not being loved by the people he loved, starting with his father.

Nor did I understand, at the time, the connection between his politics, and his reaction the day after the party, when I told him what Sakemoto had revealed to me.

'He's got a photograph of a married British government minister in bed with a Persimmon girl. That's what he thought I was looking for.'

'Good God. Who was it?'

'Not Tsubaki or –'

'Not the girl! The minister.'

'I don't know.'

'Sorry, Han. Of course you wouldn't … and how was this photograph taken?'

This, too, I couldn't answer. While I went on peeling and chopping onions for a lunchtime soup, Nith speculated on the layers of deviousness involved in obtaining such an image. With the Mama-san's complicity, Sakemoto might have set up his camera in the corridor outside the room, the door opened at an opportune moment and the shutter clicked. All this would have taken careful planning, a blackmail plot worthy of the pages of Conan Doyle. 'Of course, we still don't know who's behind Sakemoto, but to be honest, Han, I approve of their choice of target, if not their method or motive. If it became public, then the proof that we have a government of hypocrites would advance the workers' cause at a stroke!' He watched me, eyes smarting from the onion, as I scraped it into the pan to join the cabbage and potatoes, ingredients they had requested for a homelier flavour. 'So,

Sakemoto thought Her Majesty's government sent you to steal the offending image? The whole thing is farcical beyond belief!'

His flippancy was starting to grate on me. Could he not see this was serious, his country at risk of humiliation? I set the heat and began stirring the vegetables with a wooden spoon.

'He wants me to take a copy of one of the photos to the British Embassy. He said it will set the wheels in motion.' I repeated the English phrase Sakemoto had used. Intrigued, Archie stroked his upper lip where his moustache was starting to grow back.

'I wonder what wheels those are. Some form of diplomatic compromise, no doubt. Christ, Han, have you stumbled on something that could bring down the government? Now, I wonder if Murchison would ...' He tailed off, lost in thoughts that didn't interest me. What did I care about Britain's internal political struggles? It was no skin off my nose if the Prime Minister himself was photographed naked with every woman in the Persimmon, and those pictures appeared on the front of the London *Times*. I reminded Archie that our priority was discovering how Tsubaki had died, and told him the insight I had arrived at the previous night.

'Tsutsumi! Are you losing your cogs, Han? Just because she threw you in with Dowd's carp? Aren't you forgetting she was at work that night? You more than anyone should remember that!' He raised an eyebrow significantly, and I recalled the image through the doorway of him with Bara, but I had already considered this argument.

'Yamato and I had left. She could have met Tsubaki after. She could have –' Nith cut me off.

'Aye, she could have. So could just about anyone. Or has it crossed your mind that Sakemoto might have invented this whole story of spies and photographs to throw you off the scent?'

He was right, of course. I felt foolish and angry with myself, but disinclined to admit the yawning gaps in my logic. I fell silent, concentrating on adding the fish stock and slowly bringing the soup to a simmer, doing the work I was paid to do.

Thirty-three

In the days between that conversation and the trip to the Hotel Hokusai, I withdrew into myself. I didn't respond to Sakemoto's offer and shunned Archie's offers of company. Instead, I went on long walks alone; up the bluff and along to Honmoku, down to the coast road at Negishi, and back along the waterfront, not returning to the lodging house until late. It seemed that Dowd had timed his gathering well, for the temperature dropped in those days, and I enjoyed the sharpness in the air which now came with the evenings. It made me think of lonely forests and crisp fallen leaves, like the paths on the mountain behind our village. My thoughts turned often to Mother and Yoona, and again, I considered going to the port and enquiring after a passage home.

One afternoon, while tidying the house as the artists painted in the garden, I found a slim book lying next to Archie's futon: *Shakespeare's Sonnets*. The Reverend Hare used to quote lines from Shakespeare, and in school once, he had told us the story of *The Tempest*. 'Full fathom five thy father lies! Those are pearls that were his eyes.' He had made us copy out the lines and repeat them. I opened the book and read the first poem that my eyes fell upon:

When I consider everything that grows
holds in perfection but a little moment

When I finished the poem, I immediately understood why Nith would keep this book close to him. It had made me think of Tsubaki and my family, somehow heightening the sadness of their loss, but at the same time, lightening it. Leafing through, I found that the whole book was composed of poems of the same brief length. Some were surrounded by scrawled annotations, which were all but impossible to decipher, though I knew they must be Archie's. Lying back on his bed, I stared at the ceiling and recalled a time not long after the Reverend Hare had moved in with us, when I had gone into his bedroom and found the Bible in a drawer of his desk. I could barely read any English words then, but I could see that every margin had been filled with pencilled notes, and wondered if God minded these additions. The Reverend himself had taught us the Bible was so sacred that only a man trained in the church could read it. When I asked him later if it was allowed for a church man to write on its paper, I aroused his anger and received a beating for sneaking around. But then, as often happened after he released his wrath, he spoke to me as if I was older than my age. He explained that it was a pastor's job not just to read the word of God, but then to interpret it. I did not then know the meaning of the word interpret, and he explained it in a very clever way, by walking me out to the garden and picking a stem from the rice field planted next to our house.

'The whole plant, son, is the wurrrd of God, but when I interrrpret it, I find only the meaning which is good for you to eat.' So saying, he pulled off a grain between his finger and thumb and popped it between my teeth still raw.

When Archie came in, I asked him about the notes he had made around the sonnets, expecting his reaction to be very different from the Reverend Hare's. But he responded with an uncharacteristic loss of patience, telling me they were private and I should not have looked at them.

'Are you investigating me now as well?' he snapped. Seeing my hurt expression, he was immediately regretful. His blood was up, he explained; he had just been arguing with H and H about taking me with them to the Hotel Hokusai. Both had objected, not because they didn't like or appreciate me, but on account of the extra use of funds. Even just two nights at this establishment did not come cheap, and the dealer who was funding them expected a rigorous accounting of expenses. Archie, however, had eventually prevailed, and it was now agreed that I would be joining the three of them on the trip. Assuming Tsutsumi was right, I might have the chance to speak to Tsubaki's sister, and perhaps this would finally shed some light on what had happened to her.

Regarding what Nith had said in the heat of the moment, of course I was not investigating him as well. But after my illogical conclusions about Tsutsumi, I was trying to think more seriously about the art of investigation itself. It had dawned on me that I was far from the hero of Baker Street, and I began to consider, from a practical perspective, what might be the best way to reach the truth. On my long walks, or as I performed housekeeping chores for the artists, my mind was running through abstractions and forming principles. It was this, rather than any sense that Archie was hiding a secret, which led me to the sonnets. Now that I think about it, they may have been underneath his pillow rather than beside the mattress, but all I was doing was experimenting, translating into practice a notion that I had written down, which I can still read now in my sixteen-year old's hand:

Learn how people are.

I had more of these tenets, another of which was:

Write down everything.

And yet another:

Think in others' heads.

Was I aware when I wrote these that they could also be advice for becoming a writer? I certainly knew that my writing and my investigation were bound up together, believing then that words had to have some relationship with action. I wrote down all that I knew about Tsubaki and the sequence of events on her final night. Then, instead of lying in my bed awaiting visions, I put on my shoes and slipped out of the lodging house to retrace the steps of her final journey from the Persimmon to the docks. The first time I did this, I imagined she had made up her mind before leaving exactly what she was going to do. As I walked along, past the banners flapping in the wind on the eerily silent Isezakicho Street, I wondered if a strange calm might have descended on Tsubaki as she realised that whatever miseries had been blighting her life could be taken away. Might she not have seen death as a promised land of release at the end of a long, hard captivity? Trying to think myself right into her, I decided that being brought up in the same tradition as Yamato, she might have climbed the Hundred Steps for a final prayer at the shrine. After a last look in the direction of home, the hills that were only dark shapes against the night sky, she began the descent, and the last walk towards the sea. No matter what peace the decision had brought her, with each step closer to the water, her body made its rebellion clearer, her breathing growing shallow, the blood pounding thickly in her head. By the time she emerged onto the quayside, she was dizzy with nausea. It was deserted and dark, apart from circles of gaslight pooling in the doorways of the brick warehouses. The only sounds were the slopping of waves against the seawall, and the odd distant drunken shout from a boat out in the harbour. She forced herself to walk up to the very edge, looked over it down into the water, a rhythmic shifting of inky blankness. She imagined the chill she would feel on plunging in and instinctively stepped back.

The next night, I retraced Tsubaki's final journey again, but this time I imagined her fleeing from the Persimmon in blind desperation. Perhaps the hero of *Chushingura* had inspired her with his decisiveness, making her realise she could not stay there any longer. This time she did not walk calmly along Isezakicho, but clattered at a half-run in her *geta* sandals, keeping close to the buildings to avoid some rowdy sailors walking arm-in-arm up the centre of the street.

The flapping banners were like the arms of ghosts trying to grab her and drag her back, but her only thought was putting distance between herself and that place. Reaching the junction at the end of Theatre Street, she faced the choice of going left towards Noge, where Yamato lived, right towards Motomachi, or straight on to the harbour. It was not hard for me to imagine myself into Tsubaki's shoes at this point, and I was sure that her first thought would have been to go back to her family. It was home, the place she had grown up, and even if her father had sold her to the brothel and her mother was powerless to stop him, at least she had her sister, whom Tsutsumi said had visited her just a day or two before. But what if they had argued? The one member of her family who she thought would support her wish for freedom had been against it? Then going home was not an option, and she couldn't stay in Yokohama where she would soon be recognised and brought back to the Persimmon. She had to get out of town quickly, find somewhere she could disappear and survive by herself. Standing in the shadows at the side of the junction in the middle of the night, I thought: where else would a girl in Tsubaki's position make for but Tokyo, the capital? It was not far away, and though I hadn't been there, I knew it was large enough to swallow anyone into anonymity. I turned left and started walking north, more calmly now, towards the station. Perhaps Tsubaki had enough money with her to get the train, but there were no trains during the night so she would have had to wait until morning when the station opened. If this version was correct, it was in these quiet streets around the station where something unexpected and terrible had befallen her, which had ended with her murder.

Nith did not accompany me on these nocturnal investigations, but I kept him informed about them and the theories I was developing. He was aware that I was writing things down more and more, a habit of which he and the other two artists approved and encouraged. After I had finished washing the lunch dishes, I would sit down with my notebook at the kitchen table, where my daily wages would be placed down beside me. It was almost double what I had earned before, and Archie worried whether I had a safe enough place to keep my money. I told him how for every five *yen* I amassed in coins, I would go to the bank to change them for a note, then fold these into a pouch I had made in the back cover of my copy of Treasure Island. I left this in plain sight beside my futon, reasoning that any thieves would not be interested in books and search instead under my mattress or in my chest. He remarked that I was obviously learning to apply the art of bluff beyond the limits of card games.

*

I remember that a couple of times in that week before we went to the Hokusai, the earth shook enough to make the crockery rattle in the cupboards. I had told the artists about the Reverend Hare's explanation for earthquakes, and KG made a joke of it: 'There goes Old Horney again!' That was how I learned that Hornel shared his nickname with the Devil, which shocked me even though I knew they did not believe in religion. With them, more than the tremors, it was Mrs Hawk whose appearances set the seismometer needle bouncing. The day before the trip, she turned up again unannounced, and just like on the day of the card game, I saw how the force of her personality altered the way the three men behaved. It was as if on seeing this Hawk they became feathered creatures too and couldn't help displaying their plumage.

We were all in the kitchen sharing a pot of tea which I had made, when she changed the course of the conversation: 'Gentlemen, do you realise how rude it is that you have known me this long and still not shown me your paintings? Honestly, I would have every right to doubt whether you are really artists at all!' She then suggested a game – it was always games with her – in which they each had to find one of their best canvases and place them side by side in the living room. She would wait here with me, and when they were ready, they were to call her in. From looking at the pictures alone, she bet them that she could guess whose painting was whose. 'I fancy I'll be able to divine the link between your personalities and your painting styles. And if I can't,' she called after them as they hurried off to do her bidding, 'the fault is yours, not mine!'

This left the two of us alone in the kitchen, where I had been in the middle of writing some more of my notes when she had appeared. She asked me about the notebooks and showed an interest when I gave her the convenient explanation: that I was writing a story. She asked me to read some of it aloud and I obliged, choosing the part about Tsubaki running away from the Persimmon. She was silent for a while after I had finished. I had expected her to say something blandly encouraging, and was taken aback when she asked, quite coolly, as if we were two professionals discussing craft, how I was going to end the story.

'I don't know yet,' I said. At this point, Horney's head poked through the doorframe. Strangely, it's this image of him, dark eyes glittering on either side of his aquiline nose, which is the clearest I have of any of the three. Even Archie, whom I saw far more of.

'Well? Are you coming or not? Don't let Han trap you with his wee mysteries.' He winked at me as Mrs Hawk alighted from her chair, giving a tiny grunt of effort. I stayed where I was and heard a whoop of triumph from the other room. My commitment to investigation compelled me to join them, and I learned that her success rate at identifying the painters from their works had been impeccable. It was typical of Horney that he was the one to go further: 'Now you have to tell us whose you like the best.'

She looked alarmed. 'I couldn't possibly. I might set you into conflict. Don't you remember it was a three-way beauty contest that started the Trojan War?'

'Come on, we're not Greek goddesses.'

'Just burglars with brushes.'

Without much persuasion, she relented, but said she needed more time before reaching a judgment. The artists' banter was replaced by tension as she examined each canvas, sometimes up close, sometimes from further back, cocking her head this way and that. I decided that my own preference was for Henry's work, though I could only have framed the reason in what I didn't like about the others. Horney's colours and style were striking, but I found the innocence of his two Japanese children unbearable. In Archie's picture, though I had seen it and told him I approved, I was uncomfortable with the way it suggested that working on the eel stall was my whole personality. Finally, Arabella announced she was ready to announce her verdict.

'I'm not an art expert, gentlemen. What I do know is that you are all marvellous talents. Personally, though, as you have forced me to choose, I will say that I like Archie's painting the best. It's a wonderful likeness of Han.'

She beamed at me, almost as if the accolade were mine. KG graciously applauded the victor, but Horney's disappointment at losing out was all too obvious in his scowl. Archie, caught between delight and embarrassment, stammered a few words: how he wouldn't be here at all if it wasn't for KG and Horney taking him under their wing all those years ago.

'No need for speeches, man. It's not the RSA,' Horney muttered, gripping Archie in a hug.

KG followed with a handshake and a quip that was explained to me after: 'Aphrodite Nith, you are the most beautiful goddess!'

Thirty-four

The Hotel Hokusai was, and remains, a byword for a particular brand of Japanese luxury that caters to Western tastes. The Archduke Franz Ferdinand of Austria was a guest around the same time as our visit. But I had no idea then that it was so famous, or that for an immigrant stall-boy turned housekeeper to stay there was an unheard-of event. The hotel is nestled up in the forest-furred hills of Kanagawa, south of Tokyo and Yokohama, between the coast and Mount Fuji. As a foreigner, you had to have your pass, of course, to travel outside of the settlement, and I am still unsure how I was added to the one obtained by Nith, Henry and Hornel. Perhaps I wasn't, but it was assumed when they checked at the station that I was a Japanese servant.

It was my first time on a train, and I remember the feeling of excitement as I looked out the window and watched the houses and trees unspool at many times the speed seen from a horse-drawn carriage. The railway line ran next to the first part of the old *Tokaido,* the route between Tokyo and Kyoto, so there was ample opportunity to watch the old world pass in a blur from the vantage point of the new. But I'm giving myself the retrospective credit of too much perception. While the painters chattered, my mind was mostly fixed on the thorny problem of how I might find and speak to Tsubaki's sister. Again, I wondered about the role of the police: what had those men, who had taken charge of and even photographed her body then, done or not done? Nith had told me that once Tsubaki had been identified, it would have been their job to inform her family. An officer would go to their home to do this, then accompany them

210

to the mortuary, where bodies were kept until they could be released for a funeral service. Looking out the window, I tried to imagine Tsubaki's family, a month earlier, in a horse-drawn cart making the slow journey to the Yokohama mortuary to see their daughter for the last time. But maybe it was different. Perhaps only the father had gone, and he had accompanied the police officer on the train; or maybe the police had brought the body with them, to spare the family having to travel. I pictured an officer coming to our village to inform my family that I was dead. I saw Mother's tears, Yoona holding her hand, then my own funeral; the Reverend Hare conducting the ceremony. In the middle of his 'ashes to ashes' speech, I pushed the lid of the box open and pointed my finger at him: 'Not so fast!' I imagined Mother and Yoona's incredulous joy as I climbed out of the hole and grasped their hands in each of mine ...

'Han! Han!' Archie was shaking my shoulder. 'Horney's asking you something.' I tore my gaze away from the land rushing past out the window and looked at Horney, who was eyeing me with concern. 'What's eating you, son? We're on our way to the lap of luxury. Anyone'd think you were going to your own funeral.'

Were my daydreams written on my face, or did Horney have some supernatural gift? I was fine, I told him, only thinking.

'You can think too much,' he replied, probably the best piece of advice anyone could have given me at that age.

After disembarking in the coastal town of Odawara, we walked around for a while, the artists with their sketchpads out, recording impressions. I watched over their shoulders as they conjured things with a few pencil strokes: the castle, a *soba* seller, an old woman in a conical hat with a basket on her back. They kept remarking that this was 'the real Japan', and it was true that the atmosphere was different here. We seemed to have stepped back in time; as foreigners, we were a rare species. Most of the locals looked away when we passed, some no doubt from hostility, others from embarrassment or fear of what we represented: the unknown threat of change from the outside world.

Soon enough, we were on our way again. Back to the old mode of transport: A pair of horses pulling a carriage along a rough road that took us out of the town and up a valley beside a river that foamed and raced between rocks. Progress was slow, but the artists were in high spirits, raving over the views back down the valley which grew more impressive the higher we climbed. Surrounding us were the reds and yellows of the autumnal forest, down to the browns and greys of the town, the white-walled castle no bigger than a chess piece, then the blue ocean filling up the scene to the horizon. A scene on too big a scale for distant people to register as anything more than specks, though there was a steady traffic of carriages and carts passing us in the other direction: the Hokusai had to be supplied with all its needs for creating an environment of luxury. Nith had acquired a map of the region from the British Consulate. It showed that the road would first pass through Tsubaki's village at the head of the Hakone valley, where it divided, with the Hokusai located another mile or so along the fork that went north. Mount Fuji was another 40 miles or so to the north-west, represented on the map as a series of spokes on a wheel with its crater as the hub. We could not see its cone on the way up the valley: either it was too cloudy, or the forested hillsides were too close.

As soon as we entered the village, I had the uncanny feeling that I was returning home. It was our village, except the church had been uprooted and the Reverend Hare removed. There were the same wooden shacks with overhanging straw roofs, as if the houses, like the people, were wearing hats too big for their heads; the same stacks of firewood, rice fields, fruit trees; the same women carrying baskets of vegetables,

212

and children playing invented games like the ones I used to play with Yoona. There would be a village beauty like Jaewon as well, I thought, except probably Tsubaki had been that beauty. Was that why the village seemed sadder than ours, why there were no shouts or cries from the children? Would one of them tell me in which of the dwellings I would find Tsubaki's sister and parents? Or would they answer me with hostile silence? The village was gone before it answered any of my questions. The road out of it took us straight into forest on either side, climbing again, but gently now, planes of light sawing through the trees. We rounded a corner, and there it was on the left, as unexpected as a dragon king's palace appearing on the seabed: the famous Hotel Hokusai, glowing in the sun of a late autumn afternoon.

A pair of servants emerged as our carriage drew up, bowing as they chorused formal welcomes, then leaping forward to unload our cases and carry them in. We passed into the lobby, where a chandelier dripping crystals hung from the ceiling. To the left was the reception desk, with alcoves containing room keys on the wall behind it. To the right was an anteroom full of tables and chairs. All around on the walls were pictures by the famous Japanese artist, Hokusai. While the details of our booking were checked, the Scottish artists bantered over which of them might one day have produced enough masterpieces to open a hotel decorated entirely with their own paintings: the Hotel Henry, the Hotel Hornel or the Hotel Nith. What about the Hotel Han, I thought, an establishment whose every room contained a bookshelf filled with the stories I would one day write?

The receptionist, a tall, powerfully built Japanese man, guided us to our suite. There was an entrance space for the removal of shoes, then a step up to a *tatami*-matted hallway. On the wall on the left, there was a picture of a gigantic wave about to crash onto some fishing boats; later, I would manage to look at this properly, before it really did fall onto someone's head. To the right were two bedrooms, which had a connecting door between them, and a bathroom. The hall then described an L around the corner of the hotel, affording views onto the garden through large windows. In the centre of each branch of the L was a table with two wicker chairs. The garden could be attained directly through a set of sliding doors to which we had a key, which the receptionist showed us. Enclosed by the L – though it could be made a single space by sliding back all the paper screened doors – was the main room. This contained a low table of dark wood with four cushioned seats around it. At the side, there were alcoves in which we could find our *yukata* to wear when visiting the baths.

Electing to do this first, we changed and padded in our slippers past the reception to the bathing area. This was the artists' first time using an *onsen*, and I showed them how you took your own bucket to fill with water from the tap, then soaped and rinsed yourself, so you were clean before you went in. KG and Archie were awkward at first in their sudden nakedness, using the scraps of towels to protect their modesty; Horney was unconcerned, holding his towel at his side and letting his 'son' dangle proudly in the open air.

There were covered baths as well, but on the far side of them, a sliding door opened onto the outdoor pool – surely the jewel in the Hokusai's crown. The chatter and ceaseless trade of Yokohama was a world away. Here, sat on great rough stones, immersed neck-deep in hot water, we savoured the contrast of the chill breeze on our faces while looking out on the colours of the hillside, the sky a deepening navy blue as night approached. Silenced by the beauty of it, even the artists communicated little beyond murmurs of appreciation.

In a state of pleasurable torpor, we returned to our suite and found, on the table in the main room, the appetizer to the feast awaiting us: toasted rice crackers with bottles of beer placed in a bucketful of ice. We sat cross-legged on the cushions in our *yukatas*, drinking and marvelling at the comfort of the Hotel Hokusai. Lanterns were being lit in the garden, lending it some of the supernatural quality of the party at Dowd's. We were contemplating a stroll outside when a knock on the door heralded a maid pushing in a trolley, and the start of a meal the likes of which not even the artists had ever seen.

First was the crab, which took as long to figure out how to get into as it did to eat. We had to break off the claws, then use our chopsticks to tease out the white strings of tender flesh until only the smooth saucer of the exoskeleton remained. Less complicated was the squid soup, slurped with a spoon, the domed heads crunchy as boiled bullets. Diminutive side bowls kept appearing: fresh pickled vegetables, beans of different colours, slippery, wet seaweed. There was the salty tang of raw sea urchin, served on a bed of clean white rice. The maid returned again, wheeling in a cart with a pan into which she poured a drop of oil. She lit a flame underneath it and proceeded to sizzle thin strips of beef that almost melted in our mouths. It was a feast of infinite delicacy, and I tried to imagine the place of unstinting effort and concentration where it was all prepared. Unlike Yamato's stall, the Hokusai's kitchen was hidden from the diners' eyes. How could I have imagined then that it would become my place of work and I would one day see it from a chef's perspective?

Horney ensured our glasses were kept topped up with beer, and the conversation turned from food to plans for the following day. The artists had been recommended a spot in the hotel grounds from which to paint the autumn hillsides.

'What about you, Han?' KG enquired.

'I want to explore the forest paths,' I replied casually. I had already decided that I would go out early the next morning to walk to the village in search of Tsubaki's sister.

Horney frowned: 'I wouldn't go too far afield. Who

knows what they do to wandering Koreans in these parts.'

'I'm sure I can look after myself.'

'Aye, you're probably right, more than any of us.' Horney seemed pleased with my display of fieriness, the stoking of which may have been his aim. He leant across to refill my glass and I drank, wondering if what I'd said was true. Could I survive if I took off on foot into the hills? I spoke the language; I was young, fit, and strong; But was I underestimating the dangers? I might starve or be cut to ribbons by xenophobic samurai, the fate the Reverend Hare said had befallen the first missionaries who attempted to penetrate the country. Perhaps thinking I had to be reminded why I was here, Archie cast me a significant look.

'Maybe you could take a stroll down the hill to the village?'

How much did *he* want to solve the mystery of Tsubaki? Only a short while ago, I wrote that he only became involved because he believed in me. There are remarks in his diary that indicate his frustration with my pursuit, but this comment he definitely made at a moment when his mind had every reason to be elsewhere. Nor did he have to stay up after we'd retired to our bedroom and listen to me go over the plan for the following day, agreeing to his role, in the pretext I would use to bring our last hope of a witness up to the Hokusai, where I judged an interview was likely to have the greatest chance of success. It all makes me think that his interest in discovering the truth was greater than he ever admitted.

After so many nights in the lodging house, the soft bed was dangerously comfortable. How easy it would be to lie in late and spend tomorrow relaxing in the hotel grounds! Before sleeping, I forced myself to go to the bathroom and glug water from the tap. In the night, my bladder tugged me into wakefulness. I lit the oil lamp and tiptoed out past Nith's sleeping form to relieve myself. Instead of returning

216

to the bedroom, I moved round into the part of the hallway that looked onto the garden. Wind and rain were rattling the windows. If the weather was like this in the morning, it would be even harder to persuade Tsubaki's sister to come. I sat on one of the wicker chairs and kept vigil on the rain-lashed darkness, imagining the Tengu King from Dowd's story out in the forest. Eventually, I must have dozed off. When I awoke, a grey light was filtering in, the rain had stopped, and the lawn was shedding a fine mist. I poked my head back into the bedroom to tell Nith I was on my way. Already awake, sitting up in bed scribbling his latest diary entry, he wished me luck and assured me that he would have H and H out of the road and be ready to 'play Watson' when I returned. Putting on my shoes at the entrance, I walked back into the hall, unlocked the door into the garden and stepped outside.

Thirty-five

The sky was blue with trails of pink-tinged cloud. The air smelt fresh, like how Nith always described his own country, a slight breeze sharpening it. I crossed the stream and joined the path that traced the garden's edge against the forest. Spiderwebs jewelled with droplets were slung between low branches: in several of them, great yellow and black spiders sat, from one leg's tip to another as long as a man's hand.

The path curved round the back of the hotel, coming out near the end of the driveway. There was a rough wooden shelter, under which carriages and carts were lined up. As I was passing, a woman walked out of a side door carrying a bucket and sweeping brush. I turned and hurried onto the road so she wouldn't see my face.

For the time it took to walk down to the village, I forgot my mission and enjoyed the fact that I was here, on the other side of the horizon of purplish hills that I always used to gaze at from the sweat of the quayside. Compared to the hazy heat of the settlement, everything up here was sharply in focus. When I emerged from the forest, I could see all the way back down the valley. My eyes followed the ribbon of the road as it coiled back on itself down to the cluster of grey roofs that was the town, and the blue strip of the ocean beyond.

Entering the village, my spirits began to ebb. No one was about, not like in Yokohama at this time, when the waterfront would have been bustling already, and there would have been plenty of people passing from whom I could have enquired directions without attracting attention. A couple of crows heckled me, but otherwise, it was silent. I was almost out the other side of the village, when I passed a boy pulling a cart up the road. He told me he wasn't from this place, but if I retraced my steps, there was another track that forked above the main road. How had I missed this? Every settlement, even the small ones, have their points of focus where people come together. In this village, it's the crossroads with the temple opposite the well, where two young women with babies strapped to their backs were talking, but fell silent when they saw the stranger, me, approach. I wished them good morning and they bowed, offering mechanical replies. One of the infants started to cry, a sound so familiar to me now that I can interpret its different causes, whether down to hunger for Yuki's milk or something that even I might provide. But that morning in the village, the baby's wail struck me as the height of desolation, and I couldn't bring myself to address the young mothers. I walked on, until I saw two conical hats bobbing among rows of radishes in front of a house. I tried my good morning again, and the weathered faces of the Nakamuras looked up at me brightly.

'I'm looking for Kurama-san's house,' I explained.

Mrs Nakamura gripped my arm and pointed up the hill. 'It's the last one, on the edge of the forest.'

This is the house where we live now, where Yuki grew up. It's set some way above the others, hunkered tight against tall, straight cedar trees. We've made improvements, but back then the decay was obvious, even from a distance. Straw was poking loose from the bindings on the roof, and logs were scattered haphazardly in the yard. I knew that I had been right: after tasting life in the city, there was no way Tsubaki would have wanted to come back here, any more than I could imagine returning to our village to live under the Reverend Hare's roof.

Startled by a sudden movement, I looked across into the trees and wondered how I had managed to miss the man with the axe sitting on a stump, watching my approach.

Unkempt hair hung around a face lined and hardened by the years. Archie would surely have wanted to paint Yuki's father, for he looked like a worker, although some devil in his head stopped him working, and he preferred making his wife and daughters do that for him. He's dead now, and I don't think anyone is sorry, certainly not me. He was only ever an obstacle, someone to get past, like the guards on the Persimmon's gate. He muttered something unintelligible, and I called across the gap between us:

'Good morning.'

He stood up and walked towards me, the axe raised threateningly as if I were a chicken to be killed or a log to be chopped into pieces.

'Kurama-san?' He stopped and gave the smallest of nods, a concession that by knowing his name, I had earned some right to be treated as a person. Suspicion still smouldered in his eyes as he stared me up and down. I couldn't help letting my gaze linger on the livid scar crossing his cheek. I swallowed and made a silent prayer before delivering my condolences for his daughter. Bowing, I waited for the axe to hack down into my shoulder, but instead, he spoke to me in a local accent that was not impenetrable. It was a disgrace, he said, that he had not received compensation for her loss. My master agreed, I assured him. He had been a great admirer of Tsubaki and wanted to offer something to her family. I knew that the whims of rich foreigners would be far beyond his ken, and when I explained the one condition to the gift, he beckoned me after him into his house.

After the view from outside, I was struck by the neatness and industry within: a fire crackled busily in the hearth pit, licking the bottom of a pot hanging from the rafters. The sharp scent of miso reminded me of Miura-san's kitchen in the lodging house. Beyond the fire, Yuki and her mother were kneeling at a low table, producing a tapping noise like a pair of woodpeckers. I realised they were mashing soybeans into paste with heavy pestles. I thought it strange that they didn't lift their heads, though they must have heard the father come in. Kurama-san put down his axe with a grunt and ordered them to stop and listen. For a second, I was overtaken by an irrational thought that it would be Mother and Yoona who faced me. Almost as eerily, both faces contained shades and echoes of Tsubaki, but without the fiery challenge in the eyes. Yuki looked down at the bean curd while her father explained my odd request. When he reached the part about the rich foreigner who had been so saddened by their daughter's death that he wanted to give them money as a token of his sorrow, I bowed. I straightened in time to see a flicker of fear cross Yuki's eyes when her father said the foreigner was staying at the hotel, and insisted that she go there to receive the money. I tried to reassure her: 'My master often heard Tsubaki talk affectionately about her sister. He wanted to meet you and give his thanks in person.'

Clearly, I was not unthreatening enough to quell her fears. She made no move until her father barked at her and her mother whispered something in her ear. Before she was ready to let Yuki go, her mother begged me: 'Please, keep our daughter safe.'

Kurama-san spat into the fire. 'Don't be stupid, woman. The boy's not marrying Yuki.' But at the door, he promised to kill me if any harm were to come to his second daughter.

All the way back through the village, Yuki trailed a couple of paces behind me, as wary as a wildcat. I wanted to tell her that we were investigating her sister's death, that this was the real reason we had to speak to her, but it would only risk frightening her away before we had her where we needed her. I thought of telling her how much I'd admired Tsubaki's poise as she clashed with Yamato at the *kabuki*, but this would only bring back the pain of losing her sister. It might even make her resentful, hearing about Tsubaki's eloquence and grace when she was the silent, sullen one in a tatty robe. Though in fact, I thought, she was just as beautiful. She had the same high forehead and lithe figure. Realising that I didn't even know what to call her, I stopped and turned to ask her name. She froze, looking hard at me, before deciding that perhaps she had nothing to lose in sending the two syllables travelling across the air between us, improbable as the first snowflake of the year.

It was a start, and I made further ground by asking about her childhood in the village. At first, her answers came in monosyllables, but with gentle probing, they grew more expansive. Several times she mentioned someone called Umeko, and I was confused until I realised that Tsubaki must have left behind her given name when she joined the Persimmon. Umeko and Yuki had gone to school together in the village, swum together in the river, danced at the summer festival, had wild snow fights in the winter.

'I have a younger sister,' I told her. 'We used to play together too.'

'Is your sister clever?' Yuki asked.

I thought about Yoona, whose cleverness I had never considered much before. 'Yes.'

'Umeko was clever.'

I didn't know what to say, but Yuki went on, information suddenly spilling out of her. There was a school for older children in Odawara, where Umeko should have gone, but their father wanted her to stay to help in the house. This was when Umeko started to resist him and he responded with his fists. One day, she was chopping radishes while they were arguing and he'd tried to hit her – this was how he'd gotten the scar on his cheek. The next day, he travelled to Yokohama and arranged her sale to the Persimmon. The story finished, and Yuki lapsed into silence.

'You must have missed her.'

She nodded, but said no more. It seemed she didn't want

222

to think about what had happened to her sister in Yokohama. We trudged on in silence towards the Hotel Hokusai, the ranks of tall, straight cedars and pines looking down on us like sentinels on either side of the road. I imagined them in winter, heavy with snow, and saw the rest of Yuki's life stretching out here, season after season. If she was lucky, she might marry a man from the village, escape her father, and have children of her own. If I had remained in my village, I thought, if the Reverend Hare hadn't dispatched me to Japan on a fool's errand, what kind of a future would I be moving towards instead of this one? What was I doing on this road that was rapidly drying in the morning sunlight? For the first time, it struck me how utterly unlikely my undertaking was, but it was too late, far too late, to turn back now.

We were nearing the entrance to the Hokusai's driveway, and I had to think of practicalities. Yuki could hardly pass for a guest and walk in the front entrance. If we took a shortcut up into the woods, then we could skirt round the back of the outbuildings and join the path further up, leaving only a small area of garden to cross to gain access to our rooms. I pointed up into the trees.

'We can take a shortcut.'

To my surprise, Yuki did not have to be persuaded. She flew up the steep bank like a fox and I scrambled after her, holding onto roots to pull myself up. Under the trees, she seemed to know not only where we were heading, but the best route to pick through the dense bamboo clustered between the trunks. She scampered on ahead, slipping through gaps while I blundered behind. We were in sight of the Hokusai's lawn when I saw a flash of something yellow above my head and felt a sharp sting on the back of my neck. I fell to the ground with a cry, pain flooding my senses. Yuki came back and knelt beside me.

'*Dou shita*?'

223

I realised exactly what must have happened, but could only think of the Korean word. I pointed to the back of my neck and felt her finger gently touch my skin where just a few moments earlier, the spider had landed and bitten me.

'*Kumo-da*!' she laughed, a sound clear and pure that rang through the trees like a bell. 'You don't know how to move in the forest.'

Provocation made me fluent again. 'I know how to move. I don't know how to stop spiders jumping on my neck.' I got up despite the pain, and we walked slowly together through the final section of forest. I hoped no one saw us emerging onto the path and crossing the lawn to the back of the hotel.

The door was still unlocked – I had taken the key with me. I led Yuki from the veranda into the hallway. Of course, it was the first time she had ever been inside the Hokusai. Her gaze travelled across the opulent furnishings and tasteful decoration, distracting her from my cautious movements, for fear that we would run into KG or Horney, and I would need to invent some explanation as to why I had brought a village girl in here. But Archie had managed to persuade them to go out early, and our path to the bedroom was clear. I opened the door. Both beds were made up, but Archie wasn't there. Had he forgotten that he needed to be here himself? Yuki was looking at me doubtfully.

'My master will be here any moment. Please sit down,' I pointed at the bed on the far side of the room which Archie had slept in. She had never seen a Western-style bed before, and she climbed gingerly onto it, kneeling with her palms flat on her thighs. I sat facing her on the other bed, my feet on the floor. We looked like a pair of awkward newlyweds, unsure how to proceed.

'He's just coming,' I repeated, feeling foolish. But right on cue, I heard the outer door open, then the bedroom door. It was Archie, in his *yukata*, his hair still wet; he must have come straight from the baths. He seemed surprised to see us, even though he had known that this was my plan. Yuki tensed like a cat caught in a corner. Archie tried to put her at ease by introducing himself, his Japanese even clumsier than usual. Yuki looked at me for reassurance. The seed was already planted in her head that I was the interpreter, the one who would tell her what he wanted for his money.

'He just wants to find out what happened to your sister,' I explained, as Archie sat down in the chair against the wall. Yuki's eyes darted from him to the door, then back to me.

'You said he was going to give me money.'

'He will; but first, he needs to know what happened to your sister.'

'You lied to me.' Her eyes blazed, and for a second it was Tsubaki there on the bed, the same defiance that I'd fallen in love with that night at the *kabuki*.

'I'm sorry.'

'My sister jumped into the sea.'

She told me later that this was how she had explained it to herself, after she heard where Umeko had been found. Her sister liked swimming. It must have been a challenge gone wrong; an accident. So it was cruel what I said next, though it was only to draw out her testimony.

'I saw your sister's body pulled from the water.'

Her eyes widened in anguish as I layered on the details, painting the quayside with words. I described how the police had gathered round her, how they'd photographed her. 'And the reason they did this,' I went on, 'was because they suspected a crime had been committed. I heard the policeman ask if anyone had seen something suspicious. Then they decided it was suicide. That's what your family heard. But I – I mean Archie and I – we didn't believe that. Umeko's friend told us that you met her the day before she died. Did she tell you anything, Yuki-chan? Was there something she was afraid of? Someone?'

Yuki's face had set into a rigid, blank mask, but now she nodded. She looked down at her hands, and I saw they were trembling.

'Tell her there's no need to be afraid,' Archie leaned forward from his chair. I translated, and asked her to tell us everything that happened on the day she met Umeko, not missing anything out as even small details could be important.

Fortunately, Yuki has a good memory, even better than mine, and she tells a story well. Recounting the events of that day seemed to settle her, at least until she came to the way it ended. A few times I had to prompt her with questions, but mostly she talked and I only listened.

It started with a letter Umeko had written to the family. She had been earning extra money, she said, and wanted to meet her sister to give her some. Yuki should take the early morning train on the first Friday after the *obon* festival. Umeko would meet her on the platform in Yokohama. They would have lunch together, then she could take another train back to Odawara later that afternoon. The prospect of a trip made Yuki nervous, but excited. Their father did not like it, but the mention of money persuaded him to agree.

Yuki hadn't seen her sister since New Year, the last time Umeko had been home. She hardly recognised the young woman standing on the platform. Umeko wore a fine silk *yukata* and her hair was pinned back with a flower. With her faded robes and long hair trailing down her back, Yuki felt like a *yamanba*, a mountain witch. But they were still sisters, even if they had grown apart: they hugged each other in delight.

Umeko bought them bowls of *yakisoba* at a stall, and they ate them sitting on a bench by the street, watching people

226

stream past. Yuki couldn't believe how many foreigners there were in Yokohama. Umeko showed her how to tell the handsome ones from the ugly; the sailors from the land-dwellers; even the countries they came from. Those two would be from England, that one French, others from Russia, America. Yuki remembered these places from her lessons in the village school and tried to picture where they were on the map. Umeko said the men sometimes gave her things from their countries. The world was full of wonderful things, like *woduka*, a drink even stronger than sake, and *jamu*, a sweet paste made of fruit and sugar. Yuki wondered why Umeko did not mention what else happened in her encounters with the men. In that last New Year holiday, lying in their old bed together, Umeko had cried when she told Yuki what she had to do for her work.

They walked along the waterfront to the harbour, then out along the pier, past all the boats tied up with ropes. 'They're just like horses that travel on the sea,' Umeko said, but Yuki disagreed. They were ugly and made of metal, nothing like horses. Umeko laughed and called her *inakamono,* a country girl. She said the men who were sailors had told her about the boats and now she knew all the different kinds: ships with flying swords for piercing the skin of whales; ships with guns for battles at sea; ships for taking Japan's goods around the world and bringing the world's things here. And ships that did the same for people, with little rooms in them with beds and mirrors on the wall, like floating hotels. As she spoke, Umeko pointed out vessels docked in the harbour or anchored out in the bay. Yuki said she would feel afraid if she were on a ship and lost sight of the land, and what about typhoons – they would turn a ship over and it would sink to the bottom of the ocean and everyone would drown. This was not true, Umeko replied, modern ships were strong and safe. Travelling in one across the ocean to America was probably safer than the train journey back to their village!

They sat down on a bench looking towards the sea. Umeko said someone was going to meet them here, a friend. 'I'm going to make you look even more beautiful,' she said. Standing behind Yuki, she combed her hair and pinned it up with a clip. Yuki watched the passers-by on the promenade. She stared at a foreign woman perched up on a thing with two wheels, weaving between the walkers. Then a man – a foreigner, but wearing Japanese clothes – stopped in front of them. This was Umeko's friend, and Yuki's thought was that he wasn't like the ones she had said earlier were handsome. He looked more like a rich, old Japanese man, and when he spoke he sounded like one too. Umeko introduced her and she looked at the ground, nervous.

'Can she speak?' the man asked, laughter in his voice.

Umeko asked her to say something, but Yuki couldn't think of anything to say.

'She could sing a song,' the man suggested, and Yuki wondered why he needed to hear her speak or sing at all. But Umeko asked her to sing a song their mother had always sung to them when they were children, and Yuki didn't want to disappoint her. She couldn't keep the tremble from her voice, but she sang all the verses of the song. The man was smiling, but she didn't like his smile. It wasn't kind like mine was.

'Get her some new clothes and she'll be perfect,' the man said to Umeko when she finished. He patted Yuki on the shoulder, then rose from the bench with an effort. Before walking away in the direction of the harbour, he said these words: 'The time and place are the same.'

Yuki looked at Umeko, confused and frightened by what had happened.

'*Otsukare*, well done,' her sister squeezed her hand; soon, she would explain everything.

They moved to an *izakaya* on a street lined with banners,

noisy with drink and laughter. All the women wore bright *yukatas* and had painted faces. A couple of them looked at Yuki in a way that made her wish she was back in the forest. At the next table were two foreign men and two Japanese women. The women were trying to say words in a different language and the men were laughing, slapping the table with great red hands. Yuki stole glances at them, thinking of childhood stories of ogres with curly hair and horns. Umeko came back with two bottles.

'We should celebrate your coming here.' Yuki watched Umeko glue the mouth of the bottle to her lips and tilt her neck. She took a cautious sip from her own – it was disgusting.

Her sister laughed: 'I was like that at first. Tell me about home.'

Yuki wondered why Umeko wasn't telling her yet about the man on the bench, but she was glad of the chance to share news of the village. She described how certain people still shunned them – Moriyama-san had said something that left her mother in tears. But most people treated them as they always had done. The Ozawas had even started to single them out for generosity. When Yuki went to deliver *tatami* to Ozawa-san to take them to town to sell, his wife often asked her to stay and eat with them.

'She probably wants you to marry her son,' Umeko said.

Yuki laughed, but Umeko's smile had faded. She was fingering the frayed neckline of Yuki's robe, looking at the cloth and shaking her head. 'If you marry a boy like that you'll be trapped in the village for ever. Is that what you want?' She didn't wait for an answer. 'Listen. I'm going to tell you a story. Across the ocean, in a city called San-hu-ran-shi-su-ko, there lives a handsome American. His name is Okami-san, in English, you say Mister Wolf. But he's a sad wolf, not a bad one. His American wife died when she was

229

still young, before they had children. Poor Okami-san, don't you think?' Umeko put the bottle to her lips and waited for Yuki to agree before going on with the story.

'To forget his grief, he went travelling. First, he sailed to Australia. Then, to India. But he only started to feel better when he came here. He loved everything about Japan. He wanted to stay for ever, but then his father died, and he had to go back to America. You know how it is, Okami-san had to run the family business. Back home, he was a busy man, and rich, but all his sadness had returned. And now, there were two things he missed: the first Mrs Wolf, and Japan.'

Umeko lifted Yuki's bottle, which she hadn't touched, and tilted it to her lips. Yuki thought the story was finished, but Umeko continued.

'Okami-san couldn't come back to Japan because of his business in America. But then he thought, what if Japan came to him instead?' Yuki laughed. Umeko was doing what she always used to do, making fun out of the scary things, only instead of ghost stories and their father, it was the foreigners. Like this funny wolf, who believed he could drag the islands of Japan across the ocean to America. But Umeko wasn't laughing.

'Would you like to go to America and marry Okami-san?'

Yuki laughed again, but uncertain now. It was no joke, Umeko said, Okami-san wanted a Japanese wife. The man who had sat beside them on the bench was his friend. He had been checking Yuki to see if she was the kind of wife Okami would like to have. That was what he meant when he said she was perfect. Yuki stared at her sister, speechless, as Umeko went on.

'Don't you see, Yu-chan? It's the only way for you to escape. All you have to do is say yes! It's all arranged for tomorrow. I'll get you some clothes before you take the boat, but when you get to America, you'll have everything.

A house as big as a castle. Servants! I'll follow you as soon as I have enough money. We'll be together.'

Realising that Umeko was serious, Yuki stood up. 'You're crazy,' she said, and walked out into the street, leaving her sister at the table. Yuki's head was strangely clear; she knew it wasn't Umeko's fault. It was the city and her work which had infected her like a disease.

More easily than she thought, Yuki managed to find her own way back to the station and buy a ticket to return to the village.

Archie sat through this whole sad story in patient incomprehension. Maybe he understood the odd word, at least the Japanese names of foreign countries. But when Yuki finished, there was no time to translate it all, and I already knew what I needed him to do. I gave him his instructions and turned back to Yuki.

'My master is going to draw a man. All we need you to do is look at this picture and tell us if it's the man who spoke to you on the waterfront.'

Archie had already opened his sketchpad. I took it for granted now that he could translate the essential features of a person from his memory onto paper. He must have known as he sketched what the implications were, but he did not ask questions. His concern was the accuracy of his drawing, which evolved rapidly from a jumble of lines into someone we both knew. 'That's fine,' I said. 'Now show it to her.' Yuki had been growing impatient, caught between curiosity and her desire to escape. When the picture was presented, she gasped, and her hand flew to her mouth. I scarcely needed to, but I asked her to confirm that this was the man, and she nodded.

Archie had unmistakably recreated the squat stance and toad-like features of Augustus Dowd.

At that moment, we heard the main door open and

someone come into the hallway. Assuming it was KG or Horney, I put my finger to my lips and whispered to Archie: 'We're finished. Just give her the money.'

Then the bedroom door was flung open, framing the same tall receptionist who had shown us our suite. I had not gone unobserved smuggling Yuki into the hotel. A complaint must have been made, and a minor investigation carried out. A description of me had led him here, and now he had caught us red-handed. There is no doubt what he would have suspected was going on, and the scene must have confused him: a peasant girl kneeling on one bed, me on the other, and the foreigner with a sketchpad sitting on a chair. Stony-faced, he took it in, then pointed at Yuki and said in English: 'She is not allowed in here.'

I'm still unsure why Nith acted the way he did in that moment. I always thought he was the type to apologise and pretend that it was all a misunderstanding. What impulse made him fling open the door connecting to the other bedroom, grab Yuki by the hand and pull her through, shouting to me to block the way? The receptionist went after them, but I did as Archie said. We grappled, but the man was far stronger and he tripped me and spun me head over heels onto the bed. Archie and Yuki had reached the door to the garden, only I had locked it from the inside, the key still in my pocket. Archie was wrenching the handle when the receptionist strode around the corner. Archie pulled Yuki close to him and darted sideways into the central room. The receptionist gave chase and Archie and Yuki ran out into the hall, back past the bedrooms to the main door.

'Stop him, Han,' Archie cried. I was in the bedroom doorway, and, like Yi Sun Shin defending the Myeongyang Strait, I hurled myself into the action. The fellow slammed into me, knocking us both off course into the walls. Behind the receptionist, Hokusai's *Great Wave* teetered on its hook and then crashed onto his head, the impact enough to shatter

the glass and knock him out cold. KG and Horney had chosen
that moment to come back from their dip in the baths.

'Not bad for a man with a dodgy stomach,' KG remarked,
as Archie and Yuki raced past them down the corridor. He
and Horney walked into the hallway to find me climbing
groggily to my feet, and the receptionist just coming round.

Our attempts to care for him, and my subsequent
apologies, were not enough. We might be the only guests
in the Hokusai's history to be evicted mid-way through a
stay. At least Yuki escaped unidentified, never to face any
repercussions from the hotel or her father. After escorting
her to the end of the driveway, Archie remembered to press a
ten *yen* note into her hand before waving her off back down
the road to her village.

He found us in the anteroom off the lobby, where we had
been asked to await the manager's verdict. I had improvised
an explanation for H and H, telling them that I had befriended
Yuki on my walk to the village. When Archie appeared, he
took the blame for her presence in our suite, saying he had
met us outside and felt it morally imperative to invite her
in. Why should a poor village girl not sample the fruits of
luxury for once? Horney was angry, and on the carriage ride
back down the valley, he continued a tirade against what
he described as Nith's lunatic brand of socialism. KG was
hardly less critical, remarking that if word got back, there
could be some unpleasant headlines in the Scottish press.
Both were of the view that Archie's irresponsible behaviour
was harming the collective respectability of the group.

I said as little as I could through all of this, my thoughts
racing with the far more important matter of what we had
learned from Yuki. Dowd had to be our prime suspect now,
but we still had no proof that he was involved in her death.
We would have to confront him with what we knew. I was
thinking about Yuki as well: how she had told me everything;
how she had trusted me; and how she would now be back in

that shack in the village. By the time we were on the platform in Odawara, waiting for the train back to Yokohama, Horney had calmed down and was even starting to find the amusing side to what had happened. What had the girl really been doing in our room, he asked me with a knowing wink. When I equivocated, he said: 'I can't imagine Archie wanted her for *that* purpose. You on the other hand ...'

No, I told him, she reminded me too much of my sister.

Thirty-six

Being dropped at the lodging house came as a rude return to reality. My brief stay at the Hokusai had made me sensitive to my stained and sweat-encrusted bedclothes. But even more than the clean sheets, in that sleepless night I missed the peace of the forest. Here, noise pursued me at all hours: chatter and snores in the dormitory; shouts, clatters and clangs from the street outside. Once the investigation was over, I thought, I must find somewhere better than this to live. I tried to picture some small but private quarters, something between Dowd's servant's room and Holmes' flat in Baker Street. In my mind, I furnished it with a bed, a table, chairs, a bookcase and a writing desk. There would be a window with a view onto the ocean, or trees moving softly in the wind.

It was that night, thinking about the trip to the Hokusai, that marked the end of my illusions about where my investigation and my writing were taking me. Scales fell from my eyes, and I saw the limitations of who I was. I constructed a simpler future, inspired by Yuki's face as she bent over me in the forest laughing at my spider bite. Archie thought my pursuit of the truth was always pure and selfless, but he was wrong. Discovering Tsubaki's fate had given me something to fasten onto, to stop me drifting, like the bollards the ships were moored to on the pier. Now I could see beyond it, to another horizon equally difficult to attain. Like Umeko, who had become Tsubaki, I dreamed of rescuing Yuki from her grim father and his chains of poverty, of one day teaching her English and giving her decent clothes to wear. She might never have a castle and servants, but with me she wouldn't have to leave Japan; I would make this land my home, as much as it was hers.

By the time the morning light filtered through the gaps in the shutters, I had set the tiller on course for the rest of my life. First, I would have to find stable work in order to leave the lodging house. I knew a little about how marriage worked, and certainly Yuki's father's mind: the savings I had enclosed in the back cover of *Treasure Island* would have to be multiplied many times.

I did not mention any of this to Archie when we met on the bridge that morning as arranged. Our talk was of more urgent matters. After I had explained all that Yuki had told me, we discussed how to proceed. For once, I was the cautious one: was Dowd guilty? We still had no obvious motive. Could Tsubaki's failure to provide Yuki for the American really have spurred him to drown her? But Archie was adamant that a crime had taken place whether Tsubaki was murdered or not.

'You cannot trade in human destinies, Han. That's barely a rung down from slavery!'

He made plain his disgust at Dowd, even if, as he said, the man might be only indirectly responsible for Tsubaki's death. I could see that Archie was angry at himself for trusting this man against his principles. He began to talk of politics, of morality and capitalism. I was beginning to understand something of this, but felt compelled to counter with an argument that had been nagging at me.

'What if Mister Wolf had treated Yuki well?'

'And what if he hadn't? What if she was to end up in a Persimmon in San Francisco? But whether she was meant to slave in a brothel or be a millionaire's wife is irrelevant. He can't sell women like they're paintings or silks.'

Archie was right, of course. But what about the Reverend Hare, who had cast me off without a penny paid? Was there a difference between an inhuman deed committed for money,

236

and the same act done for some other reason? Raw experience had prepared me for these kinds of betrayal. Archie was shaken far more by the revelation of Dowd as villain. It was also, of course, because he had placed his faith in the dealer to help Bara, and the idea that he'd delivered his rose into the clutches of a criminal was sickening to him. Yet when we came to the plan, he returned to true form: an accused person always had the right to tell their side of the story. We were not to go to the authorities until we had granted Dowd this chance. It would be a confrontation between gentlemen, disguised as a social call, on an ordinary afternoon while the settlement ticked on in its well-worn grooves.

It is easy for me to forget that I knew Archie Nith for a mere three months. We had met in the summer, and though autumn was now in clear evidence, on the day we had to confront our villain the climate itself had regressed. It was hot, almost like a summer's day, only lacking the teeming screech of crickets. Yet, change was coming everywhere. In Samoa, Stevenson was starting yet another novel, not knowing it would be his last; And after lunch that day, with the four of us round the table for the last time, KG explained their plan to go north at the start of November. It had nothing to do with our disgrace at the Hotel Hokusai, he said. He had been tapping doors at the consulate for weeks, and they had finally arranged a sponsorship for the artists to spend two months in a town in the north. I knew enough about how they worked to see that a change of scene would give them fresh inspiration: a land blanketed by snow, with mountain shrines, tree-clad backdrops, and peasants bent in the fields.

'Maybe you'll find the real Japan there,' I said.

Horney laughed at my comment, but Archie was looking at me with concern. On top of his fears for Bara, he was consumed with another layer of guilt for me. KG went on, patiently explaining the practicalities: 'We'll have to give our notice on this place, Han. The plan is to leave the day after Arabella's play, just in case Horney here has to play the monster. That's in a couple of weeks.'

It was only when Archie did not say anything that I realised he would be going too. He had to, I understood. Painting was his living, and he was part of a brotherhood of painters. Cutting himself adrift from KG and Horney would be a foolish thing for him to do. I got up from the table.

'Don't worry about me. I'll be fine. I'm sure I can find some other work.'

Horney had asked me to wash his brushes, and I went out to the garden to retrieve them. The cat was there basking in the sun, and I bent to stroke her, feeling a new affinity. What would happen to Tsuki? Would she be passed on into the care of some new residents?

Back at the sink, my fingers squeezed oil paint from the horsehairs. I watched the water gushing over my hands, turning many colours before spiralling into unseen pipes. Laying the brushes out to dry on pages from the newspaper, I painted a picture in my head of Yuki flitting through the forest, bright and happy like one of Horney's canvases.

After I had finished, Archie and I walked out together. He began to apologise, but I stopped him. What I had said was true, I told him: I would have no trouble locating another position. The important thing now was to focus on Dowd. He nodded, and with emotion in his eyes, told me that I was 'an admirable boy.' As we walked down the hill onto Motomachi Street, past the bakery and Sakemoto's studio, we turned again to the facts of the case. By the time we turned along the coast road at the French Consulate, camellias blooming on the lawn behind the railings, we had decided our angle of approach. For the rest of the short walk, we did not speak. We were two men with a purpose, passing carriages and bicycles, chattering teahouses, the ocean glittering on our left, the bluff high on our right. The sun beat down overhead,

238

and I remember Archie rolled up the sleeves of his white shirt and tied a cloth around his head. This time when I saw Dowd's villa, even more impressive in daylight, its white walls reflecting the sun, I thought about how the money had been made to build it.

Thirty-seven

We rang the bell and waited. The door opened to reveal Dowd's housekeeper, and I thought I glimpsed recognition, perhaps even the tiniest of smiles, behind his eyes.

'We were passing and thought we would call on Dowd-san. Is he in?'

The old fellow bowed and retreated into the house to inform his master. Archie and I exchanged glances, wondering what we would do if Dowd refused to see us. Maybe, like a doctor, he was only available by appointment. But the servant returned and asked us to follow him, escorting us through the corridors out to the veranda. Dowd was on the lawn near the edge of the stream, painting at an easel. He must have been aware of our presence but carried on dabbing at his canvas as if we were not there. Archie called across to him: 'Good afternoon, Mister Dowd. Sorry to drop in on you unannounced.'

'You've caught me at a bad time,' Dowd growled, not looking up.

We exchanged glances. Could he already know why we had come?

'I didn't know you painted yourself,' Archie said.

'Because I didn't tell you.' Dowd paused his brushwork and cast his gaze towards us. In his gold and green robe shimmering in the sunlight, he seemed to blend into the colours of the garden. 'I see you've brought Sancho Panza with you again. Well, come over here, would you and have a look.'

Archie and I moved obediently across to the easel. Only

when we reached him did Dowd grace us with his benevolent smile. Had his ill humour been only a performance, to show that he was not to be interrupted lightly in his own domain?

'Come on then, what do you think? Not bad for an enthusiastic amateur? Or should I burn my brushes now?' The questions were for Nith, but I appraised the painting too, searching not for artistic qualities but signs of moral corruption. There were none in evidence, though it was obvious even to me that Dowd was an amateur artist, his figures somehow flat and unconvincing. The canvas depicted a red-haired woman and a young boy sitting on a bench on the veranda of his own house. The boy appeared to be pressing himself forward onto the woman's lap. She was in profile, looking away as if distracted by something.

'An intriguing subject matter,' Nith observed. 'You've composed it well.'

Dowd grunted in acknowledgment of the praise. 'I'm glad I've learned something from all the pictures I've acquired. But come on, man, be blunt. What are its failings?'

'You want me to be blunt about your failings, Mister Dowd?'

'Look!' the dealer held up one of his forearms, pinching the flesh between finger and thumb. 'Thick skin!'

Surely, I thought, now was the moment to come straight out with our accusation. Instead, Archie stepped back from the canvas and closed one eye, using his fingers held away from his face as a measuring tool. Nodding slowly, the professional critic, he turned back to Dowd.

'I'm afraid you have a problem with your perspective. I wish I could say it were easily rectified.'

Dowd frowned: 'My perspective. I thought the composition was good?' He moved sideways to examine the picture from where Archie was standing.

'I thought so too at first, but then, when I looked closer, I saw that it was off kilter.'

Realising what he was doing, I caught Archie's eye.

'Where?' Dowd growled.

'Not in this picture,' Archie drew breath before going on. 'I mean your perspective on a certain Tsubaki who worked in the Persimmon. The young woman who was found drowned in the harbour. That's what we came to talk to you about.'

The dealer's face had taken on its most amphibious aspect, eyes bulging and nostrils flared. There is a species called the cane toad, a successful coloniser, which is capable of spraying a lethal venom to defend itself against assailants. Had Dowd possessed this natural mechanism, he would, I am sure, have unleashed it on us then. The only weapon he had to hand was a paintbrush, however, and powerfully built though he was, the two of us would have been more than a match for this. His fury receded, settling into a cold, hooded resentment as he looked at me, then back to Nith.

'Talking of the Persimmon, I was going to tell you some good news. I've found a buyer for Bara's pictures.'

I had been growing impatient with my secondary role, and chose that moment to step in.

'What about the buyer you found for Tsubaki's sister?' To my satisfaction, I saw incredulity flicker in his eyes; a flash of panic, quickly masked. If he had been hoping that our suspicions were vague and lacking substance, now he knew otherwise.

'I see. If we're going to talk business, we had better sit down.'

Dowd placed the brush down beside his palette and directed us back to the veranda, where two chairs and a table were already set out. He called the housekeeper to bring out an extra chair for me, also requesting some sake. We did not begin the interview until the old servant came back, bearing a tray with a vase of the clear liquor and three cups.

'One of the advantages of a large garden, besides hosting theatrical events,' Dowd said as he poured, 'is that you can hide from the world when you need to. You're both odd fish like me, you'll understand that.'

I could see what he was doing: trying to create a bond of sympathy between us, so we would judge him less harshly. I thought of Tsubaki and despised him for it.

'Just tell us what happened to Tsubaki, Mister Dowd, or we'll go to the police.'

'Remember that we could have done that without coming to you first,' Archie added.

Dowd tapped his finger on moist lips, his first cup of sake already emptied. Ever the businessman, he was considering his options, searching for a way to regain the upper hand.

'Very well. I will tell you everything, but first, you must tell me what you know.'

It fell to me to describe our progress from ignorance to a knowledge that far exceeded what the police had discovered about Tsubaki's death. Several times, Dowd interjected to comment on our persistence, or ask me to explain a leap of logic. Archie said little, and I could not help but feel pride that I was demonstrating the manner in which a detective should lead out a confession. I concluded by telling Dowd that Yuki was our witness and that she had identified him: we knew the reason Dowd had met Tsubaki and her sister on the waterfront that day.

Archie pointed a finger at Dowd then. It seemed that he had been gathering his anger, and now his voice quivered with a barely suppressed rage that I had never heard from him before.

'Commerce is a stressful game, is it not, Mister Dowd?

You said so yourself when you told me about your silkworms and how they frustrated you. I suppose it's the same when you're dealing with people. When they don't do what you want them to, you become angry.'

Even Dowd seemed to flinch from the hatred in Archie's eyes, shaking his head in vigorous denial.

'I am not a monster, Mister Nith. I assure you I never intended to harm Tsubaki.'

Sniffing the beginnings of a confession, I opened my mouth to speak, but Archie raised a hand to stop me. 'If you will listen to me, I'd like to tell you my whole story, from the beginning,' Dowd continued, his face now wearing an expression of honesty and contrition. Archie and I looked at one another and agreed, not understanding what Dowd meant by 'the beginning'. Once he had started, we were obliged to hear him out, and despite what we knew, as we listened, our estimation of him surely changed. There are few stories as persuasive, or as untrustworthy, as a man's version of his own life. The more smoothly they roll off the speaker's tongue, the more this is probably true, yet the fact remains that I have no account of Dowd's life to offer other than his own, subsumed into a history lesson, as he told it to us that afternoon.

He was born in Dublin, Ireland, into, as he put it, 'a family of comfortable means but conflicting parts'. His father was an English Protestant, a judge who travelled around the district courts dispensing justice. His mother was from the west of Ireland, a lapsed Catholic inclined to mystical poetry and unsatisfied yearnings. When Dowd was four, she died in childbirth along with her second son. It was the two of them, his mother and unborn brother, whom he had imagined together on the canvas we had seen.

At six, his father sent him across the sea to an English boarding school. In this philistine prison, his fascination with art in all its forms set him at odds with the mass of crude, savage little beasts, not to mention their masters. To survive, he began to develop his talents for adapting and outflanking his opponents. He developed 'this thick hide of his', yet he was not a happy child, and towards the end of his schooling, a period of black introspection overtook him. Against his father's wishes, he was permitted to return home for a spell of recovery. It was during this period that he started to understand 'the nature of the world' and the power that controlled it. In defiance of everything his father stood for, he became an admirer of the cause of Irish independence.

He returned to England and finished his school exams, but rather than follow his father into studying law, he insisted on going into overseas trade. Relieved to be rid of him, his father found him a position in the East India Company, and Dowd sailed to Shanghai to take up employment. He was exhilarated to escape, and anxious to prove himself amongst the other young traders. Most of them shared his skills in negotiation, but what made him stand out was his willingness to take risks and bend the rules in ways that the company tacitly encouraged.

Still only in his twenties, these qualities earmarked him for selection to forge a new and more uncertain trading relationship. Japan, closed to foreigners for centuries, had in theory been open to trade for a decade. The reality was less clear, more dangerous. Dowd arrived in Yokohama in the same year that a cocksure visiting merchant refused to move off the road for a local lord and was hacked to pieces for his disrespect. The incident triggered the British navy to demand reparations, then bombard the seat of the samurai clan. Talks were eventually brokered by those merchants who had already formed trade links with the samurai. Though not long established in Japan, Dowd played a modest role in these. The samurai duly entered negotiations, and Britain agreed to back their rebellion against the shogun's crumbling authority. Success came swiftly, with the Emperor restored as a symbolic leader.

As a long-time supporter of the new power, Dowd found himself in a privileged position. He set up as a trader in his own right, independent of the Company, soon gaining a reputation for his interest in Japanese art and culture. He had seen the potential of the silk trade and invested in importing modern methods of production. These were not proof against nature's fickleness: one year, a disastrous spring cold snap destroyed the entire crop of mulberry trees. It took him years to recover his fortunes, but recover he did, establishing himself as one of Yokohama's leading silk exporters, as well as its primary dealer in arts and curios to the burgeoning Western market.

Archie and I interrupted more than once while all this history was recounted, impatient to question how it was connected to Tsubaki's fate. Dowd assured us that its relevance would become apparent, yet now I see that much of it was not, and I realise again how cunning he was, constructing his own character defence to show us that he had earned everything he now had through his own endeavour. This was the image of himself, a defiant hero repelling thunderbolts hurled at him by the gods, that he cultivated and wanted others to admire: no wonder he had decided to play Cu Chulainn on the stage.

And it all came back to those roots of his. Though he would, in all likelihood, end his days in Japan and be buried in the foreigners' cemetery on the hill, Dowd had never forgotten his dream of Irish independence. For years he had followed the Republican movement's progress, joining a network of supporters whose members were scattered across the globe. In the summer of last year, at a race meeting at the Negishi course, he had fallen into conversation with a young American from California. He soon discovered that as well as a passion for gambling, the two of them shared Irish roots.

Dowd guided the conversation towards the possibility of an Irish free state, an idea the American had never considered, but with which he was instantly enamoured. We already knew of this man, a certain John Wolf, in Japan on a travel cure after the death of his wife. Under Dowd's wing, Wolf's pride in his Irish roots grew in proportion to his admiration for all things Japanese. Wolf was still in Yokohama, staying at Dowd's house, when his father died suddenly and he was forced to return to the United States to take over the family business.

Dowd received the unusual request just after the New Year: Wolf wondered if he might be able to locate a young Japanese woman, untainted by the ways of the West, who would be willing to travel to California to be his bride. Business was good, Wolf added. If Dowd could help him with this, he would see his way to providing the kind of financial support that an Irish uprising would require.

Dowd, by his own account, was shocked at the idea. He was a silk and art dealer who may have once dabbled in opium. Slavery, the sale of human beings, appalled him. Yet, the more he considered it, the more he realised this proposal was different. If the girl was selected carefully, it could bring about positive results on all sides. He had replied to Wolf, promising to do his utmost to fulfil his end of the deal. He did not think at first, that it would be too difficult to locate a Japanese girl happy to move overseas to marry a rich American. It was only when he considered the practicalities that the delicacy of the situation became clear. What kind of father would agree to have his daughter put on board a ship to marry a man whose very existence could not be verified? Perhaps, Dowd reasoned, the same kind who would sell his daughter into a brothel. That was the logic which had sent him back to the Persimmon, a place he had never thought to enter again. Perusing the photograph of the girls on the steps, he had chosen the one whose pose for the camera had failed to mask her deep unhappiness. Tsubaki was the type of girl he wanted to offer the chance to escape, and who cared if she was more experienced in the ways of the world than the American wished?

He had made the proposition to her in her room at the Persimmon. At first, she was distrustful, but he won her round and they parted, arranging to meet again. At the second meeting, she had bombarded him with questions about Wolf and the life she would lead in San Francisco. Dowd's answers pleased her, and she accepted his proposal to sail on a ship whose captain he knew, on the route between Yokohama and the American west coast. Dowd wrote to Wolf to tell him everything was agreed. Then Tsubaki came back with a negotiation of her own: would it be possible for her sister to marry Wolf instead? Dowd baulked at the idea, but Tsubaki had persuasive skills of her own. Her sister would match the American's demands more closely than she would. Yuki was purer, untainted by knowledge of foreigners, and like Tsubaki, she was desperate to escape their tyrant of a father, none of which Dowd could deny. They arranged a brief encounter on the waterfront for Dowd to assess her suitability himself. As we were aware, this meeting had seemed to go well enough, and Dowd had left it expecting that Yuki would be the one to board the ship the following night.

Here, he paused in his story. We had been sat at the table for so long listening to him that the afternoon was now turning into evening. The air had lost some of its earlier heat, and I could feel the muscles of my legs and backside growing stiff in the wooden chair. At last, I thought, we were coming to the heart of the matter.

'So what happened to Tsubaki?'

Dowd nodded, acknowledging that I now had the right to interrogate him. He bowed his head before continuing, his words emerging slowly, ballasted with sorrow and regret.

'She came alone to meet me that night, at the place where we had agreed. She was distressed. I could see that straight away and guess the reason. I tried to calm her. I told her that it wasn't the end of the world if Yuki had refused to go. "You're here, aren't you?" I said. I remember the look she gave me. Such ...' he shook his head, as if the word or its English translation eluded him. 'Then I said something I shouldn't have said. This was in Japanese, of course.' Dowd stopped again and looked up at Archie. 'You're much safer for not speaking their language, you know.'

'What did you say?' I pressed him.

'I told her that Wolf wouldn't know the difference between them anyway; And just for that, she flew at me. Holy Christ, I hadn't been attacked like that since my schooldays. We were walking right by the water. I managed to fight her off, but she came at me again, claws out, like one of those cats your Bara draws. I moved out of the way, and she lost her balance.'

'You mean she fell in?'

Dowd nodded, his hand over his mouth. 'It happened so fast. There was nothing I could do.'

It was plausible, I thought, remembering Tsubaki's reaction to Yamato in the *kabuki*. In the darkness, the edge of the quayside was easy to miss; there was a drop of half a dozen feet into the water. Then I recalled something Yuki had said.

'But she could swim.'

Dowd rubbed at his temples as if trying to activate the memory within.

'There was a tugboat tied up below the place she fell in. She must have hit her head off the side of it before she went under.'

Archie looked at me: was this possible? I had walked by

the harbour often enough to know that there were plenty of small boats bobbing against the foot of the seaweed-glazed wall. I nodded, and Archie addressed Dowd again: 'You could still have tried to rescue her.'

'There was a set of steps down to the water. I ran down them. Maybe I could climb across the boats to reach her, I thought. But the gap was too wide. I'm afraid I'm not much of a swimmer. It would have been suicide to try.'

'So, what did you do?'

Dowd sighed heavily, lifting his palms in a gesture of helplessness. 'Believe me, I have asked myself many times whether I *could* have done anything ...' He trailed off, leaving us with the squalid image of this man-toad squatting on the slimy bottom step in the darkness, seawater lapping over his feet while, a few metres away, a young woman was drowning. For a few moments, no one spoke. I felt hollow, cheated somehow that Tsubaki's life, like my father's, had ended as the result of a stupid, needless accident. Dowd was guilty of many sins, but if what he had told us was true, and we had no grounds to doubt it, then murder could not be counted among them.

'And you just walked home?' Archie broke the spell.

'No. First, I had to talk to the captain and his mate. They were waiting to take her across to the ship.'

'So you told your accomplices, but no one else. Then you sat tight and let everyone believe the convenient explanation that she had killed herself.'

'What good would the truth have done? It would only have destroyed my reputation, everything I'm trying to build here. When you appeared with Bara's pictures, it seemed the gods were giving me a chance to atone. And I have confessed to someone else. You recall my actor friend? He happens to be a police inspector.'

These last words hung heavy in the air, their implications

sinking in, like the red sun, dropping to the horizon over the hills to the west. Corruption as a shared cultural value. Archie spoke abruptly:

'Well then. There seems to be nothing more to say beyond what we've already heard.' He looked at me for confirmation and I nodded. We both rose to our feet. Dowd asked what we intended to do.

'We shall have to consider that,' Archie replied.

The dealer escorted us back through his house, holding the door open as we stooped to put our shoes back on. Performing what he would normally have left to the old housekeeper, there was no subtlety in his last attempts to win our favour.

'You will let me know first, if you decide further action is necessary?'

'I can't promise that,' Archie said shortly, not looking back. We left Dowd in the jarring absence of formal courtesies. Instinct gave us both the desire to put a decent distance between ourselves and that mock samurai's castle before we spoke.

Thirty-eight

The sky was cobalt blue, the brighter stars already visible. To our right, between the line of pines fringing the bluff, dozens of vessels were dotted across the canvas of the bay. Some were going out, some coming in; others hanging at anchor. We followed the gentle slope back down the hill. I could hear the music emanating from the French Consulate before we reached it: a seductive interweaving of violin and piano. Electricity in the windows, lighting up another social occasion in full swing. As we passed the railings, partygoers were spilling out through the wide steps of the front entrance onto the lawn: men in top hats and tails, women in flowing dresses. Peacocks parading their finery. How many of them would even care, I wondered, if they knew what we did now?

Archie stopped as we walked past the gates – I think perhaps he had seen someone he recognised. I followed his gaze through the gaps in the railings and saw flutes of champagne being swiped off silver trays. Recalling the relaxing effect of the fizz I had enjoyed at Dowd's party, I pointed out that the gate was open and there was no obvious check in place. Could we not just stroll in and act the part of invitees? We could talk everything over with glasses in our hands. But Archie vetoed the idea, and instead we walked on, to an isolated bench looking out over the ocean.

'Is he telling the truth, do you think?'

It was impossible to be sure, I answered, but from my close knowledge of the waterfront, the layout of the quayside did fit with Dowd's account. Also, what we knew about Tsubaki suggested she might have lost her temper and rushed at him in an impulsive rage. Archie listened, bent forward, his hands clasped, the pose the Reverend Hare used to adopt when he was leading us in prayer. He said nothing for a while, and I became aware of the crying of gulls and the waves lapping against the sea wall.

'Let's say we believe him, then. That doesn't change the fact that a crime has been committed, even if it isn't murder. Two crimes, if we include the deliberate cover-up.'

'So what should we do?'

He bent lower, plucked two blades of grass from the foot of the bench, and turned back to me holding them.

'If we go to the authorities, there are two possibilities.' He lifted one of the blades between his thumb and his index finger: 'One. They listen to us. Dowd is arrested. We have to give evidence in his trial. Yuki as well.' He let the implications of this sink in before holding up the other blade: 'Two. They say we are mad. A pair of fools making baseless accusations. Either because they think we are, or because they're Dowd's friends, or he's bought them off.' He tore both blades of grass in two and tossed them away in the sea breeze.

'Are you saying, then, that we shouldn't tell anybody?'

Archie sighed heavily and stood up. 'I don't know, Han. It's as murky as those waters down there, and we might be out of our depth. But I suppose I ought to be the one to decide. You are very young still.'

I protested against this sleight on my capacity for moral judgement, and Archie apologised. He was tired, he said; it was probably for the best if we took a night to consider before reaching our decision. We traced the seafront path and then the streets back to Chinatown. As we walked, he asked me further questions on my opinion of Dowd's motivation. I think this was his way of apologising, but if I had not been tired before, I was after hearing about the convoluted politics of Ireland's relationship to Britain. By the time we reached the bridge over the creek, darkness had fallen. We agreed to meet the following morning at the foot of the Hundred Steps. I was about to turn and go when, to my surprise, Archie gripped me in a tight embrace.

'We've done as well as we could, I think, Han.' These were the last words he spoke to me before turning and walking back over the bridge to the European side. I watched his angular silhouette pass under the shopfronts, lit by the glow of gas lamps, until he disappeared out of the frame around the corner of the steep lane leading up onto the bluff.

Thirty-nine

If our attempts to investigate Tsubaki's death did arrive at some kind of solution, I am afraid the same cannot be said for the question of what happened to Archie that night. Until a year or so ago, I would still be plagued sometimes by the thought of how little I did to uncover the truth. Guilt, like a creeping rust, ate away at me for years, corroding the blade of my soul. Oddly, though, it also served to drive me on, forcing me to oil the blade with relentless work, to climb the ladder to where I am now, a respected chef in the Hokusai's kitchen. So, what changed? Several things, certainly, but one was understanding that, by writing again, I might, in some form, resurrect Archie Nith. I could remind people of who he was beyond the sensation he became: 'The Artist who Vanished', several weeks' worth of front pages in the *Japan Mail*, and maybe even the odd headline further afield.

When he failed to appear at our meeting point the following day, I walked directly to the artists' house. KG and Horney were in, already concerned because Archie had not returned the previous night. They had hoped that I might know something of his whereabouts; and perhaps at that moment I should have told them a little of what we had been up to. But thinking of my own habit of nocturnal wandering to help me reach a decision, I said nothing. I reasoned that Archie must have preferred to be alone in order to think and decide what to do. Initially, my reaction towards his absence was not so much worry as annoyance. I had been prepared to insist that we report Dowd to the authorities, and wondered if he was trying to prevent that in the interest of protecting Bara's sales.

That evening, still with no sign of him, KG and Horney must have gone to report his disappearance. The following morning, Miura-san came clattering up the stairs in a panic: there were two men who needed to see me. I descended to find a European and a Japanese, the latter a familiar face. It was the same face which had scanned the crowd of onlookers on the quayside around Tsubaki's body; the same one, presumably, which had hidden behind the mask in the performance on Dowd's veranda. The other man explained that he was an official from the British Consulate. They needed me to go with them, to answer some questions about my relationship with Archie Nith. Although he did not say so, from his attitude it was clear that I was a person of suspicion. I was taken by carriage to the consulate, into a back entrance and up some stairs, the British official in front, the Japanese policeman at my back. The official led the way into a small, windowless room, and just before I followed, the man behind me leaned in and whispered into my ear in Japanese.

'Don't mention Tsubaki and everything will be fine for you.'

This command still echoed in my head as I stumbled through an account of the friendship I had formed with Archie. I told the official about the sketches he had made of Yamato and I, the invitation to the artists' house, and my eventual employment as their housekeeper. I gained fluency as I explained how I came to be in Yokohama, even giving a brief sketch of the Reverend Hare and his deception. The official, however, was not interested in this, and asked me instead what I could tell him of Archie's movements on the last night I had seen him. All the while, the Japanese man said very little, though his eyes did not stop boring into mine for a second.

We had gone walking together as was our habit, I replied, describing the route along the coast road to Honmoku and

256

back, omitting any reference to Dowd's villa, but dropping in the detail of the party at the French Consulate. I ended with a truthful account of how we had parted at the bridge over the creek, at the entrance to Chinatown, including the fact of Archie's embrace, which I said had surprised me.

'Why did it surprise you?'

'It was unusual. It felt like he was saying goodbye.'

The official scratched a note on the paper in front of him, which I could not decipher. The Japanese officer, whose eyes had been fixed on me throughout the interview, gave a barely perceptible nod. The Englishman raised his head again.

'You say that you and Mister Nith were in discussion on this walk. What was it that you talked about for three hours?'

Again, I did not have to lie in order to produce a convincing answer. I simply related what Archie had told me about the politics of the United Kingdom and Ireland, the complex history of religious division. He was often educating me about history and politics, I explained, adding that he held strong political views of his own. This was the cue for another note to be scrawled on the paper. The nature of these views turned out to be of great interest to the official, and I found myself attempting to summarise Archie's socialist beliefs. It quickly became evident that the official disapproved of these, and he even began to argue with me as if I were representing them myself. By the end of the interview, it was no longer clear whether Archie was being investigated as the potential victim of a crime, or as a criminal himself. In any case, the official's attitude to me had shifted. I was permitted to walk out of the building, with the one caveat that I should inform them if I changed my place of residence, in case they needed to speak to me again.

I was aware, in the subsequent days, of a search being carried out along the creek, from where it met the sea to the point upstream where it flowed out of the wide river that came down from the hills. This was when the *Mail* had Archie on its front page, and I continued to keep house for KG and Horney, both of whom were often out at the consulate, pursuing the hunt for their friend and fellow artist. In the times when I saw them, naturally we did little else except speculate about what might have happened. It was in these conversations, holding back everything I knew, that the red stain of guilt started to spread in my soul. Proclaiming my ignorance, I only listened and commented on their theories, over which they would argue, in characteristic fashion, while drinking bottles of beer.

Horney, impatient with all the time they were wasting in pointless contact with officials, was first to voice the idea that Archie might have chosen to disappear, had set off on foot, without a pass, into the unexplored provinces. Why would he do that, KG objected, when they were due to go together anyway? Why go alone, in the middle of the night, without taking anything with him? But Horney even had an answer for this: 'Maybe because everything he owns is made by capitalists. He's probably in some forest now, wearing animal skins and whittling his paintbrushes out of sticks.'

This image provoked a bitter laugh from KG, who then admitted to his own wild speculations: 'I was thinking, in fact, about those monks we saw in Kamakura. He may have joined a temple and now intends to devote the rest of his life to chanting sutras. What do you think, Han?'

Wiping the table with a damp cloth – I still had to earn my wages – I shook my head and said that I had no idea.

I do not think anyone can blame them for leaving, as they had planned, for the north. It was evident that there was nothing else they could do to help find Archie, and if he reappeared he would do so on his own terms. Before they left, on my final day as housekeeper, they presented me with a box of his books and a few clothes. He would have wanted me to have these, they said. I suppose neither of them knew that pressed flat underneath the books at the foot of the box lay his diary, with all the secrets it contained.

Secrets and guilt. I have not yet explained the half of mine. Through the murky turmoil of my thoughts in those days, one jewel shone bright: Yuki, and my plans for the future. This brought me back to the reality of my present predicament: my wages about to dry up, and I still had not found another source of income. The idea, when it came to me, was frightening, but the risk was part of its appeal. There were few people in the settlement as well connected as Augustus Dowd, and as he had said himself, connections were everything. I wrote him a letter, reminding him of what I knew, and delivered it to his house. In the days that followed, I walked the streets of the port on high alert, expecting to meet a knife-wielding assailant or abductor sent to quietly dispose of me. A week or so later, a letter arrived for me at the lodging house. It was a curt reply from Dowd, instructing me to present myself at the kitchen of the Grand Hotel and ask for the head chef. This *monsieur*, a Frenchman named Dutort, was sceptical of his new apprentice at first, but quickly grew to respect my cooking and language skills. My soy-battered eel on a bed of rice was the first of my own dishes to make it onto the menu, renamed with due respect, *Anguille au Yamato*.

Forty

My ingredients are nearly all used up, but there is one remaining morsel I can offer to anyone who still hungers for the truth about Archie's disappearance. A couple of years later, a few months after I began working at the Hokusai, I took the train up to Yokohama on my day off. In truth, set though I was on my purpose – and by this time I had already re-established contact with Yuki – I missed the international feel of the port, the smell of the sea, and the company of the painters. Most of the day I spent wandering the waterfront and the streets in the centre, my mind lost in recollections. Later in the afternoon, I happened to wander into an *izakaya* near where Yamato used to live, intending to have a single beer before taking the train back down the coast.

There was a friendly atmosphere, however, and I ended up staying longer than I had anticipated, falling into conversation with the fellow next to me at the counter. By then, I could speak Japanese without the slightest trace of an accent, and when I let on that I worked at the Hokusai, he was all ears for the stories I could tell of the famous foreigners known to stay there. As the drinks flowed, I told a few, and then mentioned that I was familiar with the demands of foreign clients, having worked earlier in my career as a live-in housekeeper for three Scottish artists. Not expecting the fellow to recall the case, I said that one of them had disappeared under mysterious circumstances. At this, the man's eyes lit up. He remembered the incident well, and he had heard a rumour that it was tied up with all sorts of scandalous activities of the type that the foreigners were liable to get up to. A fellow he knew, who had been working as a servant for the British consul at the time, swore blind that a man matching that artist's description had turned up at the consul's house on the very night on which he was said to have gone missing. The servant had let him in, but never seen him leave, and while there was no telling what had happened, he thought it was all connected to the consul's wife cavorting around with different men.

'You know what they're like, these foreign women, they'll jump into bed with anyone,' he added with a conspiratorial grin, obviously expecting me to share his opinion. When I told him that I disagreed, our camaraderie faded.

'So, what's your theory then, son? Have you got another one?'

I did, of course, though I was not about to tell him. Despite Dowd's express denials that he had anything to do with Archie's disappearance, what else did the facts point towards? Only now, alone with my thoughts on the last train back to Odawara, piecing together what my companion of the afternoon had said, and with some of the entries in Archie's diary, a different explanation emerged. Could Archie have gone to the consul's residence after we parted, in spite of what he had told me, to reveal the truth about Dowd? Could Arabella Hawk's husband have killed him there, on an impulse, because he believed they were having an affair? Or had he done so because he too was protecting Dowd, unaware of the dealer's intent to betray his country?

What is certain is that the Jollity Players' performance of *Frankenstein* was cancelled at the eleventh hour, and Arabella left her husband soon afterwards to return to Britain, an event which caused no end of tongue-wagging in the Grand Hotel's dining room. I would like to report that she gave birth to a son called Archie, and has since taken him to Glasgow to see the streets where Nith became a painter. The truth, however, is that I have no idea what became of her. It is only my hunch that the two of us remain connected by our feelings about Archie Nith; that we both believe he was a man who should not be forgotten.

I have played my part in that now, and thankfully, there is not much more for me to write here. I must reply to Yoona's letter and assure her that soon I will come to visit her again at the college in Busan where she is studying to become a nurse. Yoona has never quite forgiven me for the length of time it took me to establish correspondence after my arrival in Japan, a period in which Mother had almost given me up for dead; And I have already caused Yuki more than enough frustration, sitting at this desk while she suckles our daughter to sleep at night. If I were to offer a final piece of advice to any younger man reading this, I would say it is unwise to begin writing a long account of anything shortly before you become a father. Still, at least I shall finish now, before Tsubaki's first cries – not as yet in any intelligible language, let alone Korean, Japanese, or Scottish-inflected English - pierce the eye of morning.

Notes and Acknowledgements

Burritt Sabin's *A Historical Guide to Yokohama* was an invaluable source in the writing of this novel. Although I spent a fair bit of time roaming the Yokohama waterfront in 2015 – 18, I could never have attempted to fictionalise the city in 1893 without Mr Sabin's text and its illustrations. Of particular importance were the details about the Nectarine Number Nine, of which the Persimmon is my fictionalised version. For the history of old Yokohama, I also owe a debt of thanks to the staff at the Yokohama Historical Archives, who helped me locate 1893 editions of the *Japan Mail*. Nobuhisa Kaneko's *Surprise! By Kuniyoshi* gave me an understanding of Japanese *ukiyo-e,* or woodblock printing art, as well as the plot of the Chushingura and the story of Yoshitsune and the Tengu King.

In my depiction of the geography and layout of the port, I have tried to stick as closely as possible to historical fact. The Nectarine was located at the end of Theatre Street; Chinatown was separated from Motomachi by a creek, and the Hundred Steps did lead to a famous Shinto shrine at the top. Many details, however, have been invented. To give just one example, I have no idea whether that shrine contained a statue of the Dragon King; only that Ryuo and other nature spirits are integral to Shinto tradition.

Almost all the characters in the text are fictional creations, based on my understanding of the period. Scottish missionaries were influential in bringing Christianity to Korea in the late 19th century, though there is no evidence for one as corrupt as the Reverend Hare. Strong-minded women were starting to challenge the traditional male dominance over travel and exploration, Arabella Hawk being my nod to the pioneering traveller and writer, Isabella Bird, whose *Unbeaten Tracks in Japan* was published in 1878. The Gaiety Theatre was a focal point of Yokohama settlement society, and this, and other theatres, were vital parts of the rich cultural interchange between East and West. A couple of real figures do make brief cameos as themselves: John Reddie Black, the larger-than-life Fifer who established both English and Japanese language newspapers in Japan, in fact died in 1880, but I took the liberty of having him open the door to Nith in 1893. Natsume Soseki, mentioned in brief conversation with Nith, is one of Japan's greatest novelists, who in the 1890s, translated works from English into Japanese, before embarking on his own literary career. His novel *Botchan* is a short and brilliant comic depiction of the tensions caused by foreign influence in these turbulent years for Japan.

On the Scottish side, Nith is my invention, but George Henry and Edward Atkinson Hornel were very much real, and key figures among the Glasgow Boys, who were financed by Alexander Reid to make a trip to Japan in 1893 – 94. For my research on them, Roger Billcliffe's *The Glasgow Boys* was a terrific and comprehensive account of these groundbreaking artists. Bill Smith's Life and Work of E.A. Hornel added to my understanding of Hornel, his relationship with Henry, the trip to Japan, and its aftermath. An article by Antonia Laurence-Allen and Helen Whiting, 'Hornel's Photographic Eye and the Influence of Japanese Photography', gave me vital background on the link between photography and painting, while Ayako Ono's thesis, *Japonisme in Britain,* was another valuable source in understanding the appeal of Japan for these and other artists of the period. My portrayals of Hornel and Henry in Japan are informed by all these and other sources, but I have also used an enormous amount of creative licence. Apologies to any descendants of the artists who may be offended, but I hope my portrayals are, in the main, affectionate and serve to stimulate interest. A wander around the Glasgow Boys room at the Kelvingrove Art Gallery and Museum may be the best way to appreciate Henry and Hornel's talents, regardless of my speculations about how they might have lived 'away from the canvas'. Glasgow has been, and continues to be, a city that sparks creativity in a spirit of openness and experiment. It's also a city that welcomes migrants, those like Han who have had to leave their countries to build a new life in a different culture and language.

Since first conceiving the idea for a story about a migrant eel stall vendor and a Scottish artist in 1890s Yokohama, I have shown sections of this novel at various stages to several people. I would like to thank all of these readers, whose encouragement and suggestions kept me going, even when there was so much work still to do:

Doreen Nisbet, Paul Garner, Nial Sellar, Martin Law , Jill Baxter, Fearghus Roulston, Neil Stewart, Alan McMunnigall, and member of thi wurd's online novel writing class in 2021.

I would like to thank Sandy Jamieson and the team at Ringwood Publishing for seeing the potential in The Hotel Hokusai's rough incarnation and helping me bring it to a state where it was ready to enter the world. Throughout the editing process, I have been incredibly fortunate to work with Ringwood's skilled and perceptive editors, Megan Gibson and Isobel Freeman. In addition, I am hugely grateful for the time and energy of the many interns who have read drafts and provided additional editorial input. The work and advice of the marketing team, Robyn Drain, Rosie Hall and Namitha Shivani Iyer, has been tremendous, while Skye Galloway's cover design is a thing of wonder, which exactly captures the spirit of the book. Finally, special thanks go to the following people:

Milan Acosta, for his friendship during my time in

Yokohama – including the cans of *nihonshu* after I re-enacted Jack London's swim in Yokohama harbour.

The real Han, a self-possessed young Korean who I taught once in Edinburgh – a true linguistic sponge and inspiration for the Han in my story.

Kouji, Mami and Haruka Yamada, for welcoming me into their family and helping me understand Japanese culture.

Jackie Garner, for giving me some genetic facility for learning languages (Paul Garner will be the first to admit that this is unlikely to have come from his side).

Cinzia Pusceddu, for being the best language teacher I ever had.

Finally, to my wife, Yuuka Yamada-Garner and my daughter Hannah, for their constant support and tolerance of my extended sessions in front of the laptop.

Minna-san hontouni arigatou.

Other Titles from Ringwood

All titles are available from the Ringwood website in both print and ebook format, as well as from usual outlets.

www.ringwoodpublishing.com
mail@ringwoodpublishing.com

Murder at the Mela

Leela Soma

DI Alok Patel takes the helm of an investigation into the brutal murder of an Asian woman in this eagerly-awaited thriller. As Glasgow's first Asian DI, Patel faces prejudice from his colleagues and suspicion from the Asian community as he struggles with the pressure of his rank, relationships, and racism.

This murder-mystery explores not just the hate that lurks in the darkest corners of Glasgow, but the hate which exists in the very streets we walk.

ISBN: 978-1-901514-90-2
£9.99

The Carnelian Tree

Anne Pettigrew

A dead body, a disappearance, and an epic lost in time. Unrelated incidents on the surface. Judith Fraser's Oxford sabbatical quickly takes a sharp turn when she gets tangled in the mysterious murder of a colleague. With threads leading nowhere, conflicting impressions about people around her, and concern for increasing risk to her loved ones, whom can she trust? Her eccentric housemates? The CIA? Or, herself? Too many questions and insufficient answers.

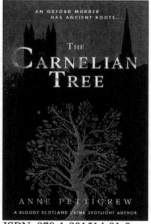

ISBN: 978-1-901514-81-0
£9.99

Cuddies Strip

Rob McInroy

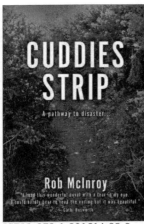

Cuddies Strip is based on a true crime and faithfully follows the investigation and subsequent trial but it also examines the mores of the times and the insensitive treatment of women in a male-dominated society.

It is a highly absorbing period piece from 1930s Scotland, with strong contemporary resonances: both about the nature and responsiveness of police services and the ingrained misogyny of the whole criminal justice system.

ISBN: 978-1-901514-88-9
£9.99

The Bone on the Beach

Fiona Gillan Kerr

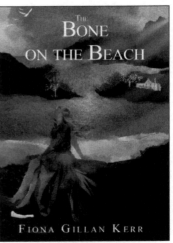

In 2002, in a tight-knit Highland community, a young woman named Deirdre mysteriously loses her life.

Fifteen years later, Meghan, a lawyer in a city law practice, arrives in the village seeking a fresh start. But when a bone suddenly washes up on the beach, she finds herself embroiled in a dark and twisted mystery stretching back to the turn of the new millennium.

Facing the residents' overwhelming reluctance to talk about the past, Meghan wonders what took place in this village all those years ago. What are the terrible secrets they have buried? Who was Deirdre and what really happened to her?

And why does it feel like she's being watched?

ISBN: 978-1-901514-91-9
£9.99

Bodysnatcher

Carol Margaret Davison

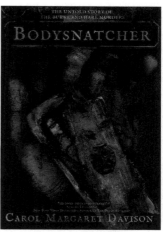

In the late 1820s, two Irish Immigrants, William Burke and William Hare, murdered 16 individuals and sold their corpses to Dr. Robert Knox, who used them for anatomical dissections. Their gruesome killing spree ended when Hare turned King's Evidence, with Burke being hanged and dissected himself.

However, the question of whether their female accomplices, Nelly McDougal and Margaret Hare, were involved, has never been conclusively determined.

In *Bodysnatcher,* Carol Margaret Davison places Nelly centre stage in this sordid story, granting a voice to a woman whose perspective has never been heard.

ISBN: 9778-1-901514-83-4
£12.99

Raise Dragon

L.A. Kristiansen

In the year of 1306, Scotland is in turmoil.

Robert the Bruce and the fighting Bishop Wishart's plans for rebellion put the Scottish kingdom at risk, whilst the hostile kingdom of England seems more invincible than ever.

But Bishop Wishart has got a final card left to play: four brave Scottish knights set off in search of a mysterious ancient treasure that will bring Scotland to the centre of an international plot, changing both the kingdoms of Europe and the course of history once and for all.

ISBN: 978-1-901514-76-6
£9.99